D1607708

HOME WILL NEVER BE THE SAME AGAIN

HOME WILL NEVER BE THE SAME AGAIN

A Guide for Adult Children of Gray Divorce

Carol R. Hughes
and
Bruce R. Fredenburg

Foreword by Bill Eddy

ROWMAN & LITTLEFIELD
Lanham • Boulder • New York • London

Published by Rowman & Littlefield
An imprint of The Rowman & Littlefield Publishing Group, Inc.
4501 Forbes Boulevard, Suite 200, Lanham, Maryland 20706
www.rowman.com

6 Tinworth Street, London SE11 5AL

British Library Cataloguing in Publication Information Available

Library of Congress Cataloging-in-Publication Data

Library of Congress Control Number: 2020932503

ISBN: 978-1-5381-3530-3 (cloth)
ISBN: 978-1-5381-3531-0 (electronic)

Dedication

We dedicate this book to Stu Webb, who began a peacemaking movement thirty years ago that has been changing the way families throughout the world experience divorce.

CONTENTS

ACKNOWLEDGMENTS

We are grateful to Kerry D'Agostino, our literary agent at Curtis Brown, Ltd., who first approached Carol to write this book. She was deeply concerned about the lack of literature thoroughly exploring gray divorce and, especially, its effect on adult children. From the beginning, Kerry championed the need for this book. Along our three-and-a-half-year journey bringing this book to fruition, she consistently encouraged us with her insightful feedback on the manuscript and provided cogent edits during numerous revisions. Her determination to make this resource available to those in need led us to Executive Editor Suzanne Staszak-Silva and Rowman & Littlefield Publishers, whom we thank for their unwavering support and confidence in this project.

Carol's beloved daughters Lara Hughes-Allen and Anja Hughes, from as far away as Siberia and Lake Tahoe, respectively, have served as part-time research assistants, proofreaders, editors, technical-support gurus, and manuscript preparers. Anja recreated the graph in the introduction and illustrated the Losses from Divorce in chapter 4. Without their assistance, this book would be only an idea.

We also acknowledge our professional colleagues in the International Academy of Collaborative Professionals, and Collaborative Practice California, who are pioneers of respectful, family-focused approaches for helping divorcing couples. We have benefited immensely from their teaching. We want to thank the many members of our local practice group for embracing our lead in listening to the voices of Adult Children of parental divorce.

Over the past seventeen years, our education and training in respectful divorce solutions came from members of these groups. We are especially grateful to our colleagues from the Leadership Team of the Collaborative Divorce Education Institute, Cathleen Collinsworth, Bart Carey, and Brian Levy, who have donated thousands of hours in meetings and training to help advance the peacemaking skills of divorce professionals. Thank you to Woody Mosten, who continually said, "You should write a book about that," and to Gary Friedman, who taught us understanding in conflict.

Beyond that, we are especially grateful to our respective spouses, Nick Allen and Yolanda Torres-Fredenburg, who continued to love and support us while tolerating our lack of availability and single focus on this book for three years. They have patiently endured the disorder created in our homes as books, papers, sticky notes, and other reference materials piled up for ready access.

We want to acknowledge Carol's therapy dog Molly, who senses when people are sad, tense, angry, or afraid, and calms them, offering her unconditional support. Bruce often "borrows" Molly and uses her extraordinary healing presence whenever a child or adult is especially distressed.

Lastly, we thank all of our clients who trusted us over the past thirty years, shared so much of their lives, and allowed us to participate in their healing journeys.

FOREWORD

When I started reading this book, I decided to take a look at my last twenty divorce-mediation cases. Lo and behold, seven of them included adult children (35 percent). I hadn't even realized it until this book focused my attention on this subject. Yet as I read further, I remembered many of the seemingly unique issues that these "gray" divorces raised.

What about the dependent adult child with special needs? What about the kids in college who were counting on now-uncertain financial support from their parents? What about the adult child still living at home whom one parent wanted to continue supporting and the other parent wanted to cut off? What about the case where the parents could barely communicate, so that their adult children had to attend the mediation sessions to help keep them calm (as they had done for years)? And there were cases in which the adult children felt pressured to take sides (some did and some didn't).

I realized that I had all of these cases but scattered throughout my caseload, so that I hadn't put together the trend that authors Carol Hughes and Bruce Fredenburg had recognized. And I hadn't really considered the depth of emotional dislocation that the other unseen adult children were going through when their parents divorced. This book has opened a new door of awareness even for me, after nearly forty years of handling thousands of divorces in and out of court.

From high-conflict divorces to "amicable" divorces to those in which the parents won't talk about it, the adult children are clearly suffering too—often alone and feeling that they have nowhere to turn. All the rules have suddenly changed, and roles are often reversed, as their parents need help instead of providing it.

As this book so well describes, adult children are not alone and are not crazy. Their situation is becoming more and more common every year. In reality, we aren't alone and can't get by without support from others. Fortunately, Hughes and Fredenburg are two therapists who specialize in the needs of the adult children of divorce. They are showing the way in this book, which will educate many other divorce professionals and will especially help those adult children who find themselves in this confusing and upsetting situation.

I hope that you find this book as revealing and encouraging as I did. The stories will pull at your heartstrings, but the wealth of information provided will get you thinking. The future of families and individuals depends on us learning how to manage all of these new transitions for everyone involved—and we can.

—**Bill Eddy**, LCSW, Esq., lead author of *Splitting*, author of *Don't Alienate the Kids*, and the training director of the High Conflict Institute

INTRODUCTION

For more than two decades, long before the idea for this book became a reality, a silent revolution has been occurring and creating a seismic shift in the American family and families in other countries. It has been unfolding without much comment, and its effects are being felt across three to four generations. It has grown so rapidly that sociologists have already coined a term for it—the "gray divorce revolution." Couples who divorce later in life after the age of fifty are a part of this cultural phenomenon.

Carol writes:

As a warm April Monday was dawning in Southern California, numerous voice messages and emails from across the United States had been arriving at my office in the hours before I did. They were from Adult Children, parents, and therapists who had read an article about my work with Adult Children of gray divorce. The voice messages and emails echoed themes that were all too familiar to me. I heard the voices and read the words of:

Adult Children: "I did not know anyone even knew about what I have been going through. Thank you for talking about this! Can you help me?"

"I feel so alone. Please reply to this email and tell me where I can get help."

"Mom is really depressed since Dad left us. I'm so worried about her and don't know how to help her."

Parents: "My adult son will not even talk to me. He is so angry at me. I left his father and have never been happier. I just want to be able to be happy and for him to be happy for me. Can you help us?"

"My daughter has been devastated by our divorce. We are going through an acrimonious divorce, and she is floundering and depressed. I had no idea our divorce would hit her like it has. She refuses to let me see my grandchildren. She says since I have left her mother, I have violated all the values I instilled in her as she was growing up. She says I am a bad role model for her kids. Everything I have tried to get through to her has failed. How can I fix this?"

Therapists: "Finally, someone is shining the light on this issue! I have been working with these Adult Children for years now. It is so difficult for them. They feel adrift because no one acknowledges what they are experiencing."

"Would you be willing to discuss with me what you have developed in your work with these Adult Children?"

THE SILENT REVOLUTION

Researchers Susan L. Brown and I-Fen Lin of Bowling Green State University were among the first to identify the gray divorce trend. Their 2012 study of the US population, "The Gray Divorce Revolution: Rising Divorce Among Middle-Aged and Older Adults, 1990–2010,"[1] found that the divorce rate for the US population over the age of fifty doubled, and more than doubled for those over the age of sixty-five. In 1990, slightly over 200,000 people fifty or older divorced. In 2010, almost 650,000 people fifty or older divorced—an increase of over 250 percent since 1990. Since half of the married population is fifty and over, Brown and Lin projected that, as the US population ages, by 2030 the number of persons age fifty and older who divorce will grow by one-third.[2] Figure I.1 illustrates this trend. Current research finds that this increase is continuing.[3] As it does, the number of divorcing parents plus their Adult Children indicates that in the United States alone, nearly a million people are affected each year by the "Gray Divorce Revolution."

The explosion of gray divorces is not isolated to the United States. The same trends are also occurring in Canada, the United Kingdom, Japan, Europe, and Australia.[4] Canada's national statistical agency Statistics Canada indicates that "grey divorce" has been consistently growing among those fifty-five and over, including those sixty-five and older. And rates are expected to increase as more people continue to age.[5] The United Kingdom's Office for National Statistics announced in 2018 that the divorce rate among those fifty-five or older, dubbed "silver splitters," has doubled.[6] In the past two decades in Japan, couples married thirty years or more have seen their divorce rate quadruple. The Japanese are calling it "Retired Husband Syndrome."[7]

Across the world, legal and financial circles have been paying more attention to the "gray divorce revolution." For example, a

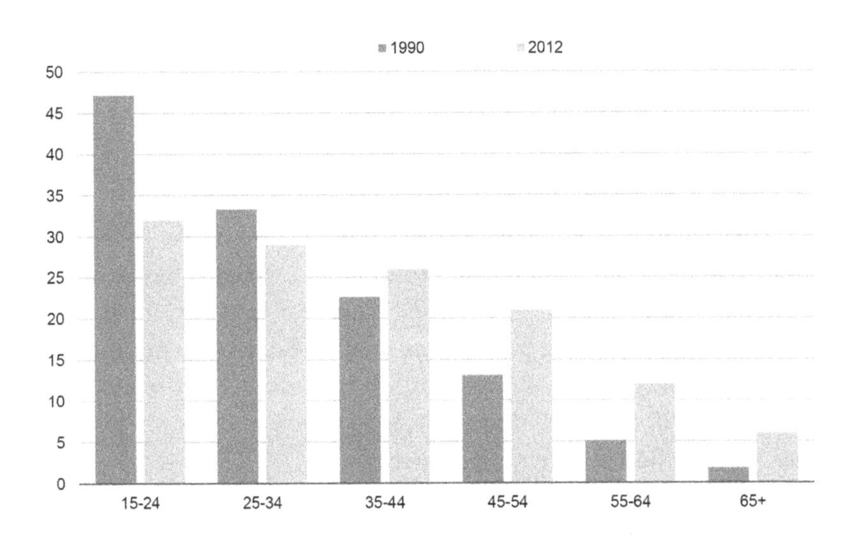

Figure 0.1. Divorce Rates by Ten-Year Age Groups, 1990 and 2012. ***Reprinted with permission from National Center for Family and Marriage Research at Bowling Green State University. Source: Centers for Disease Control and Prevention, National Center for Health Statistics, VitalStats and US Census Bureau, American Community Survey, 2012.***

2016 study found that "the feminization of poverty is evident with a whopping 27% of gray divorce women poor. Just 11% of gray divorce men are in poverty."[8] In December 2016, Martha M. Hamilton wrote in the *Washington Post*, "Divorce after 50 can destroy even the best retirement plans."[9] She suggested, "Sometimes that might mean that your first call should be to a financial planner or an accountant rather than a divorce lawyer."

That approach, though well intended, is a mistake. As important as financial concerns are, the emphasis on finances overlooks the most critical aspects of any divorce. Divorce professionals agree that, even though divorce involves money and the law, for the people going through it, divorce is primarily an emotional experience that also includes legal and financial concerns. "Yet divorce is not really about the law at all. There is rarely any dispute over the law in a divorce case. Divorces have at their heart relationship problems with a large amount of financial uncertainty thrown in," writes Stephen G. Anderson, mediator, professional practice consultant, and nonpracticing solicitor in Ipswich, United Kingdom.[10]

The same is true for gray divorce. Fear, anger, helplessness, concern about fairness and lack of fairness, abandonment, betrayal, desire for revenge, guilt, failure, and excessive anxiety are some of the many emotions that can overwhelm gray divorce couples, just as powerfully as they would those under the age of fifty.

However, there is a new aspect of divorce for couples divorcing at fifty or older that cries for attention, and it's one that has received extremely little validation to date. There is a category of family members that divorcing parents, the public, and divorce professionals consistently overlook, unintentionally damage, and relegate to the back shelf, until the harm erupts in unanticipated ways. They are the Adult Children of divorcing parents.

Their voices open this book—voices rising from the thousands of hours we have spent listening to Adult Children of divorcing parents. While presenting real-life situations, to honor and protect the privacy of our clients, we have disguised their voices and altered many details of their lives. They are the voices of men and women. Their ages range from nineteen to fifty years old. Some of them are single; some are married. Some have children of their own. All of them are in different stages of life and experiencing shock, fear, and sudden, dramatic change.

As the divorce rate for adults over fifty soars, so too does the number of Adult Children who are experiencing parental divorce. Yet, these Adult Children frequently say that they are the only ones who are aware of what they are going through, that no one understands what they are experiencing, and that they feel alone.

Throughout the following chapters, we describe relevant general research, the limited research specifically about Adult Children of gray divorce, and the deep understanding we have gained from our extensive experience during the past decades, working with these women and men.

Our goal in writing this book is to create a resource for these too-often-forgotten Adult Children of gray divorce, who so frequently say that when they talk about their emotional concerns and experiences, the most important people in their lives frequently ignore and dismiss them. We illustrate to them that they are not alone. We provide them with tools to identify what they are experiencing, and tools for moving forward with their lives in ways that strengthen their relationships with their parents, siblings, extended family, and most importantly, with themselves.

Since divorce affects the entire relationship sphere of divorcing couples, *Home Will Never Be the Same Again* is a resource not only for their Adult Children, but also for parents, extended family members, family friends, and community members.

Lastly, every year gray divorce affects millions of people and creates far-reaching impacts on society as a whole. Therefore, this book also has value to students and faculty of psychology, sociology, and public health, as healthcare providers, legal and financial professionals, researchers, and public policy makers address this societal change.

CAROL'S DIVORCE STORY

When I began my clinical practice years ago, I had no intention of working in the divorce field. Often our painful life experiences draw us toward them rather than allowing us to flee from them.

My life abruptly changed when I was a child of three and a half. My parents divorced. Barely five years old, in the middle of first grade, I became a ward of the state. County child-protective services placed me in their facility while my parents fought their bitter custody battle. It was like a scene from *Oliver Twist*. Rows of squeaky beds with vertical spindles of cold cast iron supporting the arched headboards and footboards housed the otherwise bare and cold sleeping rooms. Windows with bars that seemed as high as if giants had installed them prevented me from seeing into the outside world.

Every day, for five long days, interrupted only by caregivers moving me to various locations for breakfast, lunch, supper, bath, and bedtime, I sobbed, inconsolable, sitting on the floor at the foot of the locked door that was the exit to the offices and my freedom. Through my tiny, tear-filled eyes, I looked through the grille in the bottom of the door, watching the shoe-clad feet come and go, ever hopeful that I would see my daddy or granny's shoes. I feared that I had surely become an orphan.

Ultimately, I was "awarded" to my father and paternal grandmother. My grandmother later told me that a woman who worked at the facility told her, "That child never belonged in this place."

My father, my grandmother, and I lived in North Florida, and my mother, her new husband, and their son lived three thousand miles away in Southern California. She visited me two times during my childhood and adolescence.

BRUCE'S DIVORCE STORY

At age thirty-one, I was married and returning to the university to pursue postgraduate education to become a psychotherapist. It was then that I learned that my mother was planning to divorce my father. My parents had argued continually during my entire life, and I often thought that one day, they would divorce. Yet, when my mother confided her intention to divorce my father, I was surprised at how shocked and disturbed I was. The whole concept felt surreal and impacted me deeply.

I left my parents' house feeling anxious and guilty that she had asked me to keep her secret from my father. I felt loyal to both of them, and I worried about how I would navigate the new life that was unfolding in front of me. My reaction confused and surprised me. After all, I was a fully independent adult. I thought that this news should not so strongly affect me. Ultimately, my parents did not divorce because of my mother's deteriorating health.

Years later, in my clinical practice, I expanded my work to include families going through divorce, including the Adult Children of divorcing parents. I remembered how my parents' impending divorce had affected me, and I resonated with the experiences of Adult Children dealing with their parents' divorce.

***

Throughout this book, "Adult Children" is capitalized to emphasize this misunderstood population. "Adult Children" refers to "Adult Children of gray divorce" and "divorce" refers to divorce that happens after the children are adults. Any masculine references also apply to females and any feminine references also apply to males.

1

DIVORCE IS A NEVER-ENDING CHAIN OF EVENTS

Divorce is deceptive. Legally it is a single event, but psychologically it is a chain—sometimes a never-ending chain—of events, relocations and radically shifting relationships strung through time, a process that forever changes the lives of the people involved.

—Judith Wallerstein and Sandra Blakeslee, *Second Chances*

"It shook me to my foundation."

"I just start sobbing out of nowhere and I don't know why. Then I remember—my family is gone. My family is dead."

"After so many years of marriage, it was a shock."

"My entire life past and present changed in an instant."

"I didn't know who I was anymore."

"Had our whole family life together been all smoke and mirrors?"

"I have been questioning my ability to have a good relationship in the long term and that is causing my husband and me a lot of problems. I think he deserves a better woman than me."

"I felt homeless."

"They were the perfect couple. We were the perfect family. After thirty years . . . why divorce now? It has hit me really hard. I have been drinking too much and just don't care about anything anymore."

"My dad left Mom for one of his students. I've lost a lot of weight and am having trouble sleeping. My wife and Mom are worried about me. I'm afraid I will become just like Dad, have an affair, and leave my marriage. I just keep hearing in my head, 'The apple doesn't fall far from the tree.' Am I doomed to become like him?"

"Mom wants me to meet her new boyfriend, but that would feel creepy to me."

"It feels like the rock that was my family has been sucked into an earthquake fault."

***

There is a silent revolution that is changing the American family and families across the world.[1] It is already affecting families up to three or four generations, and it has been unfolding without much comment for more than twenty-five years. More couples are divorcing later in life, a trend dubbed the "gray divorce revolution." While coping with this change, family members are unknowingly making critical mistakes. Often, they don't see what is happening until it's too late to undo the damage.

Among the commonly recognized casualties of a divorce, besides the minor children, extended family members, and mutual friends of the couple who may be recruited to take sides, there is a seldom acknowledged group of family members who is expected to roll with it, shake it off, and get on with their lives, as if it is "just one of those things, and you'll get over it and adjust" types of experiences. Their voices open this chapter. These are the family members that we highlight in this book, so their pain is validated and understood, and they can find pathways to hope and healing. They are the Adult Children of gray divorce.

They are men and women. Their ages range from eighteen to fifty. They are single; they are married. They may have children of their own. These forgotten Adult Children often say that whenever they express their emotional concerns and experiences, the most important people in their lives frequently ignore and dismiss them.

THE SIZE OF THE PROBLEM IS GROWING

There is evidence that the problem is growing. The US divorce rate among adults aged fifty and older doubled between 1990 and 2010,[2] and it is projected to triple by 2030.[3] Across the world, more and more couples aged fifty and older are divorcing. As the older adult divorce rate soars, so does the number of Adult Children who are experiencing parental divorce, yet these Adult Children frequently report feeling that they are the only ones who are aware of what they are going through, that no one understands what they are experiencing, and they feel invisible and painfully alone. While there has been extensive research about how divorce affects minor children, the research world has virtually ignored Adult Children of gray divorce.

EMOTIONS DRIVE MOST OF THE CONCERNS IN DIVORCE

Even though divorce involves concerns about the law and money, emotions drive most of these concerns. Fear, anger, helplessness, ideas of fairness and lack of fairness, abandonment, betrayal, desire for revenge, guilt, failure, excessive anxiety resulting in mental paralysis are a few. It is especially important to note that none of these emotions support calm, generous, caring, and reasoned decision making. In fact, those who have experienced divorce, as well as many divorce professionals, acknowledge that often 80 percent or more of the difficulties arises from the emotional aspects and that only 20 percent or less comprises strictly legal and financial issues. But traditionally, most of the overt focus is on the 20 percent, often at the expense and the potentially dangerous dismissal of the 80 percent. The legal and financial concerns are important and may require professional assistance, but they are not by themselves the most important concern for a family when we view the family from the "Bigger Picture" *family* perspective.

While it is true that each divorce is different because the people are different, the circumstances vary, and the specifics are unique to each family, some things are common in all of them. Divorce brings with it myriad changes and emotions, including shock, fear, disappointment, loss, pain, anger, and sadness. Emotions in divorce are especially powerful. When we experience intense emotions, and especially when we act out of anger, fear, or anxiety, it is easy to overlook or forget our most important values and concerns. By the time we are able to right ourselves emotionally and notice how our words, decisions, and actions have affected others, damage has already been done.

THE TWO TRACKS OF DIVORCE

In most jurisdictions, there are four ways to divorce: do-it-yourself, mediation, collaboration, or litigation. Whatever way a couple chooses, divorce has two tracks—the business track and the emotional track. The catch is that these tracks are always operating simultaneously. This means that couples cannot simply address one track and then the other track sequentially. The tracks are intertwined. Even in the more peaceful divorce processes such as do-it-yourself, mediation, and collaboration, if couples do not effectively address the emotional track, it can easily knock the business track off course. When this happens, damage to the family, including the children (both minor and adult), is almost guaranteed. It is also costlier in money and time. And, of course, in litigation, the most adversarial choice, failure to address the emotional aspects can create astronomical financial cost, even to the point of potentially bankrupting a family.

There are also well-known health risks to litigation such as symptoms of posttraumatic stress and, in some cases, even physical illness. For example, in a study of physicians involved in malpractice litigation, most physicians reported symptoms of depression and many developed physical illnesses related to stress, including those who were actually successful in defending themselves.[4] This is a strong indicator that, win or lose, litigation can be harmful to health.

WHO ARE THESE ADULT CHILDREN AND WHAT DO THEY SAY?

Hans, a thirty-four-year-old machinist, married with two young children, recalls, "First, I was in complete shock! How could my parents be divorcing after so many years of marriage? Then, I began to worry if they would both be okay. Mom had been out of the workforce since my siblings and I were born, and Dad was close to retirement. How would they make it financially living apart? My two brothers took a 'hands-off' attitude, so I felt like I had lost them as well. It was very stressful on my wife and me. We felt like we were juggling the day in and day out of our own lives as well as how we were going to help my parents be okay."

Adult Children say that they worry about their parents during and after a divorce as much as they would worry about the well-being of their own children. They worry about how their parents will fare during the divorce proceedings and about their parents' future, emotionally, socially, and financially. And the loyalty binds tear at them, pulling them between supporting both of their parents and their own nuclear family.

Phillip, a twenty-six-year-old unmarried accountant, remembers, "When Dad told me that Mom was leaving him, and they were getting divorced, I immediately felt guilty being in another city with my own life and job. I felt as though I should drive home on the weekends to spend time with Dad because he sounded so depressed. I was worried that he would just waste away in that house. I felt pulled between Mom and Dad and guilty that I was spending so much time with Dad and not with Mom, like I was being disloyal to Mom."

> *Divorce is like death without a burial.*
> —Dane Cunningham, *Risky Relationships*

Adult Children of gray divorce often say that their parents' divorce hurt them as much as the death of a close family member. Indeed, divorce is like a death. Comparing divorce to a death helps parents and society understand why divorce is so painful for Adult Children. We would expect Adult Children to grieve their parents' death. Why would we not expect Adult Children to feel pain, sadness, and deep grief at the "death" of their family as they have known it their entire lives? Adult Children of gray divorce often say that "home will never be the same again."

FAMILY STRUCTURE AT PARENTAL MIDLIFE

A colleague of ours, Brian Don Levy, collaborative family law attorney and mediator, shared his experience with us. Although his practice is now dedicated solely to nonadversarial divorce processes designed to help divorcing couples reach their agreements peacefully and respectfully without going to court, for thirty years he was a fierce litigator who spent enormous amounts of time and energy in court as a hired warrior. The more he "won" for his designated client, the more he became aware that he was also helping to destroy their families without offering any remedy to repair the collateral damage to all of the other family relationships that were shattered.

He says his parents raised him to be a good person and to do the right thing. He reached a point where he was not proud of using his skills to promote outcomes that measured success by "winner take all" metrics. He has since learned how conflict, especially intense conflict, narrows focus. In the heat of battle, couples can forget all values except winning. He notes that in litigation, winning is narrowly defined as "doing what it takes to achieve a result that I perceive to benefit my client no matter the adverse consequence to the rest of the family." When parents talked about their concerns about or obligations to their Adult Children (generally eighteen years old or more in the United States if not married or legally emancipated), he explained that as far as the law was concerned, the parents had no legal responsibility for them. So, he told them that their Adult Children did not matter in their divorce. Brian says he now realizes how wrong he was and that he understands that Adult Children do matter because they can be stakeholders in their parents' divorce, and because their parents are modeling for them adult problem solving.

To what degree their parents' divorce impacts the Adult Children's emotional lives, their relationships, and possibly their finances depends on what their parents' agreements are and how they reach them. The more pain, conflict, and anger their parents experience, the more impact there will be in all areas of the Adult Children's lives. When going through divorce, many parents of Adult Children have wisely said to us, "If my kids aren't okay, I won't be okay."

Brian also says that he now understands why the parents were so quick to accept the absurd notion that there was no need to be concerned about their Adult Children. He realizes that parents want to believe their children, both minor and adult, will be okay, so they are happy to believe that they don't need to worry about them. After all, what parent doesn't want to believe that their children will be all right in the end? And, during a divorce, most couples already have so much to worry about it can be a relief to be assured that worrying about their Adult Children's welfare is not something they need to think about.

PARENTAL DIVORCE AFFECTS ADULT CHILDREN

American novelist Walter Kirn writes,

> My parents stayed together for the sake of the children. When the children were grown and settled, my parents divorced. . . . My brother was 25 . . . I was 27. . . Because Mom and Dad had decided to tough it out (29 years in all), we faced their breakup not as vulnerable kids but as self-sufficient adults. You'd think it would have been easier that way. . . . You'd think I'd thank my parents for their decision. Here's what I learned, though: when

> the rug is pulled out from under you emotionally, it isn't necessarily an advantage to be standing on your own two feet. Nothing is quite so shocking. . . . In fact, six years afterward, my parents' breakup still gnaws at me. No more holiday feasts. . . . And the question of whether I'm thankful they held on long enough to undermine me as a man rather than wound me as a boy seems insoluble.[5]

Let us take a closer look at how unrealistic and harsh it is to expect Adult Children whose parents are divorcing to simply shrug it off and adapt as if the experience should not trigger an avalanche of emotions. The first step to help someone who is in pain is to identify where the problems lie. We need to look at what's really going on beyond our initial assumptions.

As with all the other stages of life, families are experiencing many changes and challenges when the parents reach midlife and the children transition from adolescents to adults. These changes occur over the span of a few to several years, depending on the age of the parents and the number and ages of their children. Independence does not happen overnight. Despite any legal definition, there is no magic age for the transition from dependent child to independent adult.

In most families, even when young adults are able to gain full independence, they are still connected to their parents, sisters and brothers, grandparents, aunts, uncles, cousins, and other extended family. Families usually celebrate major holidays together, even when separated by geography. It is common for everyone to return to the family home or join the others at another relative's home, such as the grandparents' home. Families have their traditions that are familiar and valued by most or all members. It is also important to acknowledge that many parents continue to help their children financially even as they enter new careers and marriages, and when the Adult Children themselves become parents.

It is not too difficult to imagine the significant impact parental divorce would have on a young adult who is in the middle of transitioning into her independence but is still not there yet. Or the impact parents' divorce has on Adult Children whose own children look forward to being with their grandparents together during important family traditions and holidays. Those grandparents may play significant relational roles in their grandchildren's lives. In addition, we should not overlook that Adult Children who have achieved independent lives, married or not, with or without children, will be emotionally impacted, as they find themselves confused and conflicted when suddenly dealing with urgent and ongoing questions. Common examples are how to be supportive to one parent while feeling loyalty and connection to the other, or feeling angry, or hurt, or stuck in the middle while resenting a parent they also feel obligated to help emotionally. In addition, when the divorce creates financial need, Adult Children experiencing parental divorce may question whether or how to help one or both parents.

The idea of a parent dating or remarrying is also a common worry for Adult Children of divorcing parents. For some Adult Children, the specifics are already clearly in place if one parent was in a secret relationship or quickly jumps into a new relationship. The reality of having to consider the new significant other's children living as a family with his or her parent would reasonably and predictably create emotional responses and questions:

"What will the new significant other be like?"

"How will this impact my other parent?"

"What if I can't stand the new person? How will that affect my relationship with my parent?"

"What if I like her or him and that hurts my other parent?"

"If my parents have been helping me financially, will they continue, or will this new person control my parent so that he or she will not help me financially? If not, what will I do?"

"How could all of this affect my inheritance and that of my children?"

"Because of my parent's focus on this new person, will I be sidelined from my parent's life?"

"Do I have a right to be angry? Is it immature or selfish of me to feel angry?"

"Am I hurt, numb?"

"Do I ally with my other parent?"

"How will all this affect my children's relationships with their grandparents?"

And the list goes on.

ADULT CHILDREN ARE IN DIFFERENT LIFE STAGES

Every stage of life is a time of acquiring new and more effective skills. At first, we are not very good at the newly acquired skills, no matter how much we want to master them. Think of learning a new skill, such as learning to drive. The intention is clear, but still, it can be difficult for a longer time than we had hoped. Struggling with new and essential life skills can cause anxiety, even under the best circumstances.

A young adult who is in the early stages of transitioning to becoming an independent adult has different challenges than an older adult child who has completed that process. She is still learning all of the practical skills she will require, such as learning how to support herself, managing finances, engaging in and building new social networks, and focusing on herself while enjoying the protection of the family relationships she has depended on her entire life.

Divorce disrupts this process while at the same time creating an intense focus on the parents' needs. Until the divorce, the Adult Child of divorcing parents naturally expected and counted on support from her parents as she navigated each stage of her growth. Now, just as that support is falling away, she can find herself under pressure to provide emotional or financial support for one or both parents. While she is coping with the losses ensuing from her parents' separation and divorce, at the same time, she may have also lost some or all of their support and guidance. These disruptions can cripple her ability to complete certain stages of development needed to become a successful adult. Of course, this will rarely be identified, much less understood, while it's happening. As the most dependable and familiar parts of her life disintegrate, feelings of confusion and shock create a general sense of not being grounded.

Again, this experience seems similar to the death of someone who has always been in her life. Major landmarks of her life, a family structure that "just is," and parental reassurance about who she is and where she belongs have vanished. She realizes that the life she learned to trust and depend on is no longer there.

It is common for her to have feelings of being abandoned and lost. She may not be able to name what she is feeling. She may feel afraid, angry, betrayed, and abandoned. These feelings create anxiety and can erode her previous sense of security and confidence in her present and future life. For someone who had enjoyed dedicated parental support, it can all feel devastating. There are now many, many things to figure out without enough life experience to do so. And her support system now requires more support from her than ever before, while at the same time, it is offering less to her. It should not be surprising if she really doesn't feel okay.

An older Adult Child can find himself reevaluating his history. His family had simply "been there" his entire life. Before he was born, they were there. Of course, during his life there have been ups and downs, but he accepted his parents always being married with the same sense of certainty as the sun setting at night and rising in the morning. The idea that his family could just "be gone" never entered his mind. If he has children and they have relationships with the grandparents, his parents' divorce can change everything. It can seem surreal even if he sometimes thought his parents fought too much and should get divorced. Many Adult Children living through their parents' divorce report that the reality of living through it is much different and more difficult than the imagined event.

Suddenly there are new demands to support one or both parents emotionally and possibly financially as well. There is a change in how he thinks of his parents. If sides are taken, conflicts with his brothers and sisters can emerge or increase. He may start questioning the permanence of his own marriage and worrying about how this uncertainty can affect his children. These are not minor concerns that are easily shaken off. In addition, he may be feeling a responsibility to support a parent who is depressed, hopeless, and angry. Under the weight of these new demands, he can believe that his feelings are unimportant. Assuming he won't be affected, those around him usually reinforce these feelings. He might suppress his feelings to avoid noticing that he is experiencing normal feelings of pressure, fear, anger, and sadness. When these coping methods become the "new normal," he can lose his ability to cope with responsibilities to, and relationships with, the other important people in his life. There can be a change in obligations so that he now has the responsibility to organize extended family functions with the constant worry of preventing potential "blow ups" between family members. This can create more stress and potentially more pressure on his own nuclear family.

Many Adult Children find themselves having to care for depressed, ill, or aging parents. They may find themselves mediating between their parents, becoming constantly wary of not getting caught in the middle of their parents' battles. Challenges can arise about how to keep a relationship with the parent who has become the family's designated "Bad Guy" while not being perceived by other family members, or even by himself, as disloyal to the other parent. On a related note, one of the most difficult challenges may be when, if, and how to forgive the person who decided to divorce—especially if that person has become the designated antagonist.

The worry that all of these stressors will become the Adult Child's "new normal" becomes a realistic fear.

As you read this book, you will discover what happens when the experiences and feelings of Adult Children going through parental divorce are neglected, overlooked, or in the worst cases dismissed entirely. The damage can trigger an avalanche of emotions and can send shock waves through three to four generations of the family. This book is about the experiences of Adult Children of gray divorce, their pain, loss, anger, confusion, fear, isolation, and the lack of understanding and support they receive.

If you are an Adult Child who is experiencing your parents' divorce, if you are the parents of these Adult Children, if you are the friends, family, or community members of these Adult Children or their divorcing parents, we want you to know that there are solutions. The end of family, relationship tension or destruction, identity crisis, guilt, and divided loyalty do not have to ensue from divorce. We will help you understand the complicated familial and relationship dynamics before, during, and after divorce. We will also provide you with tools to successfully navigate these difficult family transitions so that you can preserve and even empower what is most important—your family relationships.

2

IT'S ALL ABOUT THE RELATIONSHIPS

Relationships are the most important part of our having well-being, in being human. It's that simple. And that important.
—Daniel Siegel, MD, professor of psychiatry at UCLA Medical School, author and founding codirector of the Mindfulness Awareness Research Center at UCLA

When you hear the word "relationship," what comes to mind? For many, perhaps even most of us, we imagine the feelings we associate with romantic partnerships, whether warm and loving or painful and heartbreaking. Yet, as Dr. Louis Cozolino in his book *The Neuroscience of Human Relationships* informs us, the field of interpersonal neurobiology is one of several emerging fields of scientific study that understands humans as individuals who are born into relationships, and it is through myriad relationships from birth to death that we develop and live our lives. The research supports that being in all types of caring and meaningful relationships with family, friends, marriage partners, coworkers, and others can alter the structures and biochemistry of the brain.[1]

Echoing Doctors Siegel and Cozolino, Dr. Amy Banks states that a new field of scientific study that she terms "relational neuroscience" indicates that "our brains and bodies are hardwired to help us engage in satisfying emotional connection with others . . . [and that] the human brain is built to operate within a network of caring human relationships."[2] She describes how included in this hardwiring are four neural pathways, which we will examine later. Among several studies that she recounts about the health benefits of relationships, below are two that are pertinent to Adult Children of gray divorce.

Beginning in the 1940s, a study of 1,100 medical students at Johns Hopkins, who were all healthy at the beginning of the study, revealed that fifty years later, those who had developed cancer in the intervening years were less likely to have had close relationships with their parents than those who did not have cancer. Especially noteworthy as the strongest predictor of cancer was a poor relationship between the male student and his father.[3]

Another study that began in the 1950s asked male Harvard students, who were all healthy at the beginning of the study, to describe their parents, as well as the warmth and closeness of their parents. Thirty-five years later, 29 percent who had described their parents in positive terms and who had good parental relationships had developed illnesses, while 95 percent of those students who described their parents in negative terms and who had poor relationships with their parents had developed illnesses.[4]

For over thirty years, the psychological and family sociological empirical research and theories regarding families of later life have indicated that the parent–child relationship is important to both parents and children throughout their life spans. Dr. Debra Umberson found that the quality of Adult Child–parent relationships is associated with the psychological functioning for both generations.[5] Another recent study by Dr. Joleen Greenwood found that Adult Children's parent–child relationships are just as likely as those of minor children's to be affected by parental divorce, and that the age of the Adult Children at the time of their parents' divorce did not seem to influence whether or not the parent–child relationship was affected.[6]

Throughout the coming chapters, we will interweave more detailed results of the research about the effects of parental divorce on the relationships of Adult Children of gray divorce, and how this research provides paths for healing. For now, let's peer into the lives of two Adult Children of gray divorce, twenty-year-old Maria and forty-two-year-old Daniel, so we can see firsthand through their eyes what they are experiencing.

Maria and Daniel are each meeting with Carol at her office for the first time. By the time Adult Children of divorcing parents meet with a therapist, many of them have been resisting talking with family and friends about what has been happening in their lives. They often report that no one understands what they are feeling, and that when they try to discuss what they are experiencing, people most often say, "Aren't you glad you're an adult now? Be grateful this didn't happen when you were six!" Their parental and familial relationships are rupturing, yet it seems no one is acknowledging what they are feeling and experiencing. First sessions with Adult Children of gray divorce are often very much like Maria's and Daniel's below. Because our culture does not validate that these Adult Children can and should be hurting, that they are feeling devastated and confused, the feelings and thoughts that these Adult Children have repressed for months or even years often erupt in the first sessions, like lava and ash spewing from a volcano that has been dormant for decades.

MARIA

Carol writes:

It was a day like any other day in my psychotherapy practice. When I checked my voice messages, there was a message from Emil, a friend and colleague of mine saying that he wanted to refer the daughter of a family friend to me. I returned Emil's call, and we exchanged the usual pleasantries. Emil then said, "Carol, do you have room in your practice to see the daughter of a dear and long-time friend of mine? I have told her father about your expertise with Adult Children who are experiencing their parents' divorce." I listened and jotted a few notes as he began.

"I have known Maria since she was a little girl," Emil started. "She is an only child and was always such a happy child, kind, caring, and intelligent. I have watched her grow up. She was every parent's dream of the perfect child and the perfect teenager. She was always an honors student, and for years she volunteered as a tutor for young children. She and her parents always seemed to be the happiest family one could imagine. They were picture perfect. Her parents came from humble origins and worked their way up, you know. They worked as they completed each college degree. They are still humble people—salt-of-the-earth folks. Her mom and dad went to every one of Maria's school and athletic activities—or at least one of them did if the other had to work. The three of them vacationed together several times a year. They volunteered at community events like the Thanksgiving soup kitchen and Wounded Warrior fundraisers. They were the happiest and most solid family I knew. They have quite an extended family of grandparents, aunts, uncles, and cousins."

I continued making notes. So far, the story seemed familiar. "Her father tells me that their impending divorce has devastated her and their extended family members. I can understand that because I bet that they never saw it coming. I certainly didn't see it coming. Frankly, I was in shock when her father told me they were divorcing, and I still can't believe it now. How do these things happen when no one is expecting it?" Emil didn't pause for me to answer his question. "Well, I know you can help her. Honestly, these people are like family to me. I think of Maria as my own daughter."

"Emil, you know how much I appreciate your confidence in referring Maria to me," I said. "When couples like your friends of longstanding and seemingly happy marriages announce that they are divorcing, it is usually quite a shock to their family members and friends. I would be happy to meet with Maria." I appreciated Emil's referral and told him to tell Maria to call my office. I would see her as soon as possible.

A week later, when I entered the waiting area of my office, I saw a lone young woman, sitting on the couch farthest from the front door. She was nestled deep into the corner of the couch, supported on one side by the high arm of the couch, on the other side by a large couch pillow that she had snuggled against her side. Her hands lay lightly in her lap. Her fingers were entwined like those of a supplicant, and her head was tilted slightly downward. Molly, my yellow Labrador therapy dog, accompanied me, and greeted Maria. She offered her unconditional friendship to Maria and offered her favorite soft, plush tree-trunk toy with squirrels inside that she held in her mouth. Molly's tail wagged amicable acceptance of Maria.

Negative feelings such as anxiety, stress, fear, sadness, and worry are often clients' companions on their first visits to a therapist's office. For most people, Molly's presence somewhat allays these feelings. I watched as Maria raised her head slightly, smiled at Molly, and scratched her head. Her ice-blue, fiercely intelligent eyes snuck a quick peek at me. Then she followed Molly into my office. I followed Maria. For several minutes, Maria and I sat in silence. I honored her need to be able to settle in, collect herself, and be unrushed. Maria sat stiffly on the couch diagonal to my chair, absently stroking Molly's velvety ears. Molly had instinctively placed her head on Maria's lap. Maria's face was frozen in the wide-eyed stare that therapists know portrays shock and pain.

Tear after tear gently rolled down each cheek one after another and dropped into her lap. Maria seemed oblivious to her tears. At twenty years old, she was already quite an accomplished and mature young woman, attending college three thousand miles away on an academic scholarship, yet I could already see in her the devastation that Emil had described.

After five minutes or so—though I am sure those five minutes seemed like hours to Maria—she took a slow, deep breath. It was the kind of deep breath that presages immeasurable agony arising from the depths within the psyche. She paused after exhaling a final, deep breath. Then, one shallow breath, as if steeling herself, and the words cascaded out of her.

"I'm truly in shock. I can't believe this is happening. I feel like I am living someone else's life." She inhaled another shallow breath as though gasping for air. Her eyes drifted slowly downward. Her fingers stroked Molly's soft ears as tears continued softly spilling down her cheeks. She seemed to whisper the words as though they were part of a secret—the secret she was afraid to share with herself and the world outside of her. "We weren't the perfect family, but we always had each other. Well, actually, I always thought that we *were* the perfect family. It has always been the three of us. We called ourselves the three musketeers. You know, all for one and one for all!"

I listened to the rhythm and tone of her voice. The cadence was slow and lingered on every word. Her tone seemed to question how true each word now was. She looked like she was in a trance. I knew it was the trance of shock and grief. I nodded and softly said, "I know. I'm listening, and so is Molly." Maria was still stroking Molly's ears and head. A small smile flashed across her face. Perhaps it was the thought of Molly listening too that gave her a moment of lightness.

Maria continued, "They both seem like such different people now, only focused on themselves." Though she was still staring wide-eyed at the glass doors of the bookshelf atop my rolltop desk across the room from her, I noticed that her ashen face was beginning to show more color and her body was becoming more animated. Her breathing was still rapid and shallow. Tears continued to glide down her cheeks into her lap. I patiently waited a minute or so and gave her uninterrupted time for her to realize if she was finished talking for the moment or not. She continued.

"I feel guilty wondering how or if they will still be able to help and support me when they are both going through so much pain themselves. I feel so overwhelmed, with no one to turn to. And I feel so alone. This is so sad. My life is so sad. I'm questioning everything I thought our family was. I'm questioning everything, period. Is nothing stable or constant? What else in this life isn't real? What else can't I count on? They are, well, they *were* my rock, my foundation my entire life! And it's gone! They are gone! *We* are gone! My family is gone! I can remember all that we have been as a family, yet all of those memories feel completely out of my reach! What we were is gone forever! I feel like I don't know who they are anymore. I don't know who *I* am anymore."

Her voice trailed off, becoming almost a whisper. At that moment, she seemed to regress from the mature, accomplished, young woman Emil had described to the small child she once was so many years ago. Almost unnoticeably, she began to rock gently from front to back. I thought about how we console a baby or small child when we hold it in our arms, swaying from side to side and front to back. I reassured her and said, "I am so sorry that you are going through this, Maria. I know that you are in so much shock and pain. I am here for you. I will help you get through this."

Maria's body paused its rocking and raised her head to look at me. Her lips allowed a small smile as if to say that she and I had made a connection and that my word had reassured her. I hoped that she was feeling the hope that I had offered her. She continued, "I can't imagine that our relationships, our closeness, you know, will ever be the same again. I feel like *I* need to be the strong one for *them*, but I just can't. I'm angry that I am expected to support *them*! I was not prepared for this. I don't know how to deal with all of this. I've lost my home base, my grounding. I'm sorry. I am so all over the place!"

Maria broke into inconsolable sobbing. I waited patiently in silence, not rushing her and allowing her to experience all that she was feeling. After a few minutes, she looked up. Her tearful, red eyes gazed at me. It seemed she was finished talking for now.

"Maria, I want you to know that I am honored that you are willing to share with me what you have been experiencing and feeling. All that you are describing is very common for Adult Children whose parents are divorcing." Maria's gaze was now locked on me. Her red, watery eyes were barely blinking.

"Really?" she asked, an incredulous tone in her voice.

"Yes," I replied. "When their parents first tell them they are divorcing, Adult Children report instantaneously feeling shock, disbelief, and that everything is surreal. They describe that their world begins to spin; they feel lightheaded; it is like they can see their parents' lips moving, but they cannot hear their voices. They say that it feels like the entire foundation of their lives is crumbling around them."

"That's . . . exactly . . . how . . . I . . . feel," she said. Long, silent pauses lingered between each of her words laden with the pain of grief.

"You also said that your parents seem like different people now, very focused on themselves," I continued. "I know that feels surreal too. They don't seem to be the parents you have always known. Something has shifted. And you don't feel prepared to deal with all of this. Knowing that your parents are also experiencing so much pain, it is completely understandable for you to feel guilty when you wonder if they will be able to help and support you."

Maria repeated, "I definitely don't feel prepared to deal with all of this. I feel like *I* am supposed to be the parent for *them* now!" Maria's voice grew stronger and louder. "I'm angry, you know. How can *I* be expected to support *them*? I'm still in college! I don't feel like a grown-up!" She fell silent and again stared across the room at my desk and bookshelf, though she was staring through them into another dimension.

Allowing her the space and time she needed, I said, "It's okay. There's no rush. Take as long as you need. All of this is overwhelming. It's difficult to sort out everything." Then, I too was silent, mirroring her.

She sat quietly for several minutes. Molly was now curled up next to Maria's feet, still supporting and connecting with her, yet also giving her some space. Suddenly Maria's chest swelled with a slow deep breath. Then, the words shot out, "I feel angry and guilty! I feel like a bad daughter! I feel like I am defective! Will I ever be able to have a good relationship with *them* as my role models? Why is this happening? Why do I think *I* am so special? It's my *parents* who are divorcing. *I* should support *them*. After all, they supported and raised me. Maybe I'm just selfish. But I am so angry with them too! I feel betrayed, abandoned, and alone, so alone." She leaned down to Molly and slowly scratched Molly's head. Molly also inhaled a slow, deep breath, exhaled and snuggled across Maria's right foot on the floor. Maria gave Molly's head one last scratch and sat up. She snuggled her back into the corner of the loveseat diagonal to me, pulled a throw pillow across her lap, and rested her hands atop it. She seemed to be accepting the support I was offering her. For the first time in the session, Maria's eyes connected with mine.

I began. "Maria, you are feeling so many overwhelming and conflicting feelings. I want you to know that they are all valid feelings. You are also feeling very alone right now because you have no siblings to talk with about all of this. Your friends can't understand because they haven't gone through this. Your parents, who are your usual support system, need all kinds of support themselves. And the attitude of our culture is that you should just get over it, because you are an adult now, as though to say that all that you are feeling and experiencing isn't valid and isn't real."

Maria's eyes were still engaged with mine, and her body was still snuggled into the corner of the loveseat. "It's true. What you are saying is true. I do feel so alone. I'm confused. I'm sad. I'm angry. And I'm overwhelmed all at the same time." Her voice trailed. Her eyes dropped from mine and looked at her hands on the pillow.

I continued. "I also want you to know that you are not alone in what you are feeling and experiencing. Current research indicates that half of Adult Children who are experiencing their parents' divorce have many of the same feelings."

Maria looked up, and again her eyes met mine. "Really?" she whispered. Her tone was part amazement and part hope.

"Yes, really," I assured. She was the student hearing information for the first time that was expanding her awareness. I was the teacher opening her to new learning.

Maria questioned, "You mean what I've been going through is normal and I'm not crazy? I sure feel crazy!"

"Yes," I replied. "All of what you have been feeling and thinking is perfectly understandable. Divorce is a traumatic time for everyone—the divorcing couple *and* the couple's Adult Children. You never expected to be in this place at this time in your life. It is a trauma and shock for you. You said that your parents have been your rock and your foundation. And now that is gone." I paused and let my words hang in the space between us. Her ice-blue eyes were slowly blinking, and she was intently listening.

"Hmm. Trauma and shock," she uttered, as though evaluating if the words were a fit for her. "It does feel like a trauma, and I do feel shocked. And that's what a lot of people like me say?"

"Yes," I again assured her. "During all my years in practice, I have worked with a lot of Adult Children whose parents are divorcing. Every one of them describes some or all of the same feelings and experiences. Sadly, there is very little research about Adult Children of divorcing parents. I believe that further research will show that, when Adult Children and our culture become educated about the very complex relationship dynamics that ensue from later-life parental divorce, more Adult Children will feel the freedom to talk about what they are feeling and experiencing. I think that the research will then show that it is a lot more than half of Adult Children who report such conflicting, overwhelming, and painful feelings and experiences."

Maria lifted the pillow off her lap and leaned it next to her side onto the back of the loveseat. She straightened her back, lifted her head, and held her gaze to the right and slightly upward for several minutes. Finally, she said, "This is the first time I have felt any hope that I am not crazy, I'm not completely alone, and that I may be able to get through this. I am so grateful that Emil knows you and sent me to you. I think you can really help me through this. Thank you so much."

Tears welled slightly in her eyes. They were tears of pain, gratitude, and hope.

"I too am grateful that Emil and I know each other, and that you found your way here to Molly and me," I replied.

Shortly after, we ended our first session and scheduled an appointment for the next week.

DIVORCE CREATES RELATIONAL CHANGE

Humans are relational animals. We need attachment bonds. Our attachment bonds form within our relationships. These attachment bonds ensure our survival as infants, as children, and as adolescents.

This survival is not only physical but also emotional. Maria was questioning whether the attachment bonds that she and her parents shared throughout her young life would still be there and if she would be able to count on them as her support system. Though launching into adulthood, young adults still need their attachment bonds. Indeed, attachment bonds are crucial throughout the entire human life cycle. Dr. Dan Siegel asserts that "of all the factors in human life that predict the best positive outcomes, *supportive relationships* are number one. These research-proven findings include how long we live, the health of our bodies, the well-being of our minds, and the happiness we experience in life."[7]

DANIEL

A friend of Daniel's wife Anna gave her my name as a referral for Daniel. When I returned Anna's call, she described her concern for her husband. "Dr. Hughes, I am so worried about Daniel. Since his parents announced that they were divorcing, he hasn't been the same man I married. He is irritable most of the time. He is short with our kids. Daniel and I have never been a couple to argue. Now we argue a lot about what seems like little things. He has lost weight and sleeps more than usual, though his sleep is fitful, and he says he never feels rested. Can you help him?"

I encouraged Anna to tell Daniel that she had spoken with me and to ask him to give me a call, which he did. Daniel and I scheduled his first session.

Molly and I greeted Daniel in the waiting room. Daniel rose, and we both extended our hands in greeting. As he and I shook hands, I noticed that, after brief eye contact, he quickly averted his eyes downward. His hand was cold and clammy. He was obviously nervous. I understood this because many people are often nervous on their first visit to a therapist.

I offered the usual housekeeping information—where the bathroom was, where he could find a glass of water, coffee, tea, or oatmeal bars.

"No, thanks. I'm fine," he said, although he appeared far from fine.

"Molly will show you where we are going," I said.

Daniel followed Molly into my office, and I followed him. He shuffled along, his shoulders hunched as though carrying a heavy weight. He seemed older than his forty-two years. He sat down on the loveseat directly across from me. I noticed that his hands were fidgeting. His right foot was bouncing up and down at the end of his right leg that was crossed across his left. "It's okay to feel nervous," I thought, but did not yet say. Molly was curled up on the floor next to his left foot.

I began, "Sometimes it is difficult to know where to start. Anywhere you begin is just fine."

For several minutes Daniel and I sat together in silence. Then, suddenly he blurted out, "I can't believe I am sitting in a therapist's office! I mean, I am forty-two years old, married with two kids. I have a good job. My wife and I are both teachers. We work with kids every day. I am supposed to be an adult, but sometimes I feel younger than my students. What am I doing here? I know I have been feeling depressed and irritable. My wife and I have been arguing a lot. I don't get it. What is going on?"

I asked Daniel to share with me any recent changes in his life. "The only change I can recall is that for the past year, my parents have been going through a divorce. It really hasn't been one of those hostile divorces. You know, the kind where the enemy lines are drawn, and everyone is supposed to line up on one side or the other for the battle."

Daniel fell silent again, seeming unsure where to continue from here. After a moment, I spoke again.

"Daniel, may I share with you what I know about the effects of parental divorce on Adult Children?"

"Of course," Daniel replied.

"Contrary to what to our cultural mythology says, Adult Children can experience their parents' divorce as exceptionally stressful, painful, and even traumatic." Daniel then took a deep breath and held it for several seconds. His chest swelled with the inhaled air.

Suddenly, as he exhaled, the words spewed out of his mouth, like water gushing from a crack in a dam.

"I found out that they were divorcing when my dad called me to tell me that my mom had been having an affair and wanted a divorce. They are both teachers too. He is still not doing very well. He seems depressed and tells me he misses work sometimes because he can't get out of bed, but he won't get help. He calls me instead. He asks if I see Mom. When I say that I do see her and talk with her just like I do with him, he asks if I believe what she says about him. I just say that I don't know what to believe. I wonder if I should not be so truthful with him, because I worry that maybe he will pull away from me because of what I think.

"And my mom calls me to ask for my help with money because she has never been on her own about money, you know. She has also told my sister and me that our dad has been very abusive to her since my sister and I left home years ago. My sister and I aren't getting along because she's mad at me for still talking with our dad. She is very angry with him. She says she doesn't even know who he is anymore, and I honestly wonder who he is too."

I listened attentively and empathically, knowing that Daniel needed to offload the feelings and confusing thoughts that I suspected he had been suppressing for so many months.

"Both my sister and I worry that our mom won't be able to take care of herself financially, even with whatever money she may get from Dad in the divorce. And what if Dad doesn't snap out of it and can't work anymore? My sister won't attend any family functions if our dad is there. It's like our family has completely fallen apart.

"Our family home, where my sister and I grew up and where our kids have played for years, has to be sold. Our kids don't get to see my sister's kids if our dad is around. Our mom is hurt too because I haven't just kicked my dad to the curb. Sometimes I wonder if she will pull away from me because she thinks I am siding with Dad. I tell her that I am not siding with anyone and that I love both of them. Then she cries and asks me how I could love someone who hurt her so much. I never saw my mom as the victim type, but she sure does seem like that now. She says she will never again be in the same room with Dad. I really do feel caught in the middle, so it looks like all of our family holidays together aren't going to happen anymore. I don't know how to explain all of this to our kids. What if none of this ever changes? Even though I am an adult with family, I don't have a clue how to handle all of this!

"Months ago, I told my best friend at work about what was going on. He shrugged and said, 'At least you aren't still a kid when all of this is happening. That would really be awful, right? At least you have your own life now.' My wife keeps saying that I am not the best person to help everybody and that I need to get help myself. So, I guess that's why I am here. I don't know what you can do to help though since I am the only one in my family who is willing to see you." He paused again, catching his breath. "Sorry. I know that was a lot."

I reassured Daniel, "What you are experiencing is very common. Your wife was right to encourage you to see me, so you can learn how to deal with the crisis your family is going through. I have helped many Adult Children experiencing their parents' divorce. There is hope for you and your family. There are a few things that stand out to me about what you've shared today. Do you feel able now for us to begin to talk about what is troubling you?"

"Of course," he replied. "I would like that a lot. As crazy as it sounds, I already feel better just saying all of this to you."

"I'm glad you are already feeling better. It seems to me that for many months, in fact, for over a year now, you have been trying to process and deal with the major life changes that are occurring in your family. You haven't known how to effectively deal with all that has been happening to you and your family. You have been swinging between many feelings of being sad, depressed, irritable, and then feeling like you are going to explode. These are common feelings and experiences of Adult Children whose parents are divorcing."

Tears began to fill his eyes and slowly spill down his cheeks. "Thank you for saying that! Wow! It feels so good to hear that I am not crazy!"

I smiled and continued. "You say that your parents' divorce isn't the kind where the enemy lines are drawn, and everyone is supposed to line up on one side or the other. Yet, I hear you say that you and your sister aren't getting along, because she's mad at you for still talking with your dad. Your sister refuses to attend family functions if your dad is there. Your children don't get to be with their cousins if your dad attends. Your mom will not be in the same room with your dad, and she seems to guilt trip you for continuing to talk with your dad. Daniel, it's as though you are in a vise grip with each family member squeezing you tighter and tighter to pull you to his or her side."

To depict for him how his familial relationships had been changing, I drew on the whiteboard in my office various scenarios with stick figures representing Daniel standing in the center and each member of his immediate family standing around him. I drew bold lines between his sister and father, between his father and his mother, and between his children and their cousins whenever Daniel's stick figure father was in the picture. The bold lines were like solid walls between them. Then I drew red lines from Daniel to each member of his family depicting how each family member was pulling on him to align with him or her and for him to be the responsible one to hear everyone else's thoughts and feelings while ignoring his own. The red line between Daniel and his children represented the responsibility he felt to keep their childhood as untouched by this family crisis as possible. I suspected that he knew that it was affecting his children. "Aside from my lack of artistic skills, Daniel, what do you see here?" I asked.

He stared at the pictures for several minutes. Again, his eyes filled with tears. Pointing to the whiteboard, he said, "It feels awful! It's just how I feel! These dark, black walls are blocking family members from being together, and I can't break down the walls. These red lines are always pulling on me. I am so tired of being in the middle of all of this! This is destroying all of our relationships!" He began to sob and apologized for doing so.

"You know, Daniel, our tears are the silent voice of our pain when we are feeling such loss as you are. Our tears serve a purpose.

They are just as valid as coughing or sneezing. There is no reason to apologize. When the stability of our relationships hangs precariously on the edge of the proverbial cliff, we feel what you have been feeling and experiencing. You are not alone in this."

We sat in silence while he stared at Molly's head, now lying on his lap. Finally, he shared, "This is the first time I have cried since my dad called me to tell me about their divorce. It is such a relief."

"Yes," I replied. "It helps humans to know that we are not alone and that we are not the first ones to have such feelings. I want you to know that there is help and hope for better tomorrows."

He then said, "I'm surprised how much this has helped me. When can we meet again?"

We ended our first session and scheduled the next appointment.

> *Home is the place where, when you have to go there, they have to take you in.*
> —Robert Frost, American poet

Stiff as a statue in her shock, Maria had intoned, as though chanting a funeral dirge, "Home will never be the same again." Although young adults are becoming independent and exploring their world, the attachment bonds that form during the family life cycle ensure that young adults remain connected to their parents and their family of origin, which includes their siblings and extended family members such as aunts, uncles, cousins, and grandparents. Also, their community relationships are a significant source for their ongoing support system.

It is customary for both young adults and midlife adults to return to their family home to celebrate established family traditions, such as the celebration of holidays, birthdays, graduations, weddings, births, and even celebrations of life for loved ones who have passed. From infancy to death, we define our identity within the context of our relationships. Family and community activities provide a home base from which young adults can launch and to which they can return when needed. Family and community activities ground young and midlife adults in their origins, ensuring the continuity of their attachment bonds.

Like Maria, many Adult Children of gray divorce report that they have lost that home base, "where when you go, they have to take you in." Due to their lack of life experience, they feel unanchored and adrift in the sea of an uncharted world. And, even though they have established their own families and homes, midlife Adult Children of divorcing parents like Daniel also feel deep pain from the loss of their family of origin's home base, family relationships, and family traditions.

RELATIONAL CHANGES SIGNIFICANTLY IMPACT ADULT CHILDREN OF GRAY DIVORCE

Although the research to date is limited, it indicates that Adult Children experiencing parental divorce report reduced contact and relationship closeness with both parents and extended family members, decreased contact between grandchildren and grandparents,[8] more geographic distance between fathers and Adult Children, and more severe negative impact on the father–daughter relationship quality and contact.[9]

Researchers applied the Relational Turbulence Model to Adult Children's experiences during and after their parents' gray divorce and found that Adult Children of gray divorce experience what is termed *relational uncertainty* and *partner interference*.[10] Although the research population size was small (twenty-five participants, ranging in age from twenty-one to fifty-five years old), we include it here because it is consistent with our clinical experience working with Adult Children of gray divorce. Throughout this book, using the experiences of Maria, Daniel, and other Adult Children, we will illustrate in detail their research findings. For now, let's briefly look at what they found.

Their research revealed four themes comprising *relational uncertainty*:

(1) Questioning what the parent–Adult Child relationships will be like going forward; how will the family roles, traditions, and rituals remain the same or change; what the boundaries regarding parental disclosures and Adult Children's questions about the divorce are; the common role reversal wherein the adult child becomes the giver and the parent becomes the receiver of financial, emotional, and even physical support;

(2) Questioning and reevaluating who each parent is individually; how the parent will be emotionally, physically, psychologically, and financially;

(3) Questioning the reason for and the timing of the divorce; experiencing an ambiguity between wanting to know why their parents are divorcing and not wanting to know why their parents are divorcing; wanting to know what led to their parents choosing now as the time to divorce and wondering why they did not choose to when the Adult Child was younger; and

(4) Questioning what being a family means: Who were we in the past? Were we the perfect family I thought we were or was our entire life together a lie? Was our life just a façade like the façades on a movie set? Was it all a sham? Who are we now in the present? Our nuclear family is gone. Are our happy family memories still real and valid when they seem tainted and even shattered? Who do our friends, extended family, and community members see now when they look at us? They certainly don't see our family of the past. Am I embarrassed about that? Who will we be in the future? What will our family look like going forward? What will all the family logistics be like? Where will we spend the holidays and family celebrations like birthdays, graduations, weddings, births, and deaths? Who among our immediate and extended family members, friends, and community members will be included and who will not be included?

The researchers also found that the Adult Children of gray divorce experienced *partner interference* from parents, grandparents, siblings, and spouses or significant others that caused:

(1) Disruptions to normative developmental stressors such as the Adult Children completing their education, focusing on their own romantic relationships, and planning their own weddings; and

(2) Disruptions to maintaining family relationships, such as the Adult Children feeling caught in the middle of their parents' divorce and conflicts, feeling guilty for not being able to please both parents, feeling divided loyalty to their parents. Additional examples are parents hindering or interfering with Adult Children's relationships with grandparents and other extended family members; the extended family members demanding that the Adult Children "take sides" in their parents' divorce; extended family members such as grandchildren, cousins, aunts and uncles cutting off contact with each other, "drawing battle lines," so that when organizing family traditions such as graduations, weddings, and births, the Adult Children were conflicted which family members were okay to talk to and which were not.

Let's look at how Maria is experiencing the relational uncertainties described above. She questions what her relationship with her parents will be going forward: "We always had each other." She wonders if her parents will still be her support system: "Will they still be able to help and support me?" She wonders if their closeness and contact will continue: "I can't imagine that our relationships, our closeness, you know, will ever be the same again." She also questions each of her parents' identity: "They both seem like such different people now, only focused on themselves." She is conflicted, thinking she should give emotional support to her parents rather than receive it from them: "They are both going through so much pain themselves. I feel like *I* need to be the strong one for *them*, but I just can't." Feeling the pull of a role reversal, although she realizes she is ill-equipped to meet her parents' emotional needs, she thinks she needs to parent her parents and feels guilty thinking about her own feelings and needs. Through her sobs, she whispers, "I feel so overwhelmed, with no one to turn to. This is so sad. My life is so sad. I just can't do this. I've lost my home base, my grounding."

Although twenty-two years older than Maria and well established in midlife, Daniel is also experiencing relational changes. He questions what his Adult Child–parent relationships will be with both of his parents. He wonders "if I should not be so truthful with Dad, because I worry that maybe he will pull away from me because of what I think." And Daniel questions what his ongoing relationship with his mother will be like as well. He wonders "if she will pull away from me because she thinks I am siding with Dad." Daniel is also questioning his parents' identities. He shares about his father that his sister "says she doesn't even know who he is anymore, and I honestly wonder who he is too." And he worries about his dad's psychological and financial well-being: "What if Dad doesn't snap out of it and can't work anymore?" Questioning his mom's individual identity, he also has concerns about her psychological and financial well-being: "Then she cries and asks me how I could love someone who hurt her so much. I never saw my mom as the victim type, but she sure does seem like that now." Both he and his sister "worry that our mom won't be able to take care of herself financially even with whatever money she may get from Dad in the divorce." Daniel has many concerns about what the family relationships are currently and what they will be like in the future: "My sister won't attend any family functions if our dad is there. . . . [Mom] says she will never again be in the same room with Dad. . . . It looks like all of our family holidays together aren't going to happen anymore . . . I don't know how to explain all of this to our kids. What if none of this ever changes? It's like our family has completely fallen apart."

Daniel is also caught in a role reversal. Both his parents are relying on him for advice and emotional support, and he struggles with the expectation that he should give rather than receive emotional support. He has been more focused on helping his family members cope than he has been on his own well-being, and he now realizes he is ill-equipped to meet everyone's needs: "I really do feel caught in the middle. Even though I am an adult and have my own family, I don't have a clue how to handle all of this."

GRIEVING THE LOSS OF RELATIONSHIPS

In the next chapter, we will examine the cycle of grief. For now, let's briefly look at how Maria and David are experiencing grief.

Maria's comments indicate that she is experiencing what are often the first stages of grieving: shock, denial, confusion, pain, and sadness. "I'm truly in shock. I can't believe this is happening. I feel like I am living someone else's life. I feel so overwhelmed, with no one to turn to. This is so sad. My life is so sad." And Daniel says, "I have been feeling depressed and irritable. What is going on? I don't have a clue how to handle all of this." When humans experience significant loss, it is common to feel a "psychic" shock, numbness, and confusion. "Surreal" is a word many Adult Children of gray divorce use to describe their feelings because humans are not emotionally equipped to bear the deep pain of such enormous losses all at once.

Adult Children of gray divorce are grieving because they are experiencing significant, multiple losses both immediately and over time, as the realities of their parents' divorces unfold. They lose what they have always known as permanent and constant: their home base; their intact family; their previous Adult Child–parent relationship; their own identity as it relates to family, friends, and community; their meaning of family; and their shared family time, activities, holidays, vacations, and other traditions. Questioning what they thought were constants from their previous lives, they begin to question what else might not be so constant, such as their own relationships. In addition to experiencing the deep pain that ensues from these losses, these Adult Children feel additional pain that their friends, their family members, and even their parents unknowingly thrust upon them. The pain arises from the lack of support and understanding, and the expectation that they should just be okay, shake it off, and get over it. After all, they *are* adults.

3

ATTACHMENT AND ABANDONMENT

Attachment theory offers a lifespan perspective on affectional bonding . . . It suggests a unified conception of love—ranging from love of mother, through love of grade-school classmates and teachers, rock stars and eventually a spouse.

—Lee A. Kirkpatrick, associate professor of psychology, William and Mary University

Carol writes:

Twenty-three-year-old Atsuko's parents sold the family home during their divorce. In our prior two sessions, we had discussed many things, one of which was attachment theory. It helped her understand what she was feeling and why. Wearing wire-rimmed glasses, she looked like a professor twice her age. Her manner of speaking and maturity belied her chronological age. She sat on the loveseat diagonal to me with her shoulders hunched, and Molly lay across her feet. I noticed her calm countenance slightly reddening. Intuiting this shift, Molly arose from her slumber and put her head on Atsuko's left knee. She tilted her head gently upward just enough so that as she gazed at Atsuko, their eyes could meet, as if she were saying, "Hey, Atsuko, what's going on?"

Atsuko inhaled slowly and began. "Molly has the deepest, most meaningful eyes. Has anyone ever said that?"

"Actually, yes," I replied. "Many people have said that—my clients, colleagues, family, and friends. Do you know that saying about the eyes being the windows to the soul? I guess that is one of the many reasons she is a good therapy dog, eh? My clients often say that as *she* gazes deeply into *their* eyes, she also helps *them* look deep into themselves." Molly gives unconditional attention and love to my clients. She interacts with their attachment system, providing the safe haven and secure base that they may or may not have experienced in their childhood, adolescence, and adulthood. This interaction with Molly can also activate their feelings about what losses they are suffering from their parents' divorce.[1]

I watched Atsuko's fingers slowly walk her hands from where they had been resting on the loveseat on each side of her legs. She began stroking Molly's soft ears. She seemed far away and lost in her thoughts. Her face was still red. After a few minutes passed, as though reluctantly returning from a daydream, she replied with a slow, hypnotic tone in her voice, "Yep. Now that you say that about Molly helping me look deep into myself, I realize that she does do that."

I thought to myself, "I think you have been away and looking deep into yourself right now." I noticed she was a little more energized and present in the room. She was still gently stroking Molly's ears, and her lips were beginning to curl upward into a smile. The redness had faded from her face. I wondered what the redness was about.

"You know," she said with a lilt in her tone, "when I arrive here for each session, I'm actually looking forward to seeing her run out to greet me in the waiting area. She always seems so positive and happy to see me. Somehow that lifts my spirits a bit. She is so constant and dependable, you know. Sometimes I think, 'I wish I had Molly's life.' She seems so happy. My life doesn't feel so happy, or constant, or stable."

She stared directly into my eyes for a few seconds before averting her gaze back to Molly, whose head was still on her knee.

"One day, they were what I thought were my happily married parents, and the next day, they were telling me they were divorcing!

I felt crazy! I felt like the earth had opened up, like in those scary movies, you know, and I was being swallowed up along with everything I had ever known in my life. And I was *so* angry at them. When they sold our home, I became even angrier. I remember shouting at them that they had ruined my life and that they were selfish for making me question everything that was stable and secure in my life, past, present, and even future! Looking back now, a year later, I realize that for me our family home symbolized all that had been stable in my life. It was that safe haven that you and I have discussed, that I could always return to in happy times or in times of stress and need. Once they sold it, I no longer had that safe haven. I think knowing about this will also help my parents understand why I was so angry."

As I listened to her, I knew that she had been internalizing what we had been discussing about attachment in childhood, adolescence, and adulthood. She was beginning to shift her thinking about what would help her parents understand her anger; that indicated that she was beginning to integrate her painful feelings into a larger family view that included her parents. I was hopeful about her healing and the eventual healing of her relationship with her parents, assuming they were willing to work on their relationships as well.

She continued. "We had always been so close. I have never forgiven my parents and have been estranged from them since the divorce. You've helped me understand that my anger was my reaction to my loss. That home was my secure base growing up, and it symbolized my attachment to my parents as my safe haven. I felt like they betrayed and abandoned me and discarded all the family traditions and memories that were important in my life growing up. I was so angry about that that I abandoned them by cutting all my ties with them. I hope they will understand why I have been so angry. I don't want to lose them in my life. The last year has been just awful."

"I hope so too, Atsuko. Remember that I told you that understanding is the first step to healing. If you would feel comfortable inviting them in for a family session, we could do that. Often it is a bit easier to have such painful and difficult conversations with a professional like me assisting everyone. We can discuss that later if you want to."

"I'd like that very much. I think I'll call each of them tonight and see if they would be willing to meet with you and me."

As she stood to leave, she seemed lighter. Her shoulders were no longer hunched, and her face seemed less stressed. Through her individual therapy, she had been able to drop some of the burdens she had been carrying for the last year. I wondered if her parents would be willing to meet with us.

WHAT IS GOING ON WITH MY PARENTS AND WHY DO *I* FEEL SO CRAZY?

"You mean what I have been going through is normal, and I am not crazy? I sure feel crazy!" Maria proclaimed to Carol near the end of their first session. And during his first session, Daniel shouted, "Thank you for saying that! Wow! It feels so good to hear that I am not crazy!" Like Maria and Daniel, many Adult Children of gray divorce say they feel crazy.

WHAT IS GOING ON WITH THESE ADULT CHILDREN?

In our work with Adult Children of gray divorce, we have found that educating them about attachment theory and the neuroscience research that supports it helps them understand what they and their parents may be undergoing in the wake of their parents' divorce. Familiarization with the basic tenets of attachment theory is foundational for understanding how childhood relationships with parents or caregivers shape behavior and impact future relationships across the lifespan. Understanding is the first step to better coping and eventual healing. Whether you are the Adult Child or the parent, we encourage you to reflect on what meaning your own attachment style has for you in your relationships with each other, in your other relationships, in your life, and in your healing.

THE DEVELOPMENT OF ATTACHMENT THEORY

Dr. John Bowlby, British psychologist, psychiatrist, and psychoanalyst, and Dr. Mary Ainsworth, American-Canadian developmental psychologist, shared a forty-year relationship of professional collaboration. They are credited with the development of attachment theory. Building on concepts from evolutionary biology, developmental psychology, ethology, and psychoanalysis, Dr. Bowlby introduced the basic tenets of attachment theory in the late 1950s, and he continued formulating and publishing about it for more than thirty years. Dr. Ainsworth contributed her research methodology that made it possible to empirically test some of Dr. Bowlby's theories and expand attachment theory with new concepts. In her work conducting experiments with infants, she developed the theory of attachment styles that apply to children and adults even today.[2]

WHAT ARE ATTACHMENT STYLES AND HOW DO THEY DEVELOP?

Below is a brief description of the four attachment styles.[3]

1. **Secure**: Children's parents or caregivers are available and responsive to their needs. As children, they are confident and feel secure, and as adults, they are also secure and look for trustworthy relationship partners.
2. **Anxious-Avoidant**: Children's parents or caregivers are generally unresponsive to the needs of the child or outright rejecting. These children do not expect others to meet their needs. As adults, they are autonomous and dismissing, seeking only to care for their own needs.

3. **Anxious-Ambivalent**: Children's parents or caregivers seem anxious and are inconsistently available to or rejecting of the children's needs. The children generally feel anxiety when separated from their parents or caregivers. Because the parents of these children are inconsistent caregivers, these children learn not to depend on their parents. As adults, they fear rejection and criticism, have anxiety in relationships, and require a lot of attention.
4. **Disorganized-Disoriented**: The children's parents or caregivers have been neglectful or abusive, or both. These children do not exhibit attachment behaviors, are defensive and untrusting. As adults, they are detached and angry and have very dysfunctional relationships at work and at home.

In a 1983 review of American studies on the first three infant attachment styles, researchers found that 62 percent displayed secure attachment, 23 percent avoidant attachment, and 15 percent anxious-ambivalent attachment.[4]

In the 1970s, researchers began studying adult attachment relationships, and in the late 1980s, attachment theory researchers Cindy Hazan and Phillip Shaver conceptualized adult romantic relationships as an attachment process like that of infant to parent or caregiver. Their research found that adults reported the same three attachment styles in their love relationships that Ainsworth found in infant and young child attachment and that the percentage among the three attachment styles was similar to those in the 1983 review of the US infant attachment studies. Below are very simplified descriptions of the attachment history of each style and the percentages that their research found:[5]

1. **Secure attachment** that is associated with sensitive and responsive primary care (56 percent of research subjects),
2. **Avoidant attachment** that is associated with unresponsive primary care (23 percent–25 percent of research subjects), and

3. **Anxious-ambivalent attachment** that is associated with inconsistent primary care (19 percent–20 percent of research subjects).

Confirming Bowlby's assertion that attachment is a process "from the cradle to the grave," their research also indicates that the research subjects' adult attachment styles had their roots in their perceptions of the quality of their relationships with each parent and in their parents' relationship with each other in their family of origin.[6] Though there are some differences in the age groups, their research indicates that, in general:[7]

- **Secure** subjects describe their relationship with their parents and between their parents as generally warm and supportive; they appear to be confident and open, and they characterize other people as "well-intentioned and good-hearted." They describe their most important love relationships in terms of friendship, trust, and happiness.
- **Avoidant** subjects, at least by middle age, describe their parents as demanding, disrespectful, critical, and uncaring; they characterize themselves as independent and disliked by others, and say that romantic love rarely lasts and is hard to find. They describe their most important love relationship in terms of fear of closeness, jealousy, and lack of acceptance.
- **Anxious/ambivalent** subjects describe their parents as unpredictable, unfair, and intrusive; they lack self-confidence, are prone to fall in love easily and quickly, and characterize other people as unwilling to commit themselves to a long-term relationship. They describe their most important love relationship in terms of jealousy, desire for reciprocation, emotional highs and lows, and intense sexual desire.

They also note that secure subjects' relationships last more than twice as long, on average, as insecure subjects' relationships, and that the divorce rate is significantly higher for the two insecure

groups (anxious-ambivalent and avoidant). The two insecure groups also score significantly higher on measures of loneliness.

MORE ABOUT ATTACHMENT

Attachment theory is one of the most influential and widely researched theories in understanding the emotional and social development of children and the love relationships of adults. A 2013 journal article noted that a literature search using the keyword "attachment" on PsycInfo, the database of the American Psychology Association, yielded over fifteen thousand titles.[8] Attachment theory presaged Dr. Dan Siegel's words in chapter 2: "Relationships are the most important part of our having well-being in being human. It's that simple. And it's that important."

Dr. Bowlby posited that humans have a biological predisposition to form attachment bonds that are strong, persistent, emotional ties that we develop in relationships with other human beings who are of primary importance to us. These attachment bonds ensure that we have a safe haven where we can grow and thrive, and from which we can explore. Attachment bonds also ensure that we have a secure base where we can return for comfort and support during times of need, stress, and crisis. He states that:

> human beings of all ages are happiest and able to deploy their talents to best advantage when they are confident that, standing behind them, there are one or more trusted persons who will come to their aid should difficulties arise.[9]

He describes a *trusted person* as someone who ensures a person's safety and security by providing:

1. a safe haven to which he or she can retreat in times of need, and

2. a secure base from which to explore (to learn, discover, work, play, engage in challenging activities, develop relationships with peers, and grow as an individual).[10]

During childhood, a trusted person is usually a person's parent, parents, or important caregiver. In adulthood, a trusted person is most often a person's spouse or partner. In order to foster safety and security, a trusted person recognizes and respects the other's need for a safe haven and secure base. In addition, the trusted person understands the other's need to explore and seek out the trusted person in times of need.

Dr. Bowlby stated that attachment bonds are person specific. Feelings, interactions, and memories are the threads that weave the tapestry of each unique attachment bond with each person. He stressed that emotions are strongly associated with attachment. Below he describes intense feelings associated with attachment bonds—feelings of love and affection from children to parents, from parents to children, from romantic partners to each other, and grieving, anxiety, sorrow, and anger:

> Many of the most intense emotions arise during the formation, the maintenance, the disruptions, and the renewal of attachment relationships. The formation of a bond is described as falling in love, maintaining a bond as loving someone, and losing a partner as grieving over someone. Similarly, threat of loss arouses anxiety and actual loss gives rise to sorrow; while each of these situations is likely to arouse anger. The unchallenged maintenance of a bond is experienced as a source of security and the renewal of a bond as a source of joy.[11]

Throughout his trilogy on attachment and loss, Dr. Bowlby emphasized that "from the cradle to the grave" attachment bonds ensure our safety, security, and even survival, and that the availability of responsive, dependable, and reciprocal attachment-bond relationships is critical to healthy development *from the cradle to the grave*[12] (authors' italics).

WHAT ABOUT ADULT ATTACHMENT?

Research spanning the last three decades indicates that adult attachment styles significantly impact how adults feel, think, and behave in relationships. Debra Zeifman and Cindy Hazan's research found that the majority of adults view their romantic partner to be their principal attachment figure.[13] They also found that adults who were in romantic relationships of less than two years and those without romantic partners named their parents as the people whose presence provided for them a base of safety and security and whose absence was the most distressing to them, while the majority of adults who were in romantic relationships for at least two years named their romantic partners as the people whose presence provided for them a base of safety and security and whose absence was the most distressing for them.[14] Considering this information is helpful when examining how parental divorce affects Adult Children who are in various stages of romantic relationships.

FURTHER RESEARCH THAT APPLIES TO ADULT CHILDREN AND THEIR PARENTS

One of the central tenets of attachment theory is that when the attachment figure (parent or caregiver) is unavailable, the infant or child exhibits signs of distress such as crying, calling, and seeking that can even progress to anxiety, anger, and despair.

Applying this tenet to adolescents and adults, researchers have found that adolescents and adults who suffer disapproval, criticism, hostility, or rejection by their love relationship partners often exhibit similar signs of distress and that these rejection experiences are quite close to the experience of physical pain. Functional MRI (fMRI) studies found that even when the participants experience rejection and exclusion by strangers, consistent heightened activation of the regions of the brain associated with physical pain occurs. Additional research indicates that the emotional reactions of adults experiencing the breakup of romantic partnerships can be extremely intense: loss of positive self-image, heightened physiological arousal, and negative effects on psychological and physical health.[15] Furthermore, numerous studies support the notion that when a person interacts with an accepting, loving other, he experiences a positive boost in self-esteem, and conversely, when ignored or rejected, he experiences a significant and painful drop in self-esteem.[16]

WHAT THIS MEANS FOR ADULT CHILDREN OF GRAY DIVORCE AND FOR THEIR PARENTS

Attachment bonds are strong, enduring, and resistant to change. Divorce ruptures one of the most significant and powerful attachment bonds that adults form—the bond with the marriage partner. Sadly, divorce also frequently negatively affects the attachment bonds between Adult Children and their parents. Throughout this book, you will hear stories from Adult Children and from parents about this bond being distressed or broken during and after the parental divorce.

Divorce threatens the feelings of safety, security, and survival the attachment bond has ensured, and impacts current and future relationships. It is understandable then that humans tenaciously cling to their attachment bonds, both consciously and unconsciously, and that when they experience the losses that ensue from divorce, distress and anxiety about being separated from the attachment figure arise.

> *The greatest fury comes from the wound where love once issued forth.*
> —Pat Conroy, American novelist

UNDERSTANDING IS PART OF HEALING, SO WHAT ARE YOUR PARENTS EXPERIENCING?

Studies have found that except when compared to those in the unhappiest marriages:

> separated and divorced individuals have higher rates of physical and mental health disturbances than married individuals, and often higher rates even than widowed individuals . . . separated and divorced individuals experience increased rates of acute (infectious diseases, respiratory illnesses) and chronic (diabetes, heart disease) physical illnesses, physical limitations, psychopathology, depression, suicide, homicide, violence, substance abuse (alcoholism), accidents and injuries, and disease-caused mortality. . . . Divorced individuals also report lower levels of happiness, life satisfaction, self-esteem, self-confidence, and competence.[17]

Despite the negative effects of divorce, findings indicate that even though most divorcing individuals suffer through a period of physical and emotional turmoil, most of them successfully cope with divorce and some report positive outcomes such as personal growth and life satisfaction. Additional positive news for the divorced is that although the divorced generally fare worse than those who are married, they report having higher morale, fewer physical problems, fewer depressive symptoms, and greater life satisfaction, self-esteem, and overall health than those in the unhappiest marriages. Lastly, research also indicates that those who were in the unhappiest marriages often feel a sense of relief and hopefulness that their future can be better.[18]

ATTACHMENT STYLES AFFECT THE ABILITY TO COPE WITH STRESS AND DISTRESS

Since Hazan and Shaver's 1987 research, there now exists more than three decades of research about adult attachment indicating the wide-ranging effects of adult attachment not only on human emotional, behavioral, and cognitive systems, but also on immune and endocrine systems, neurobiology, and physical health. The body of research is comprised of a variety of research methods such as behavioral observations, interviews, questionnaires, physiological and neuroimaging assessments, and implicit measures of cognitive and emotional processes. Many studies suggest genetic factors may contribute to some individual-difference variance in attachment anxiety (although perhaps not in avoidance).[19] This research supports previous hypotheses that the secure attachment style provides individuals with the best coping mechanisms to deal with stress and distress, and that the insecure attachment styles (anxious and avoidant) can inhibit effective coping and increase people's risk of serious emotional and physical problems.[20]

Specifically, adults with *secure* attachment histories are able to seek personal and social support from family members, friends and community members that helps them cope, because their relationship templates that they developed in childhood and adolescence provide them with the experience and belief that they can do so, and that they can depend on their support systems. Those with *insecure* attachment histories (*anxious-ambivalent* and *avoidant* attachment styles) generally view life's stressors as more threatening and have developed coping styles that defend them from these stressors. Those high in attachment anxiety view themselves as less capable of coping, report greater distress, and may be lacking support systems. Those high in avoidant tendencies use distancing to cope, do not turn to others for support, and report greater hostility.[21]

Attachment theory helps Adult Children of gray divorce understand why they often name shock as their first reaction upon hearing that their parents are divorcing. Why shock? When we explore the stages of loss and grieving in the next chapter, we will see that shock is often the first reaction of many people when hearing about a loss, any loss. In addition to disrupting the marital attachment bond, divorce may disrupt and even destroy another significant and powerful attachment bond—the bond between parent and child. Adult children do not expect that this bond will ever be broken.

When this occurs, it can disrupt or even destroy the feelings of safety, security, and survival that the attachment bond has ensured for the Adult Child. Indeed, many Adult Children of gray divorce echo Maria when she says, "Home will never be the same again . . . Everything feels empty. We were like the Three Musketeers, you know. All for one and one for all." Maria is describing the loss of attachment, safety, and security that her family of origin provided for her.

CAN ADULT ATTACHMENT STYLES CHANGE?

Bowlby emphasized that attachment styles are neither linear nor static, because the human attachment system responds to environmental situations during developmental stages. Indeed, research has found that adult attachment styles can change across the lifespan.[22] For example, when adults are in relationships that are more attachment secure than those during their childhood or adolescence, their attachment style can shift from insecure to secure. Conversely, if securely attached adults are in relationships with those who have insecure attachment styles, their secure attachment style can shift to insecure.

In his book *The Neuroscience of Human Relationships*, psychologist and professor Louis Cozolino writes, "Without mutually stimulating interactions, people and neurons wither and die . . . in humans it is called depression, grief, and suicide. From birth until death, each of us needs others who seek us out, show interest in discovering who we are, and help us feel safe. . . . *Relationships are our natural habitat*"[23] (authors' italics).

Attesting to the importance of the parent–child bond, in her 2012 research about parent–child relationships and mid- to late-life divorce Greenwood found that about half of the Adult Children, who at the time of the study were ages eighteen to fifty-four, reported having a strained relationship during the parental divorce with one or both parents.[24] Many of these Adult Children decided to stop communicating with their parents. Yet, eventually these Adult Children were willing to resolve the issues that led to the period of not speaking.[25] Their willingness to resolve the issues with their parents is compelling evidence of the parent–child attachment bond, even in adulthood.

Another study of college students that speaks to the benefits of intact parent–child attachment bonds revealed that students with highly involved parents excelled in many areas, including higher levels of engagement in effective educational practices in college, deep learning activities, self-reported educational gains, and satisfaction with their college experience.[26]

Carol writes:

Let's see how the strong attachment bonds between Atsuko and her parents motivated them to repair and heal their broken relationships.

Atsuko and her parents, Hana and Haruto, met with me for several sessions. I educated them about attachment theory, and how the occurrences during the divorce had strained their attachment bonds and fractured their relationships. All three were willing to do "whatever it takes" to repair and heal their relationships. I suggested that her father and mother meet individually with EMDR (Eye Movement Desensitization and Reprocessing) therapists to heal their wounds from the divorce and Atsuko's alienation from them. (EMDR is a noninvasive, evidence-based psychotherapy that helps clients heal from psychological and physical trauma.) They did so without hesitation. Atsuko also met with me for several EMDR sessions to heal her wounds from the divorce.

Our last family session depicts the healing that can occur when each family member is willing to participate in individual therapy to facilitate the restructuring of the family. Hana spoke first. "Atsuko, I realize that your father and I yanked the rug out from under you by selling our family home so quickly. I assumed that since you were technically an adult, you would not be affected by our divorce. I realize now that I was completely ignorant about how our divorce would affect you, and I understand why you pulled away from us. You must have felt that we didn't understand at all what you were going through, and that we were focused only on ourselves. I am so sorry that I was so ignorant about how our divorce would affect you."

Taking a slow, deep breath, while absorbing her mother's words, Atsuko replied, "Mom, thanks for saying all of that. It feels like you really do understand what I was feeling and have been going through."

Next Haruto spoke. "I echo what your mom said, and I'm embarrassed to say that I was so preoccupied with getting all of the tasks of the divorce done, so that your mother and I could move on with our lives, I didn't for one moment think about you. In my individual therapy I have learned how easy it is for parents to forget about their adult children, since they are not part of the legal divorce. Sadly, you have been part of the emotional divorce. I apologize for how I handled everything, and for the pain my self-centeredness caused you. I promise to do better in the future."

Tears were now gently falling down all three faces. I sensed their deep pain. I also felt that they had begun to repair their strained attachment bonds and heal their broken relationships.

Atsuko replied, "Dad, thanks for saying all of that. I love you both very much. I'm sorry that my hurt turned into anger, and I apologize for hurting you both by pulling away. You say that you plan to remain friendly with each other. It would mean a lot to me if we can still do a few things together as a family, like meeting for lunch, going to Nisei Week, the Family Festivals, and other activities at the Japanese American National Museum that we have attended every year. I want us to be still able to share our heritage together. Would you be willing to do that?"

Hana and Haruto eagerly agreed.

Atsuko's story is a poignant depiction of the pain that Adult Children experience. It also depicts how parental unawareness affects their Adult Children. Her story also illustrates what can happen when Adult Children take the first step in healing their fractured parent–child relationship.

In chapter 4, we examine how attachment style is one crucial factor in how humans grieve and heal.

4

SHOCK AND THEN GRIEVING

Divorce has many witnesses, many victims. . . . Each divorce is the death of a small civilization.
—Pat Conroy, American novelist

"It was a fine cry—loud and long—but it had no bottom and it had no top, just circles and circles of sorrow." This is Pulitzer Prize–winning novelist Toni Morrison's depiction of grief.

When we first met twenty-year-old Maria in chapter 2, she had just learned that her parents were divorcing. She was at the beginning of her long journey as an Adult Child of gray divorce. During her session with Carol a week later, Maria repeated what she had said in their first session. Many Adult Children of gray divorce report the same feelings at this stage of their journey—shock, disbelief, destabilization, loss, feeling overwhelmed, aloneness, and sadness. "I'm still in shock! I can't believe this is happening. *How* can this be happening?

"Mom picked me up at the airport last week when I flew home for summer vacation. I was so happy that I was going to be home for the summer. On the flight home, I imagined the three of us doing some of our fun summer traditions like driving up to San Francisco to visit Grandma and Grandpa; going to the outlet malls, Dad patiently going from store to store with Mom and me, picking out clothes and shoes that he thought we would like; riding bicycles across the Golden State Bridge, and having a picnic together in the Golden Gate Park." A soft smile appeared as she recounted their happy times together.

"Mom and Dad were supposed to be there, arm and arm, waiting for me to come down the escalator to the baggage claim area. When I saw only Mom standing there, I felt my smile instantly fall off of my face and crash painfully into the pit of my stomach. Mom's face was furrowed with new worry lines, all of which ran downward. She looked like she had aged ten years! The first words out of her mouth were, 'Your father's left us.' I said, 'What do you mean he left us? Where did he go?'"

I listened attentively to Maria recount the life-changing moments, and I noticed the color drain from her face and neck.

Maria continued, "Suddenly I felt lightheaded, and my chest was tightening. I couldn't breathe! I wanted to hear what Mom was saying, and at the same time I didn't want to hear it, you know? I could see Mom's face, and her lips were moving, but I couldn't hear her words. It seemed like hours passed that then became days, while I stood there looking at her but not hearing her words. It was like her words were slogging through a thick, muddy marshland. She seemed very far away. I could hear her saying my name over and over again. 'M-a-r-i-a, M-a-r-i-a . . . M-a-r-i-a, a-r-e y-o-u o-k-a-y? Y-o-u a-r-e w-h-i-t-e a-s a g-h-o-s-t!' Looking back, I realize I felt like what a ghost would feel like, you know, like in the movies—surreal, floating a bit, with no feet to firmly plant on the ground. I seemed very far away from her. It was eerie. Then I heard her repeating over and over, 'Your father's been having an affair. He has a girlfriend. He has left us forever! Your father's been having an affair. He has a girlfriend. He has left us forever! Your father's been having . . ." Her voice trailed off into an unhappy silence.

Maria sat statue still, her eyes fixed on my oak rolltop desk across the expanse between where she was sitting on the loveseat and where the desk stood on the wall across from her. I knew that she was not really seeing the desk. Her eyes had the far-off stare of a person who is physically occupying one space, though the rest of her was far away. She was blinking very slowly, as though in a hypnotic trance.

"I feel like I am living someone else's life! This is so sad. My life is so sad. *I'm* so sad! Is this normal? Why am I so sad? Some days I can't stop crying. I am not sleeping. I'm not hungry. My thoughts are scattered all over the place. I can't stay focused. How am I going to be able to go back to college this fall and focus on my studies?" She struggled to form the words that described the poignancy. Almost whispering, she haltingly said, "When . . . Mom . . . told me . . . that Dad had left us . . ." The words stuck in her throat as if the reality was too much to acknowledge. Suddenly, she burst forth, "My family, my history, and my future have changed forever. I've lost the only family I have ever known. It feels like someone has died. But no one has died! Well, actually, my family is dead!"

Maria burst into sobs, the kind that rise slowly from deep in the psyche and gush forth uncontrollably. Sensing Maria's pain, Molly awoke from her slumber and gently placed her head in Maria's lap. Maria continued sobbing while she softly stroked Molly's velvety ears and head. Minutes passed. The only sound in the room was Maria crying. I silently witnessed Maria's pain. Finally, her river of tears subsided. She inhaled deeply and again whispered sadly, "My family is dead."

> *Tears are the silent language of grief.*
> —Voltaire, French Enlightenment writer, historian, and philosopher

Divorce is often compared to death. American actor and novelist William Shatner said, "Divorce is probably as painful as death."[1] And author D. A. Wolf wondered why, even though heartbreak accompanies both widowhood and divorce, "we demonstrate more compassion when it comes to the former, though the ghosts of the latter still walk the planet."[2] Adult Children and their divorcing parents are the ghosts still walking the planet.

The *Merriam-Webster Dictionary* defines grief as "a deep and poignant distress caused by, or as if by, bereavement" and defines bereavement as "the state or fact of being bereaved or deprived of something or someone."[3] We grieve when we are feeling the excruciating loss that overwhelms us in death's wake. Grief is our response to this loss. Divorce is the death of a marriage, the death of "couplehood" and a family living together in one residence. Sadly, often divorce also includes the death of the extended family, friends, and community networks, gatherings, and traditions; it also includes the death of hopes, plans, and dreams for the future. Divorce is the rock that drops into life's lake, and the ripples of grieving wash over everyone in the family's circle.

For Adult Children of gray divorce one of the most painful aspects of their parents' divorce is the belief that the majority of people hold, that since they are already adults, they are "too old to hurt."[4] Yet, recent research found that 51 percent of gray divorce parents reported that their emerging Adult Children were "unsupportive," "somewhat upset," or "very upset" about their parents' divorce. Even among Adult Children who were supportive of their parents' divorce, the parents perceived that 67 percent were very sad and 19 percent were devastated when their parents divorced.[5] Psychologist and university professor Joshua Ehrlich writes, "Divorcing grown-ups often have no idea how to bear grief; some do not even know they *are* grieving. . . . We can think of the people, then, who approach therapists for help around divorce . . . as stuck or partially stuck around the tasks of mourning."[6] Ehrlich's book is a helpful addition to the literature about divorce and loss and he masterfully educates about the mourning process for parents and their children. Although he writes about parents and minor children, his words also apply to divorcing parents and their Adult Children.

When divorce occurs, often the last topic to be considered is grieving. And yet every aspect of divorce involves loss and grieving, and for many, it is often inconsolable loss and grieving. Our culture gives little acknowledgment to this. Grieving is the invisible travel companion on the journey called divorce—for the one who is leaving the marriage, for the one being left, for the children of the marriage, for their extended family members, and for their friend and community networks and support systems.

The grieving is inevitable. It is also invisible because most of those who are experiencing the divorce (whether it is their own divorce, the divorce of their parents, or the divorce of their extended family members, friends, or community members) do not think of what they are experiencing as grieving. Most often those touched by divorce say they are feeling shocked, angry, sad, and powerless—all feelings that arise during grieving.

GRAY DIVORCE IS A FAMILY EVENT THAT WASHES ACROSS GENERATIONAL, FRIEND, AND COMMUNITY SUPPORT-SYSTEM LINES

During separation and divorce, both members of the couple are experiencing significant losses too, although both are often unaware of grief, their invisible companion. For the parents, the losses may include the loss of their spouse, who may have been their best friend for decades; loss of their nuclear and extended family, friend, and community relationships and support systems; loss of dreams they had for their current stage of life, raising children together, weddings, births, celebrations and family traditions; loss of the family home; and loss of financial security.

For the Adult Children, the losses can feel overwhelming: the loss of their identity, as they wonder whether their childhood and adolescence were based on a foundation of lies and whether the appearance their family showed to the world was a façade; the loss of the permanence of their intact nuclear family, extended family, friend, and community relationships and support; the loss of emotional and sometimes financial support; the loss of accustomed family togetherness that they have experienced for decades; and the loss of their dreams about celebrations, family traditions, graduations, weddings, and births.

Other support-system members, comprised of extended family members—grandparents, aunts, uncles, cousins, friends, and community members, are often grieving the lost relationship connections if they feel the pull to "choose sides." They are at a loss for what to say to the Adult Children. What they do say can make the Adult Children feel worse rather than better. It's common for Adult Children to hear, "Well, look at the positive side. At least they waited until you are an adult. They didn't divorce when you were six years old. You didn't have to grow up going back and forth between your mom and dad's houses. You'll be fine. You have your own life now. It's just a bump in the road." Even professionals, who are unfamiliar with the complex dynamics of divorce, can make similar statements and be insensitive to and invalidate Adult Children's feelings and experiences.

> *Most of us think of ourselves as thinking creatures that feel, but we are actually feeling creatures that think.*
> —Jill Bolte Taylor, neuroanatomist and author

Carol writes:

Maria's face was flushed, and her eyes swollen from crying. "How could Dad do this? He has abandoned Mom and me! Why? To be with some other woman? I don't even know who he is anymore. He was always my superhero. I was Daddy's little girl. Who am I now? What is my place?" Once again, sobs overcame her.

Research explains what Maria is experiencing. Grief is a common experience in job loss and divorce, and it is not unique to just the death of a loved one. A study suggests that the experience of grief may be correlated to a loss of self-defining roles, like relationships with parents, and the ensuing process of accommodating to that loss.[7] Attachment theory, discussed in chapter 3, provides understanding as well. Maria has lost her intact family that is the secure base, that she can return to, and she has lost her father, one of her two trusted people. In addition, when a parent has been involved in an affair, it adds another layer of grieving to the losses about the divorce and can intensify the loyalty double binds that Adult Children usually feel. Often daughters have more difficulty dealing with their parents' divorce when their father has had an affair.

Maria bemoans that she has lost her intact family, her identity as one of the three musketeers, and the father she thought she had for her entire twenty years of life. Maria is now catapulted into a new role she is not prepared for because she feels more responsible for her mother, whom she sees as the victim of her father's affair. She is mourning all of these losses. Figure 4.1 depicts the losses from divorce that parents and their Adult Children can experience.

> *To love means to open ourselves to the negative as well as the positive—to grief, sorrow, and disappointment as well as to joy, fulfillment, and an intensity of consciousness we did not know was possible before.*
> —Rollo May

Psychosocial education is part of any healing process, whether people obtain this education on their own by reading books, visiting websites, and talking with friends and family, or by working with professionals such as therapists, clergy, and hospital and community educators. Understanding the many variables that affect us during life's challenging times, such as divorce, provides one aspect of what we need to heal. There are as many ways of grieving as there are people. There is no one size fits all. Next, are some of the theories of grieving that Adult Children find useful.

> *There are few blows to the human spirit so great as the loss of someone near and dear.*
> —John Bowlby, MD

THEORIES OF GRIEF AND BEREAVEMENT

Undoubtedly the most widely known grief theory is Dr. Elisabeth Kübler-Ross's five-stage theory of grief that she described in her classic book *On Death and Dying*, published in 1969.[8] While her book was about facing one's own death or the death of a loved one, the stages she described have been used to describe losses that arise from any life-changing event in which a person feels profound loss, such as divorce, loss of one's home or job, and experiencing a trauma. She later explained that she did not intend the stages to be

Figure 4.1. Losses from Divorce. ***Illustration by Anja Hughes.***

viewed as linear, one coming after the other, because people could often move back and forth between them. She described the stages as:

- **Denial** – "I'm in shock! This can't be happening to me! I'm not going to talk about this. I'd rather just be alone."
- **Anger** – "Why is this happening to me? How could you do this to me?" Often this anger is directed outward at others.
- **Bargaining** – "If I do this, maybe I can make it go away." This stage is about having irrational hope that they can change something that is unchangeable.
- **Depression** – "I give up. Nothing matters now."
- **Acceptance** – "I am willing to accept this new reality."

Less widely known, especially to the lay audience, is Dr. John Bowlby's theory of grieving, developed from his attachment theory that states that humans form strong attachment bonds with important people in their lives. Many theories and models of grief have built upon Dr. Bowlby's work. He wrote "Grief and Mourning in Infancy and Early Childhood," published in 1960 in the professional journal *Psychoanalytic Study of the Child.*[9] He asserted that adults' mourning processes were similar to the anxiety he found that children experienced when separated from their mothers. In 1969, he published the first book of his groundbreaking *Attachment and Loss* trilogy, and in 1980 he published the third and final book of the trilogy titled *Loss: Sadness and Depression.* Bowlby's theory emphasized the survival purpose of attachment bonds, and this provided a plausible explanation for grief responses like searching and anger. Separation, divorce, and death break attachment bonds. Bowlby explained that when attachment bonds are broken, adults respond to the separation and loss, and that grief is the natural reaction.[10]

Grief psychiatrist Dr. Colin Murray Parkes joined Bowlby at his research institute in 1962. Dr. Parkes states in his book *Bereavement: Studies of Grief in Adult Life*, which sets forth his grief theory, "From that time until Bowlby's death in 1992 our collaboration was close and I made use of many of his ideas . . . I am no longer sure which of us deserves the credit (or blame) for originating many of the ideas that make up the overall theory on these pages. All that I can say, with confidence, is that my debt to John Bowlby is great."[11]

In 1970, Parkes and Bowlby published their theory on the four phases of grief:[12]

- **Numbness** that allows a person to cope initially with the loss: "This is unreal! I feel numb."
- **Searching and Yearning** that includes a variety of emotions such as anger, anxiety, uncertainty, guilt, sorrow, restlessness, and confusion. The person searches for meaning and why the loss has occurred: "I yearn and search for the comfort I had before this loss occurred. Why has this happened?"
- **Despair and Depression** that causes the person to feel that everything is surreal, and nothing feels right. The person may want to be alone, withdraw from activities, feel hopeless, and lack self-care: "I have lost all hope. Nothing will ever be the same."
- **Reorganization** wherein the person begins to realize the reality of the loss, accept that her old reality is gone forever, and have increased energy and interest in activities. The person still has moments of grieving, but is moving on with life: "I will find ways to integrate this loss and the memories we shared into my own identity and life."

Bowlby stated that these phases were not discrete and that individuals may oscillate back and forth between any two of them, and he noted that for grieving to result in a favorable outcome, the bereaved person must be able to express his feelings of yearning, anger, sadness, fear of loneliness, desires for sympathy and support, and that the person may need the support of another trusted person.[13] Contrary to Dr. Bowlby's assertion that in order for grieving to result in a favorable outcome, a bereaved person must be able to express his feelings, Dr. George Bonanno, a psychology professor at Columbia University Teachers College, found that many bereaved individuals will exhibit little or no grief, and that these individuals are not cold and unfeeling or lacking in attachment but, instead, are capable of genuine resilience in the case of loss.[14]

Many people ask how long should grieving take. The answer is that there is not one answer that applies to everyone because many variables affect the grieving process. Because of these variables, sometimes people experience what is known as "complicated grief" that feels like being in an ongoing, heightened state of mourning that prevents a person from healing.[15] Nevertheless, as early as 1964, Dr. Parkes's study of widows found a sharp rise in the number of psychiatric complaints in the first six months of their widowhood, and that thereafter their distress returned to a level similar to his control group of nonwidowed women.[16]

Findings similar to Parkes's 1964 study come from a 2019 study by Dr. Paul Maciejewski of Yale University School of Medicine, and his colleagues. They found "that in the circumstance of natural death, the normal response involves primarily acceptance and yearning for the deceased . . . all of the negative grief indicators are in decline by approximately 6 months postloss. The persistence of these negative emotions beyond 6 months is therefore likely to reflect a more difficult than average adjustment."[17]

Another grief theorist, Dr. J. William Worden, professor of psychology at Harvard University, developed four tasks of mourning theory that provides a motivational framework for grief. The tasks are designed to help the person work through grief:

- **Acceptance** that the loss has occurred.
- **Experiencing the Pain**, during which the person works through the pain of grief by talking and acknowledging the loss and how he feels physically, emotionally, and spiritually.
- **Adjusting** to the accompanying losses such as loss of family home, loss of identity, and financial losses.
- **Letting Go** and investing his energy in his life, activities, and relationships.[18]

Like Bowlby, Parkes, and Kübler-Ross, Worden reminds us that grief is not linear, nor are the tasks intended to be linear, and that a person may revisit a task as needed.

Dr. Bonanno also states that there is now strong prospective evidence that associates resilience to loss with the experience and expression of positive emotion.[19] His research supports the idea that many individuals will exhibit little or no grief, and that they are not cold and unfeeling or lacking attachment but, instead, are capable of genuine resilience in the face of loss. Almost half of the participants in this study had low levels of depression, both prior to the loss and through eighteen months of bereavement, and had relatively few grief symptoms—for example, intense yearning for the deceased spouse—during bereavement.[20]

Although not specifically about grieving, the research of Dr. W. Thomas Boyce, professor and chief of the Division of Developmental Medicine at the University of California–San Francisco, echoes the research of Dr. Bonanno and his colleagues. In Boyce's 2019 book *The Orchid and the Dandelion*, he writes about his almost four decades of research as a developmental pediatrician and describes his discovery that genetic makeup *and* environment shape behavior. His research indicates a pattern that appears to be true for children around the world and continues into adulthood: bbout 15 to 20 percent of children experience over half of psychological illnesses, while the remaining children are comparatively healthy. He calls the approximately 80 percent of children dandelions, who are healthy, hardy, and resilient and can thrive in any environment. The other approximately 20 percent of children he calls orchids, who are fragile, sensitive, and susceptible, but who can thrive more than other children if given the right environment.[21] Perhaps his research findings explain the varied reactions and coping capabilities of Adult Children and their parents to the losses that ensue from divorce. Maybe the "orchids" are the Adult Children and parents who have the most difficulty dealing with their emotional reactions to parental divorce, while the "dandelions" continue to adapt and thrive in the new divorce environment.

Specific to divorcing couples is the work of Dr. Robert Emery, professor of psychology at the University of Virginia and respected expert in the divorce field. He differentiates grieving an irrevocable loss like death from grieving a revocable loss like divorce, where the possibility of reconciliation remains for the former spouses and the children. Based on his case observations and research, he developed a cyclical theory of grief in divorce that describes the cycle of grief for the divorcing couple. He postulated that the emotions of the spouses swing between feelings of love, anger, and sadness, diminishing over time. In our work with Adult Children of divorcing parents, we see that they often swing through cycles similar to what Emery found. He also stated that the uncertainties associated with divorce mean that grief in divorce can be delayed, interrupted, repeated, prolonged, and unresolved.[22] Applying his findings beyond divorcing couples to their Adult Children indicates why it can be more difficult for Adult Children to process and accept what they are experiencing during and after their parents' divorce.

There are other grief theories that are beyond the scope of this book that Adult Children of gray divorce may find helpful.[23]

HOW THESE THEORIES OF GRIEVING CAN ASSIST ADULT CHILDREN OF GRAY DIVORCE

Remember that understanding is the first step in healing—for you and your family. Assess how the grief theories help you understand what you have been experiencing and where you are in your grief process. Also, ascertain where your nuclear family and extended family and support-system members are in their grief process. You are all on your own paths of grieving and eventual healing, and the paths and timeframes are likely not the same. Grieving takes time, sometimes a lot of time, and it takes its own path. Although it is often difficult to maintain an attitude of hope while grieving, hope is essential to help us heal in the grieving process.

Next, we explore the stages of adult development and the experiences of Adult Children in each stage.

> *Some people think that it's holding on that makes one strong; sometimes it's letting go.*
> —Author unknown

5

STAGES OF ADULT DEVELOPMENT

The secret of change is to focus all of your energy not on fighting the old, but on building the new.
—Socrates, Classical Greek philosopher

One in three parental divorces take place postchildhood,[1] and a significant number of divorces occur when children reach late adolescence or early adulthood. When parents reach midlife, they are often experiencing what is known as the "empty nest" phenomenon. Their children are becoming more independent, leaving adolescence, and entering young adulthood. It is a time when parents may be reflecting on their own lives and reevaluating their life goals. Their marriage may not have been the happy one they had imagined during their courtship. Whether or not they have fully acknowledged it, they may have remained married "for the children."

During the early decades of marriage, families establish traditions and rituals for holidays, birthdays, graduations, and weddings that create a sense of continuity and predictability. As the years go by, celebrating these traditions and rituals make family members feel connected to the family. Later-life divorces disrupt these decades-long family patterns, and family members may begin to question the stability and continuity of the family.

Divorce is the second-highest stressor in adult life, second only to the death of a spouse.[2] If this is true, why is it so common for divorcing parents to assume that their Adult Children are "okay," simply because they are adults? In the midst of their parents' later-life divorce, Adult Children are navigating their own life stage transitions. What they are experiencing during and after their parents' divorce can stress and even impede their adult development.

THE STAGES OF ADULT DEVELOPMENT

Several theories of human development incorporate adult development.[3] Of course, it is impossible to categorize humans into discrete stages based solely on their ages, although the descriptions below provide a framework of adult development across the lifespan and can clarify what Adult Children of gray divorce who are navigating various stages of adult development may be experiencing.

Early Adulthood: Late Teens/Early Twenties to Forties

Subsumed within this stage are two stages—Emerging Adulthood and Young Adulthood. Two recent trends now extend emerging adulthood to twenty-five years old or older, specifically, late teens through twenty-five-plus years old: the trend for Emerging Adults to obtain additional training and education to offer better employment opportunities in work and professional markets and the trend to delay marriage.[4] Emerging Adults aren't yet fully independent adults, and the current trends have extended Adult Children's dependence on parents.[5] In fact, between 1960 and 2010, the number of young men eighteen to twenty-four years old who lived at home increased from 10 percent to 57 percent, and there was a similar increase for young women aged eighteen to twenty-four.[6] Payne found that in 2010 about half of Emerging Adults eighteen to twenty-four years old live with a parent.[7] High-school graduates and college-age Adult Children are especially vulnerable during this stage because they are transitioning from adolescence into the embryonic phase of adulthood. Their culture views them as "adults," and expects them to cope as "adults" with the shocks and aftershocks of their parents' divorce roiling through every facet of their lives.

Yet it is likely that these Adult Children are still emotionally and financially dependent on their parents. Residing with or being dependent on one or both parents can create loyalty conflicts for them, and they can feel caught between their parents.[8]

Research has consistently indicated that interparental conflict is harmful to children in all family forms, whether in two-parent families or in divorced families.[9] Moreover, being pulled into interparental conflict and feeling torn between contentious parents are risks factors for children of divorce. The gender of the Adult Child plays a role in loyalty conflicts in that females are enculturated to be kindship keepers. Research found that daughters of all ages were more likely than sons to report feeling caught between their parents and suggests that parents are more likely to put pressure on daughters than on sons to take sides in parental disputes.[10]

Emerging Adult Children often feel torn between wanting to assist their parents and other family members and starting their own career and personal relationships. They may feel loyalty conflicts when they attempt to balance the amount of time they spend with each parent. Loyalty conflicts are common among Adult Children in all stages of development. They can feel conflicted, drained, and exhausted when they return home because the stable home life they once knew has vanished. The emotional turmoil of their parents' divorce or postdivorce relationship can impede their ability to focus on their friendships and studies. Making life-altering decisions can be extremely difficult for them, especially considering the kinds of decisions high-school graduate and college-age young adults are facing: first jobs, first homes, first long-term significant other relationships, and more. It is also a time when they may be searching to find their lifelong relationships with a significant other, yet, in light of their parents' divorce, "they are haunted by powerful ghosts from their childhoods that tell them that they, like their parents, will not succeed."[11]

Maria in chapter 2 is also an Emerging Adult. She is an accomplished twenty-year-old college student, who is still dependent on her parents emotionally and financially. After describing the shock that she felt when her mother told her that her father had left them, she describes the conflict and guilt she feels, wondering if her parents, who are going through so much pain, will still be able to help and support her. Although she feels alone and overwhelmed in her grief at the loss of her "home base," she thinks she should be able to be the strong one for her parents. She is also in a loyalty bind. Although she was "Daddy's little girl" and she loves her father deeply, she is angry at her father for abandoning her mother and her. She feels drawn to supporting and protecting her mother, whom she believes is the unwilling victim of her father's actions. Feeling unstable and disoriented, swirling in the sudden changes in her young life, she wonders how she will be able to be focused on her studies when she returns to college in the fall. And, like many Adult Children of gray divorce, losing the stability and security that her parents' marriage provided her—the one constant in her ever-evolving new life—she has begun to question her ability to have a healthy and lasting love relationship. In this stage of her young life, she doesn't feel prepared "to deal with all of this."

Phillip in chapter 1, a twenty-six-year-old unmarried accountant, is also an Emerging Adult. He talks about feeling guilty that he was living in another city, moving forward with his own life and job. He felt compelled to drive home on the weekends to spend time with his father because his father sounded so depressed. He feels guilty that he was spending so much time with his dad and not with his Mom, "like I am being disloyal to Mom."

Young Adulthood: Twenty-Six to Forty Years Old

Adult Children who are graduating from college or from specialized training, or living in another city, moving forward with their lives and jobs, may begin to question the meaning of commitment and family more seriously. It may be difficult for them to take steps toward career and marriage when their familial foundations feel shaky. Like Adult Children who are in the Emerging stage of adult development, Adult Children in the Young Adulthood stage can also feel caught between generations. They often feel a responsibility to assist their parents and other family members, while at the same time, they need to focus on their lives, starting or advancing their careers, and meeting their responsibilities to their nuclear families and personal relationships. They often report that it seems that just as they are coming to terms with the reality of growing up, moving forward away from their family, and becoming established in the world, they realize that the foundational reality they knew growing up no longer exists, and it shakes them to their core.

Hans, introduced in chapter 1, is a thirty-four-year-old machinist in the Young Adult stage, married with two young children. After describing how shocked he was that his parents were divorcing after so many years of marriage, he describes his concerns about how his parents will be able to "make it financially living apart." He also shares that when his brothers took a "hands-off" attitude, he felt alone and unsupported. Then, he talks about how he and his wife felt torn between meeting their responsibilities to each other and their children and helping his parents "be okay." He adds, "My wife and I have even been having serious discussions about the permanence of our marriage, you know. We are both still a bit numb about all of this and wondering if we will come out the other side of it with the good marriage that we always thought we had. I mean, if my parents bailed after all these years, how do we know that we aren't destined to do the same?"

Middle Adulthood: Forty to Sixty Years Old

Adult Children who are well established in adult life, married with children, and have a home and career, may experience that their current life that is rooted in their familial past may no longer feel so firmly rooted. Like those in the Emerging and Young Adult stages of adult development, haunted by the painful awareness of their parents' failed marriages, they can begin to reflect on their relationships and wonder if they are inevitably bound to experience the same failure. They can feel pulled between their responsibilities to their own nuclear families and the additional responsibilities they may now be assuming for the well-being of their divorcing parents and other family members, like their siblings, grandparents, aunts, uncles, and cousins. The accumulating pressure from such responsibilities brings them overwhelming stress. Because these Adult Children are in such a "mature" stage of adulthood, their worlds may not offer support to them about how to cope with their parents' divorce. The underlying message from their culture is to deny the distress and pain they are undergoing and just march through it.

In chapter 2, we met Daniel, a forty-two-year-old teacher, married with two teenage children. Although he is in the Middle Adulthood stage of adult development, he says he sometimes feels younger than his students. The family dynamics arising from his parents' divorce are causing him significant stress, so much so that he has become depressed, sleep-deprived, and irritable with his wife and children. Like Phillip, Maria, and Hans, he worries whether his parents will be okay mentally, emotionally, physically, and financially. He struggles with loyalty conflicts in a tug of war between his mom, his dad, and his sister, as each one attempts to form an alliance with him against the other. He worries that his dad may pull away from him. His mom and sister won't be in the same room with his dad. His sister refuses to let her children be with Daniel's children if their dad is around. Although he is competent and accomplished in his professional life, he proclaims, "I don't have a clue how to handle all of this!"

Carol writes:

Jerome is another Adult Child in Middle Adulthood. On a warm April morning, I checked my office voice mail. "Beep. You have one new message," and then an articulate, baritone voice announced, "Hello, Dr. Hughes. My name is Jerome. I just read about your work with Adult Children of gray divorce." After an extended silence, he continued, struggling with each word. "I'm one of them. I never thought I would be, but I guess I am." I heard deep pain in each word. "I would appreciate you returning my call."

I returned his call. "Thank you for calling. Honestly, I haven't known what to do or where to turn. What I do know is that my life feels eerily surreal. I have never experienced anything like this before. I am fifty years old, a CEO of a successful corporation and my parents are divorcing after fifty-two years of marriage! My seventy-year-old mother has been having an affair, if you can believe that!" He was barely pausing to take a breath. The words tumbled out. I heard the despair in his voice. "Dad is so angry with her he has been attempting to get my wife Karen to align with him against Mom and not allow her to see our children—her grandchildren! This is crazy! Karen is distraught because she loves Mom and Dad and doesn't know how to handle all of this. Our kids are asking us what is happening with their grandma and grandpa. I am distracted and having a lot of difficulty focusing at work. Both Mom and Dad call me at work, complaining about the other. Mom even calls and keeps inviting me to have dinner with her and her 'boyfriend.' That's what she calls him! Her 'boyfriend'! Is there a word other than that? It's crazy!" He paused for a moment, then concluded, "I travel frequently to Southern California on business. Could we schedule a time to meet next week?"

"You know, Jerome, what you are experiencing is understandable. It sounds like your parents' impending divorce has come as a complete surprise to you. It might help you to know that you are not alone. Parental divorce surprises Adult Children of all ages. You probably don't know that since 1990, the US divorce rate for those sixty-five and older has tripled." "You're kidding!" He sounded as shocked by that statistic as he was by his mother leaving her fifty-two-year marriage. We scheduled his first appointment for the following week.

Late Adulthood: Sixties until Death

When Adult Children are in this stage of adult development, they are often sandwiched between their children, perhaps their grandchildren, their aging parents, and other kin. They may feel responsible for assisting with the needs of all of them while trying to take care of themselves as well. Though some parents like Jerome's are still vibrant intellectually, physically, and sexually, some are not. While Jerome is dealing mainly with emotional issues, many Adult Children in this age group are leaving their own first, second, or third marriages. They may have multiple children from various marriages, and these children's ages can range from young children to midlife adults. There may be sets of children who are siblings, half-siblings, and stepsiblings. There may be two or more former spouses and myriad former in-laws, such as grandparents and grandchildren from the various marriages, aunts, uncles, cousins of the blood, half-, and step- variety. As we will see in chapter 11, the family dynamics can become overwhelmingly complicated. Balancing all the kin while going through one's divorce creates added stress for Adult Children in this stage of life.

Even if their aging parents have an estate plan for their final years, these Adult Children must find long-term care facilities for their aging parents. Or sometimes they move their parents into their own family residences, and either become their parents' caretakers or have to provide caretakers for them. Adult Children in this stage usually have little experience with these life transitions. Juggling their family's needs as well as the needs of their aging parents causes them unexpected stress, as does dealing with their parents' eventual death. Of course, this life transition involves the grieving process we discussed in chapter 4.

ADULT CHILDREN ARE STAKEHOLDERS IN THEIR PARENTS' DIVORCE

Carol writes:

Almost two decades ago, Bart J. Carey, a collaborative divorce family lawyer, mediator, and adjunct law school professor, and I were attending a collaborative divorce[12] training in Arizona. He said to me, "You know, Adult Children are stakeholders in their parents' divorce." This one sentence became the seminal concept for my future work with and writing about children who are adults when their parents separate and divorce. When I was conceiving the ideas for this book, I knew I wanted Bart to share some stories from his practice that would illustrate how Adult Children are stakeholders in their parents' divorces.

Bart writes:

It began like any other consult. A woman in her late fifties called to make an appointment to inquire about mediation services. We inquired if her husband would be able to join us. She would ask but doubted it. At the appointed time, she appeared alone. However, as she was filling out an information sheet, in trouped two young men with a determination that spoke of a sense of mission. These were her sons. One was twenty-four years old, and the other was thirty-one. They had followed her to our office.

One of the sons was married, and the father of the family's only grandchild. The other was a recent college graduate still living in the family home as he attempted to launch his career and pay down student loans. And they were adamant to speak with me.

First, they wanted to be sure I wasn't a shark who was going to influence their mother to get into a litigation that would devastate the family finances—money they were sure she was going to need because, secondly, their father was to blame for all this, and was going to abandon her in midlife and leave her destitute. She needed protection and they were going to do everything they could to protect her from their father.

While their mother remained in the waiting room, I brought the sons into the mediation room to hear their concerns. I reframed the concerns about their mother's future and that of the family, removing the judgment and blame they were expressing for their father. I focused instead on the uncertainties and questions that their mother and father would have to answer for the *entire* family, while developing a statement for their hopes for everyone to make the transition through divorce with a financial safety net and the family intact. I assured them that, if I were privileged enough to be their parents' mediator, their concerns and hopes would be shared.

This was a bit more dramatic than we typically see but serves as an example to illuminate the concerns that their parents' divorce can raise for Adult Children—concerns that they harbor, sometimes quietly, sometimes not, but that infect the whole family. After all, Adult Children are affected by every major life transition that their parents experience. When their parents divorce, they are not in control, not decision makers, but they have a stake in the journey and the outcomes.

Adult Children are stakeholders. Parents mostly recognize this, but in the fog of war, they may still lose sight of the impacts on the family.

On occasion we get referrals from attorneys and judges. These can be the most challenging cases, because the couple may have been battling over rights and entitlements through the court system for one or more years and may be entrenched in the war. As former U.S. Secretary of Defense Robert McNamara reflected, in the fog of war, perspective may be lost, affecting our perceptions and judgments.

One such referral brought a couple to our office on the eve of trial. Both were in their early sixties, married for thirty years, breadwinner father and homemaker wife, with little more than their cars, family home, and husband's retirement. Their shared mentality of scarcity was supported by the realities they were facing. They were instructed by a settlement conference judge to try mediation and instructed by their attorneys to attend. They sat in my waiting room in unhappy silence.

I invited them to join me in the mediation room. The wife was the first to speak. She informed me that her husband didn't feel the need to negotiate anything because he was going to win at trial, so we'd be out of there very quickly. I asked her husband if this was true. He confirmed her statement and went further, saying he would "win everything" at trial. Asked what "everything" means, he informed me it was his car, all "his" house, his social security, and "all" of his retirement. Asked what his wife would have, he said her car and her social security check. How could he be so sure? His attorney assured him of these outcomes so, no, there was no point to continuing our meeting. I asked him if he'd give me five minutes. He agreed.

At this point I asked his wife to kindly allow us to speak alone for five minutes. She returned to the waiting room.

A couple of questions confirmed that the husband was certain, despite my skepticism, his attorney had assured him of the outcomes at trial. So, instead of discussing rights and entitlements and the uncertainties of trial and community property acquired during a thirty-year marriage, I asked him if they had any Adult Children. They had two: a single daughter up north and a son (clearly a favorite child) living close by. He had a five-year-old grandson, who was his fishing buddy. His retirement plan was to spend a lot of time fishing with his grandson and being involved, as he grew up, in other sports, camping, and other activities with him. We bonded over how great it is to be a grandparent. Then, we were coming up to the end of our five minutes so I asked him, before his wife came back into the room, to again confirm that she would only have her car and social security. I observed it didn't seem possible she could live on that. "Her problem," he said.

"One more question," I said. "Assuming you get 'everything,' as your attorney has assured you, it seems improbable your son would not step up to help his mother. So, how's that going to work when you show up at his house to hang with your grandson or take him fishing, and she answers the door?"

In the fog of war, he had forgotten to consider how "getting everything" would impact his son and perhaps his plans with his grandson. He quickly became open to "some flexibility" and our five minutes became a much longer joint session.

I hope these examples from our work speak to the impacts of parents' divorce on their Adult Children and the power of bringing their voices and concerns into the process, while parents make decisions about not only their own future, but the future of the *family*.

ADULT CHILDREN IN ALL STAGES OF ADULT DEVELOPMENT ARE STAKEHOLDERS IN THEIR PARENTS' DIVORCE AND THEY EXPERIENCE MANY LOSSES

Although the above Adult Children are in different stages of adult development, their experiences are similar, and their stories indicate that Adult Children of all ages can struggle with their parents' divorce.

As we described in chapter 3, Bowlby emphasized that "from the cradle to the grave" attachment bonds ensure our safety, security, and even survival, and that the availability of responsive, dependable, and reciprocal attachment bond relationships is critical to healthy development across the lifespan.[13]

When we listen to Adult Children of all ages describe what they are feeling, it is clear that they are experiencing the loss of the reciprocal attachment bond relationships with their parents and family members that attachment theory asserts are critical to healthy development *across the lifespan*. This causes them to feel a loss of safety and security provided by the family attachment bonds and can cause them to question how they will survive emotionally, physically, mentally, and financially.

THE IMPACT OF PARENTAL DIVORCE ON ADULT CHILDREN IN VARIOUS STAGES OF DEVELOPMENT

Adult Children of gray divorce at all stages of adult development report feeling "outside the norm" and alone, so educating them about what studies have found helps them realize that they are neither "abnormal" nor "alone." In addition to the research in previous and future chapters, the findings outlined below describe issues common to Adult Children of different ages.

In her review of the few earlier studies that investigated the impact of parental divorce on Adult Children in various stages of adult development, Dr. Joleen Greenwood found that Adult Children's first response to finding out about their parents' divorce included shock, disbelief, anger, and a sense of loss. She found that the most common theme was role reversals, where the Adult Child became the "parent" to the parent and even assumed familial tasks such as maintaining family traditions, holidays, and birthday gatherings. Additional themes were Adult Children feeling stressed from being pressured to take sides, being caught in the middle of their parents' emotional needs, coping with their parents' demands for help with legal and financial issues, and acting as a mediator between their parents.[14]

In her own research, Greenwood found similarities to and differences from the previous research. Her research sample was comprised of forty Adult Children in various stages of adult development, whose parents divorced after they were eighteen years old. Their ages ranged from eighteen to fifty-four years old. Twenty-five of the Adult Children had experienced their parents' divorce within the past ten years, and for the other fifteen, more than ten years had passed since their parents' divorce.[15]

She found similar results to Bonanno's grief research described in chapter 4, in that only about half of them reported struggling initially with their parents' divorce. Whether they were in the half that struggled initially or in the half that did not, when they described their initial responses to their parents' divorce, six themes emerge: surprise or shock; holidays altered; loss of family home; financial ramifications; parental divorce as an additional source of stress; and being put in the middle.[16]

She found that about one-third of the Adult Children were surprised by the news of their parents' divorce. Others reported being relieved by the news because they knew that their parents' relationship was a conflicted one. Regarding holidays, some reported that they missed the "old holidays," splitting the holidays was stressful, and they hated the holidays for many years afterward.[17] For many, the loss of the family home that represented the way their family life used to be was difficult, even for those who reported not initially struggling with the divorce.[18] Some reported that dealing with the financial ramifications of the divorce included seeing their family's financial situation change, their loss of financial support for college tuition, their parents and siblings struggling, and feeling a responsibility to take over and make sure that the family was managing financially.[19] Some reported that dealing with the divorce overburdened them because they were dealing with their own lives, while others reported that being busy with their own lives helped them during the divorce because they didn't have time to deal with it.[20] Lastly, being put in the middle of their parents created a strain on their parent–child relationship, and negatively affected their well-being.[21]

In her study of Adult Children who were between the ages of eighteen and thirty-four when their parents divorced, Greenwood found that Adult Children's parent–child relationships are just as likely to be affected by a parental divorce despite the age of the Adult Children at the time of the separation. Her study indicated that about half of these Adult Children reported a strained relationship with one or both parents during the divorce, but that for many the strained relationships healed over time.[22] The results suggested that certain factors made it less likely that the relationship would be negatively impacted, including the following: parents did not force the Adult Children to take sides; parents did not put the Adult Children in the middl; Adult Children did not blame one parent over the other; and the parents tried to make the process a smooth transition for the Adult Children.[23]

Additional complications can arise when Adult Children and even their parents are in their second or third marriages. Past statistics indicate that in the United States, 50 percent of first marriages, 67 percent of second marriages, and 73 percent of third marriages end in divorce.[24] There may be children and grandchildren from the various marriages, half-siblings, stepchildren, step-grandchildren, as well as various combinations of extended family members. Holidays, gift exchanges, and celebrations such as graduations, birthdays, and weddings can involve many people who are related by blood, marriage, or previous marriages. There are myriad relationships. It is often difficult for the couple and the family members from previous marriages to adjust to the relationships that comprise "blended families." A blended family is one where at least one parent has children that are not genetically related to the other spouse or partner. If families become mired in mental and emotional confusion trying to figure out all of these relationships, it can be helpful to seek professional assistance from experts in blended-family dynamics. We discuss blended families in more detail in chapter 12.

Next, we examine effective communication and how it benefits all family members.

6

COMMUNICATION

When we generate compassion for the difficult people in our lives, we get to see our prejudices and aversions even more clearly. It can feel completely unreasonable to make compassionate a wish for these irritating, belligerent people. To wish that those we dislike and fear would not suffer can feel like too big a leap. This is a good time to remember that when we harden our hearts against anyone, we hurt ourselves.
—Pema Chodron, American Tibetan Buddhist

While you and your family are going through this crisis, you might have moments of overwhelming anxiety or sadness. To help you through those moments, there are tips in this chapter with instructions for specific things you can do immediately to calm yourself and lower your worry and fear or anger.

Many families cannot talk easily about difficult, emotional issues. Some family members are less open to seeking professional help for a family crisis. Different understandings of what is considered "normal" can arise from ethnic and cultural differences, as well as individual family norms based on the unique experiences of individual families. What family members and friends say and do can influence how the divorcing coparents make decisions that increase or decrease the difficulties of their divorce. Divorce professionals refer to these others as the "Greek chorus."

Bruce writes:

John sported a dark blue golf shirt, designer jeans, and running shoes. In contrast to his casual dress, his demeanor was both formal and reserved. I invited him to sit and prompted him to begin. John started in straightforwardly as if giving a report. He explained that his wife of thirty years wants a divorce. He added that they have three children.

He then paused.

"My divorce lawyer wants me to get a divorce coach. Why would I want a divorce coach? I'm practical, a businessperson. What is the bottom line on this? I look at a problem and gather what I need. I need a lawyer. I get that. I can understand why a financial person could be helpful, but why a divorce coach? We already tried a marriage counselor off and on for a year, and that didn't work."

I replied, "Most people think that divorce is mainly a legal and financial event. What makes divorce so hard is that it is actually an emotional experience that includes legal and financial concerns, and for most people, fears about money now and in the future."

I then explained, "Divorce has two tracks—the business track and the emotional track. They operate simultaneously. You can't do them separately. You can't do first one and then the other, because everything is happening together. The business track involves lawyers and financial specialists. What most people overlook is that if they do not handle the emotional track well, it will knock the business track off course. When that happens, it can damage your family, including your children, both adult and minor. On top of that, it can cost you a lot more money and time."

He said, "Okay. My lawyer said something about that, but exactly what do you do?"

"I will help you and your wife communicate better. By the time a couple has decided to divorce, their communication has usually deteriorated. If you don't change that, it will be hard for both of you to agree on the necessary business and family decisions. Better communication helps you and your family have a better outcome, and it can save you money and time. Exactly how I do that depends on whether you choose me as your divorce coach or as your family's neutral child specialist. As your divorce coach, I will help you improve your communication and manage your emotions."

John interjected, "It's hard for us to talk about any of this. We either don't talk, or we fight."

I replied, "I don't know the particulars about your situation and your family. I know that whatever is happening, this is not what you were planning when you got married. I know that while every divorce is different, there is usually anger or sadness, and disappointment or fear. Most people experience all of those feelings during a divorce. When it is time to make decisions, most couples fight over two things, money and children. You have both. If you are angry or afraid, that is the worst state to be in neurologically. The part of your brain that can make the best decisions is 'offline' when you are angry or afraid. During a divorce, most people are feeling both."

John said, "My kids are grown now. My lawyer mentioned a child specialist, but I don't think we will need one."

"That is a common mistake many people make," I said. "They think that because their children are adults, their divorce won't affect them. You will be surprised how much this will impact their lives. Their family is coming apart. How this affects them is going to affect you and your wife. In fact, your wife isn't going to be your 'ex,' because each of you will always be your children's other parent. How the two of you interact will always affect them. There will be weddings, graduations, and grandchildren. Most of us know a family that did a divorce badly. A bitter, angry divorce. When weddings or grandchildren's birthdays are pending, there is tension. In some families, the anger and hurt make everyone cringe."

"Yes, I know," John agreed hesitantly.

"John, a lawyer or financial specialist can tell you the value of an asset, like a retirement account or a house. But what is the value of being able to dance at your children's weddings or attend a graduation without feeling like you don't belong, or having someone get upset?"

We talked some more about the different divorce processes available in California, where I practice. I gave him a handout prepared by a family lawyer that said in part:

> In this state, the two most common ways to divorce are "Do It Yourself" or litigation. Litigation is what most people think about when considering divorce, and it is the most adversarial approach. In addition to those options, there are two more peaceful, less destructive approaches that are less well known, but offer many advantages for families: Divorce Mediation and Collaborative Divorce.

I also gave him an information packet that included intake questionnaires to take home and review.

John called a few days later. He said he had decided to work with me as his divorce coach and scheduled an appointment for two weeks later.

This time, he was dressed in a white freshly pressed business shirt with an open collar, no tie, a dark blue blazer, light gray slacks, and highly shined, black leather shoes. He sat down and without any prompting, began speaking in a soft voice.

He recited information he had answered on his intake questionnaires. He and his wife Wendy had been living together in the family home in a local upscale beach community. He had recently moved into an apartment near the beach in the same city. She wants the divorce.

He told me, "I am living in a dumpy apartment." He added, "She gets to stay in the house."

He paused and continued, "Maybe it's better that way so the kids have a home to come to, but . . ." his voice trailed off. Another pause, then he resumed. "Our youngest daughter Brittany is twenty, and in her second year at Boston College. She lives in a dormitory. We rarely see her, and when she flies home, she wants to see her friends. Her mom gets to fly up there two or three times per semester but . . ." He stopped.

John looked out the window behind me for several seconds and then turned his face back toward me and said, "Brittany and I have always had a good relationship, but she has always been closer to her mom. I guess it's a mother–daughter thing. Ever since she learned about the divorce, Brittany does not talk to her mom as often as she used to, and she doesn't call me at all. She only texts me when she needs something, and she doesn't get back to me when I text or email her. Calling her is a waste because she rarely answers her phone or voicemails. I understand that Brittany is busy with school," he hesitated for a moment and said quietly with a forced smile, "but I would like her to call or text me more often."

After another brief silence, John then continued as he had in our initial meeting as if giving a report. I learned that their son James is twenty-three, a recent college graduate, and working locally as an engineer. He plans to work and maybe travel before going to graduate school. James had always done well in school and was a good athlete. John was closer to James when he was younger, and John attended his soccer games and track meets. James, like Brittany, is closer to his mother. He and John do not speak often but have always gotten along well. Now that James is on his own, although he lives locally, John doesn't see him very often, and they only talk when James stops by. Since John moved into his apartment last month, he has not seen James in person. John assumes that James will not be affected by the divorce because he has been out of the house since he went away to college five years ago. Their oldest child Anne is also an adult. She is twenty-six, married with two children, a girl and a boy, and lives nearby. John enjoys his grandchildren and now wonders how often he will see them. Anne is closer to her mother, too, but before the decision to divorce, she and John never had any friction in their relationship.

John paused again and shifting said, "Anne is the one most angry about the divorce. She has complained to me about my decision to move out. I think she is having trouble with her marriage to Tony, but she has not talked about it. Tony and I have always gotten along. We have a good relationship. We have a lot in common, and he comes to me for mentoring sometimes. Anne used to invite us over to their home a lot, and Tony and I would watch sports on TV, or just talk about business. Since Wendy told Anne that we are planning to divorce, I have not been invited over there, and she has not spoken with me since I moved out. Tony has not reached out to me, so I don't know how he feels about it. I have hesitated to contact him because Anne seems angry with me. I told her it was their mother who wants a divorce, but . . ." and again his voice faded before finishing.

He briefly smiled again, just with his mouth, but not with the rest of his face or eyes and said, "I feel lost. My wife doesn't want me anymore, but she still wants my money. I feel sad and don't even know how to talk to her. I don't feel angry, just stunned and sad. I don't know how to talk to my kids, and I don't think they want to talk to me, especially about this. I don't know what to say when my parents ask what happened or how am I doing. They have always liked Wendy and don't know why we are divorcing. My brother and sister take my side and think I should really 'let her have it.' I am not mad at her, just numb."

John's experiences are not unique, but that doesn't make them any less painful or confusing. He can barely handle his own sadness and confusion, let alone understand what is happening to his Adult Children, extended family, and friends. This point is very important for John and Wendy to realize about themselves. John and Wendy are experiencing first-hand that being an adult does not shield them from the confusion and distress caused by the disintegration of their world. Because they are overcome with their own feelings, they could easily overlook how much it will affect their Adult Children. They need to understand and expect that the divorce is creating similar shock and distress for their Adult Children as well. It is also helpful for their children to understand this about themselves and their parents.

When a family is going through parental divorce, they will get questions from well-meaning, or sometimes not-so-well-meaning, family members and friends. Some people won't know what to say and will avoid any meaningful conversation. Sometimes it will be a relief that others don't ask, and other times, it might feel like being abandoned.

Tip: It may be that by now, you are still anxious or becoming a little anxious. So here is something you can easily do.

Say to yourself, "I'm all right, right now."

You can do this anytime you are feeling worried.

Here is why it's important: It is true. You are all right in this moment.

Your brain is continually scanning for possible trouble. At times it will lock on to the worst possible outcome and flood you with adrenaline as if it was happening right now. A good first step to turning that off is to find a way to interrupt that internal self-talk, and then use it to shift your attention to something easy and useful. Unless someone has a loaded gun pointed at your head this very second, you are all right, right now. They haven't pulled the trigger, so it's true. You probably have shelter right now. You likely have food in the cupboard, or the ability to get it. And you are still breathing. Your mind can't honestly deny it when you say in this moment, "I'm all right, right now." In times of overwhelming anxiety, simply say to yourself, methodically, silently, or aloud, over and over, "I'm all right, right now," for as long as it takes to calm down. Five minutes or twenty minutes. Whatever it takes. This works. Mark this page so you can find this when you need it. Many clients have reported that this has been very helpful to them when dealing with even the worst family crises.

The first step to solving a problem is to recognize that there is one and then correctly identify what it is. Here are some points to keep in mind. The more you and the rest of your family and friends understand and remember these points, the better you will be at being compassionate and gentle with each other in times of crisis. Of course, that does not mean it will be easy, just that you will be better equipped to improve your ability to stop yourselves from making things worse.

COMMUNICATION WITH OTHERS IS COMPLICATED

The details of what makes communication so complicated are complex. It can be challenging even in good times. It's easy to think that other people see, experience, and think about life in similar ways that we do. There is a saying, "If only you were more like me how much better the world would be."

We all see, hear, feel, and interpret life events through our unique perspectives, shaped by our individual experiences, and whatever meaning we took from those experiences. This impacts not only how we talk to others, but also how we interpret others' communications to us. Our social class, level of education, the culture we were raised in, the culture we now live in, our gender, and our expectations of another's gender influence our expectations and interpretations of the communication of others. Added to that are all of the quirks we absorbed while growing up in our family of origin. If you can recall the first few times you stayed overnight at the house of a friend or cousin, it was evident that the other family had their own rules about how things were done.

TWO FACTORS THAT AFFECT COMMUNICATION

1. Brains have a negative bias
2. Genders have different psychosocial programming

It is important for you to understand these. Your family is in crisis. Better communication is needed now and going forward.

The Brain's Negative Bias

Our early experiences, good and bad, affect our emotions. Although adverse events can be deeply impactful, at those times, we lacked the experience to understand what was happening accurately. We may not consciously remember many of the happenings. Our negative interpretations of and the meanings we attached to those experiences may not be exact, whether we are consciously aware of them or not, but they can and do instantaneously trigger our emotions.

The resulting physiological changes can impact our facial expressions and voice. This means they influence how we are communicating. Even when we don't notice our own emotional state, other people do see the resulting physiological changes, and we see theirs. Readily observable changes include the rate and volume of our speech, a flushed face when embarrassed or angry, a clenched jaw, a slumped posture, and teary eyes. Others consciously and unconsciously notice those telltale changes. Those changes are a form of communication and affect other people. Others may accurately interpret the meaning of those changes or might get it wrong. Either way, this affects our relationships and reactions, whether we are the one talking or listening.

"Early environments and experiences have an exceptionally strong influence on brain architecture. As a neural circuit is maturing and beginning to function, a child's environment and experiences, good and bad, can significantly impact that circuit, causing adjustments in its genetic plan, and changing its architecture in fundamental ways. Brain development has 'sensitive periods'—periods in which certain neural circuits are very receptive and grow dramatically."[1] High-level neural circuits build on the earlier ones, and they can be limited by any damage done to the earlier-developed circuit.[2]

Early humans lived in a world filled with physical dangers. Research shows that negative events impact human brains more powerfully than positive ones.[3] Needing to scan constantly for possible danger created a brain with negative bias. That is how our ancestors survived. Our brains pay more attention to something bad, no matter how unlikely, nor actually happening, than they do to good things that are present right now. Today, there are not many wild predators to be aware of, but our brains react the same way to possible emotional threats. Those automatic emotional and physical reactions can distort how we receive the words from another person, and how we communicate to him.

In order to minimize the communication distortions resulting from these automatic emotional and physical reactions, it is important to learn practical techniques to counteract the "fight, flight, or freeze" response. You also need to learn strategies to overcome your brain's negative bias. Otherwise, you risk increasing conflicts and misunderstandings between you and the people you care about.

Gender Differences

Gender differences significantly impact communication. They affect how we communicate and how others receive our communication. Yet most people only vaguely understand how this works. It is helpful for Adult Children and their parents to understand how these differences routinely distort communication between women and men. This includes husbands and wives, daughters and fathers, mothers and sons, and brothers and sisters.

Talking about gender differences and how they affect communication is often controversial, especially when trying to explain to what degree biology (nature) and culture (nurture) shape how men and women experience life and communicate differently. Physiologically, sex differences do exist, but it remains unclear how much the physiological differences affect how we communicate. Gender differences *do* exist and affect how we communicate. Men and women experience life differently.

A BRIEF LOOK AT NATURE VERSUS NURTURE

Nature

Solving the complex problems experienced by Adult Children during their parents' divorce is difficult, but it can be done. We cannot just ignore physiological differences, so we will take a short detour and discuss our findings about that before moving on to psychosocial influences.

Some of the popular ideas that laypeople have about the brain are not conclusive. Neuroscience lacks consensus about significant differences between men and women's brains. While there are physical differences between women and men that do affect the way we experience life, whether a person is born with a "female brain" or a "male brain" is not necessarily sufficient to make a person into society's version of a man or a woman. The debate about whether these differences are even the main factor is inconclusive. There remains a lot to learn about the neurological differences between men and women.

Researchers in neuroscience argue and counterargue that the physical differences in our brains are the major cause of differences between men and women. Below are two specific examples from respected academics that illustrate the contentious debate raging in neuroscience on this issue. Each one adamantly claims that he or she has the correct answer, yet they contradict each other in significant ways.

> 1. On CNN's website on March 25, 2010, best-selling author Dr. Louann Brizendine, a member of the American Board of Psychiatry and Neurology and the National Board of Medical Examiners and author of the books *The Female Brain* and *The Male Brain,* concludes that certain physiological differences in female and male brains account for much of our differences. She emphasized the idea that men's attitudes and behaviors are driven and controlled by testosterone and a larger amygdala (the alarm system for threats). She also asserted that the "I feel what you feel" part of the brain—mirror-neuron system—is larger and more active in the female brain, so that women can naturally get in sync with others' emotions by reading facial expressions, interpreting tone of voice, and other nonverbal emotional cues."[4]
>
> 2. In a *Washington Post* book review of *Delusions of Gender: How Our Minds, Society, and Neurosexism Create Difference* by Cordelia Fine, PhD, the reviewer asserts that Dr. Fine challenges the above assumptions, and questions how much our differences are really biologically based, or whether other factors are involved. The review states, "the academic psychologist and writer, a Full Professor of History and Philosophy of Science at The

University of Melbourne, Australia, continues to advance her ideas that there is no 'male brain' or 'female brain' . . . cognitive psychologist Cordelia Fine offers a fairly technical explanation of the fMRI, a common kind of brain scan . . . everyone is familiar with these head-shaped images, with their splashes of red and orange and green and blue. But far fewer know what those colors really mean or where they come from. . . . In other words, being male or female isn't enough to make you into your society's version of a man or a woman. There is no 'male brain' or 'female brain.' But as soon as your maleness or femaleness is recognized, other people start to treat you in ways that form you into a man or a woman, with the support of toys, books, role models and a million other subtle nudges."[5]

Nurture

This chapter, however, is not primarily about our physical differences. They exist. Since there are so many varieties of communication around the world, the influence and psychosocial conditioning of the particular culture and the individual's family plays a significant role as well.

The rest of this chapter concentrates on the psychosocial aspects of communication. Psychosocial differences in how men and women are raised explain differences in attitudes and behaviors.

TWO CONCEPTS THAT HELP US UNDERSTAND MEN AND WOMEN

Here are two concepts from different sources that, when taken together, provide a unique perspective for understanding both men and women. These ideas will help you better understand your fathers, mothers, sisters, brothers, and yourselves. Understanding each other in new ways will, of course, help all of you to communicate more effectively with each other.

Different Cultures

For more than three decades, best-selling author and professor of linguistics at Georgetown University Dr. Deborah Tannen has contributed a useful perspective on relationships between women and men by presenting female–male programming as cultural differences.[6] Despite how it looks on the surface that we are learning the same values, language, and customs, Tannen emphasized how these cultural differences result in unique communication patterns and purposes. Men, being raised to perceive the world in terms of vertical hierarchy and competition, use conversation as a battle. In the male world, communication is used as part of the struggle for dominance. On the other hand, according to Tannen, women have been raised to downplay overt excellence, and the battle for status is hidden behind a mask of sameness. Conversations are expected to be a participatory event with everyone taking a turn, whereas males give each other orders to gain higher status. Girls dislike the "bossy" girls.

Tannen says that for girls and women, talking about problems is an expected norm in contrast to men, who learn as boys that talking about their problems risks their being seen as weak. Therefore, when men hear a friend (or spouse) has a problem, they attempt to fix it as a way to nurture and restore equality. Women say that is ignoring their feelings and putting them down. When men and women are viewed as being raised in different cultures, we can see there are many differences in our respective purposes for and structures of communication, making it easy for us to misunderstand each other. Tannen provides many instructive examples that illustrate the problems our separate cultures create. She helps us make sense of our misunderstandings. She teaches us how these misunderstandings lead each gender at times to attribute malice toward the other when the problem actually stems from cultural ignorance about each other. We have consistently found that when clients take these ideas seriously, their communication and relationships with the men and women in their lives get better.

Different Primary Fantasies—Women Want Heroes and Men Want Something Else

In his books *Why Men Are the Way They Are* and *The Myth of Male Power*, Warren Farrell, PhD, offers the concept that men and women are taught to seek and value two very different primary fantasies about what to want from life.[7] Like Dr. Tannen's, his books are well researched. He proposes that we grow up in very different worlds and explains these differences from another useful and unique perspective. Farrell describes how, historically, men have been programmed to suppress feelings, and sacrifice developing relationships with their young children in order to further careers, and that women have had to deal with daily "beauty contests" since early age. Simply put, he argues that men are judged by how well they compete and earn status, and women by their looks. One of his most important points is that neither gender understands how much this programming harms the other. Farrell argues that both need to get a better deal.

Farrell believes that girls and boys are programmed to have different but equally damaging primary fantasies. Girls have been encouraged to seek what he describes as some version of *Better Homes and Gardens*. The perfect house, children, a good career, and complete with some type of male "hero." The hero is vaguely defined as someone who is ready, willing, and able to make a lifetime commitment and is confident, secure, and most importantly, a successful competitor in the marketplace. This generally means he has a good job. Typically, a lot of weight is given to his ability to convincingly portray himself as confident and sure of himself. Not having an acceptable job is often a deal-breaker as a potential partner. Farrell challenges that, if you doubt women have been programmed to value a man's status or potential status, ask yourself, "How many women doctors do you know who are married to male nurses? How many women executives are willing to marry a male clerical support worker?"

When most men choose a woman, that she has a suitable job is not essential. Farrell says boys are trained to have a different primary fantasy. It is to have sexual access to as many attractive women as possible. Fulfilling the vague criteria of qualifying as the hero is the means to fulfilling it. There is nothing in this fantasy about houses, kids, or commitment. As an adult, Bruce recalls being surprised to learn from women he interviewed how much time many girls spent thinking about and planning their future wedding. He says he has never met one man who gave any thought at all to the subject.

Both programs are destructive. As silly as it sounds, many men subconsciously keep waiting for some version of "Wonder Woman" to show up some day, dressed in appropriately suggestive clothing ready to rock his world sexually. This makes it difficult for some men to commit to real-life women with whom they could have healthy relationships. We see how these primary fantasies guide us, lure us, perhaps, into making poor choices in the important areas of our lives. We did not choose them, but due to our cultural imperatives, they dominate our criteria for selecting our mates or deciding whether we should have a mate. They can be training to get divorced. They influence career choices and our relationships with friends and family. Absorbing these fantasies automatically affects our approach to marriage and parenting, and it likely influenced your parents, and you, their Adult Child. These largely unexamined fantasies deserve closer inspection.

Despite all of the attention given to this subject over the past fifty-plus years, as a culture, we still offer the same destructive cultural programming to boys and girls, and men and women, as though we haven't learned anything. It isn't that the situation hasn't improved at all. It has. The changes are neither as wide nor as deep as many of us might think or want. Traditional programming can result in men and women having different feelings about marriage and divorce.

The concepts presented by Tannen and Farrell help us understand that a lot of the basic assumptions we have about life and ourselves as men and women are only roles that we absorbed from our culture, so they are changeable. How changeable are they? For those of us who are adults, only so much change can be expected.

These roles and beliefs are deeply part of our personalities and core identities. It feels like they are who we are, not simply roles we assumed because they were the only choices offered. We can soften the roles, improve the good parts, and blunt the effects of the programming and choices that no longer serve us well.

Tip: Don't Be Too Hard on Yourself

We all need this reminder more than once. Be kind to yourself. Remember, you are reading this book to improve your life. Give yourself credit for taking action and give yourself the gift of kindness.

This Is Why It Is So Important

There is no problem so big it can't be made worse by adding some guilt. Whether you are an Adult Child whose parents are divorcing, or you are a divorcing parent, whatever mistakes you may have made, this book is not about blaming yourself, or anyone else. It is about learning new perspectives and practical steps you can take to change your life for the better. So, be kind to yourself.

ADDITIONAL THOUGHTS TO HELP YOU WITH COMMUNICATION

Tip: Too Much Anxiety Affects Communication

Notice your inner conversation and thoughts. We all have a constant, inner conversation that affects how we experience our life. As you read and think about the ideas presented here, start deliberately and consciously noticing your thoughts, beliefs, and feelings, and your inner monologue. Notice whether your self-talk is supporting your hopes or your fears. Too often, people discover that their self-talk creates and amplifies anxiety.

This is why it's important. Bruce writes:

The first step is awareness. You can't change anything until you are aware it is happening. The simple act of noticing your self-talk can improve it. Someone I know wondered whether he was sabotaging himself. He did an experiment. On his regular morning walk, he took a note pad and recorded how many negative thoughts he had. He was surprised by the high number. He repeated it the next morning and was surprised again. The number dropped significantly. The next day it stayed low. He surmised that by simply noticing the negative messages he was giving himself, the awareness itself caused him to change. Since then, other people who have tried this report similar results. As you do this, think about how you can apply in your life the concepts you are learning here.

When you are going through a difficult time, increased anxiety is common. When you reach higher levels of anxiety, it can become overwhelming. This causes poor decisions that not only do not solve the current difficulties but also add more problems. This includes an increase in misunderstandings and harsh words that cannot be easily taken back.

Using the tips and understanding the ideas in this chapter will help your communication in all areas of your life.

7

BOUNDARIES

I also understand that I cannot make other people change the way I want them to. I am only able to change myself. It is true that when I change, others may change in response but that is not to control. They have their lives and I have mine.
—Jane Claypool, American author, *Wise Women Don't Worry, Wise Women Don't Sing the Blues*

The term "boundary" indicates or fixes a limit or extent. In her book *Healthy Parenting*, Janet G. Woititz, EdD, writes that personal boundaries involve an individual's right to his thoughts, feelings, possessions, space, and body.[1] Adult Children of gray divorce suddenly find themselves in the midst of changing or changed interpersonal boundaries with their parents, siblings, and others. At such a disturbing and confusing time, genuinely concerned friends and relatives can intrude into Adult Children's boundaries. Whether Adult Children like it or not, they may become participants in their parents' divorce. However willing or unwilling they may be, many are drawn into the role of primary emotional support person for parents. Difficult choices are thrust upon them, such as whether to keep a parent's affair secret, or whether to provide financial support to a parent, and if so, how much. Family friends and relatives, including siblings, grandparents, aunts, and uncles from both sides of the family, may choose sides, and then openly or covertly pressure Adult Children to side with the "good parent" against the "bad parent." Adult Children can feel trapped into listening to others disparage a parent.

Understanding interpersonal boundaries can help you minimize the intensity and frequency of such awkward situations and conversations. After you are clear what healthy boundaries are, you can become empowered to discuss with family members and others what boundaries you want going forward. Although as an Adult Child you do not have a choice whether or not your parents divorce, you *do* have a choice about whether to simply react, or thoughtfully respond.

GWEN

Bruce writes:

Gwen is a twenty-year-old therapy client who has been seeing me for two months. Six weeks ago, her parents announced they were divorcing.

She arrived on time for her appointment. Even before sitting down and without prompting, she began to speak. In a slightly angry and complaining voice she said, "I am getting so worn out by this. If I was a kid and my parents were divorcing, everyone would try to shield me from their battles and make sure I was okay. But when you're grown, your parents look to *you* to help *them*. They expect my sister and me to support them emotionally, and they feel free to tell us horrible things about the other."

She paused as she settled into her usual spot in the comfortable, well-cushioned high-backed armchair facing a bank of windows behind me. She resumed in a softer voice. "I feel sorry for Dad, because he doesn't really have anyone to talk to, and the divorce kind of blindsided him. I'm not used to seeing him this way, and I find myself getting mad at Mom. I am also angry with Dad's relatives for not helping him. I know it's not right, but I even get angry with him for not having better friends. I didn't ask for all of this. My family is collapsing. I guess I'm not a good daughter."

She continued, "It's putting a strain on my relationship with my parents, and family members are expecting me to side with Dad against Mom." Gwen's plight illustrates that divorce affects other relationships besides the one that is breaking.

ROGER

Ron, a colleague who knew about my work with Adult Children of parental divorce, referred twenty-two-year-old Roger to me. When Ron called to make the referral, he shared that Roger was dealing with the challenges of trying to support one parent emotionally, while sympathizing more with his other parent, and simultaneously doing his best to maintain a balance with his older and younger siblings. He felt resentful about these conflicting obligations and guilty because he did not think he was being helpful enough.

Roger sent me the completed intake paperwork ahead of time. He arrived early for our appointment. As I entered the waiting room to greet him, he rose from the chair and introduced himself. Roger was casually dressed in shorts and a golf shirt and was wearing comfortable boat-type shoes without socks. He seemed like a friendly and confident young man. "I hope you can help me," he said.

He declined my offer of water, coffee, or tea, and gestured to show he brought his own water bottle. I directed him to my office. He chose a chair facing away from the windows, while I took a seat directly across from him. I told him what I knew, based on the referral and his intake papers, and prompted him to begin wherever he liked.

He said, "My parents started their divorce three and a half years ago, and I have been dealing with all of this ever since. The divorce has taken over three years!"

"Three plus years is not unusual for a litigated divorce," I said, "and the process is hard on a family."

He looked down for a brief moment, then raised his head and eyes and replied. "Mom is a mess. I guess she was a teenager when they got married. I have an older sister. She's twenty-six. My parents never really said anything about it, but lately Mom has talked about how hard it was to be pregnant and have to get married. My grandparents were respected in our church, so she and Dad felt that they had to 'do the right thing' and get married. Mom's parents, my grandparents, don't believe in divorce, and no longer want anything to do with Dad. They also act like I should be on Mom's side. I can tell that Mom gets hurt when she thinks I have seen Dad, like I should be against him."

Plaintively he asked, "What should I do?"

"That happens a lot when couples divorce," I informed him. "Your mom is hurt. I don't know her except through what you have described. It's common for people to want their family and friends to be angry with someone who has hurt them. She may simply be making the mistake of temporarily forgetting that you are allowed to have your own relationship with your dad, and that it is a different relationship than she has."

I then asked, "Who initiated the divorce?" "Dad," he answered. "How do you feel toward him now?" He quickly replied, "I feel sympathetic toward Dad, even though I wish that he hadn't done this. They have not been happy for a long time. Maybe they never were. I love Mom, but she is hard to be with because she has always been kind of helpless and needed lots of support. My sister is married, and our parents' divorce has affected her more than me. I have a younger brother Dale, nineteen, and a sister Angie, seventeen. They were young when the divorce started, and it hit them hard. I feel like I am the only one who has kept it together during the past few years."

"Your situation is difficult, and your reaction to it is understandable," I offered. When people are in crisis, it helps to assure them their distressing reactions are understandable, as were Roger's. He has never been in a life situation like this and needed someone to trust to tell him that he was okay when he feared he was betraying one or both parents.

I educated him about boundaries and how the concept of boundaries can help him. I told him that if what he is telling me is accurate, it is unreasonable for any family members to assume the right to deny him having a relationship with both of his parents. I reminded him that his dad did not divorce him, that his parents' relationship is about *their* relationship, and that their relationship is separate and different from his.

I reminded him, "You asked me what you should do," and then I asked, "What do you WANT to do?" He replied, "I don't know."

In later meetings, I helped him understand the value of learning to view his family from a multigenerational perspective. When Adult Children view their family from a multigenerational perspective, it helps them better understand their family, including extended family—grandparents, aunts, uncles, and cousins. This understanding can help heal present and past emotional wounds.

We ask clients, "How would you describe your grandparents?"

"What do you think it would be like to have been raised by your father's parents?"

"What about your mother's parents?"

Often, they can see their parents through a new lens. When we review some of the traits they describe about their father or mother, Adult Children are able to speculate about how those traits could have emerged from being a child in that family. They can see how their parents, aunts, and uncles became the people they are today. It helps them see how, under the right circumstances and with guidance, they can change early family programming. Many times, they say that they can see how much better their life was for them, and how their parents "raised the bar." They also say that they can now see their parents and extended family members from a more empathetic and even sympathetic perspective. Many report that such understanding empowers them to feel determined to break dysfunctional intergenerational patterns and set boundaries that will work for them.

A CLOSER LOOK AT HOW CLEAR BOUNDARIES CAN HELP DECISIONS ABOUT SOME OF THE COMMON CONCERNS OF ADULT CHILDREN OF GRAY DIVORCE

1. It's hard not being able to turn to my parents, because everything has changed.

This can be a significant loss for children, adult and minor. In most families, the parents share mutual goals and values. When both care about the other, their interests are united, and each's decision making includes weighing how much every action affects the other. After a divorce, their respective goals, aims, and intentions might be mutually exclusive. When the conflict is high, some parents feel that any affection or interest that their Adult Children show to their other parent is a betrayal. Some parents are so blind with feelings of hurt, rage, and betrayal that they assume an attitude of "if you are not for only me then you are against me." Often when the anger extends so broadly, it is because it is linked with carry-over emotions and beliefs from events earlier in their own lives. Divorce easily triggers and amplifies feelings that originated in their past. Ideally, that parent will seek professional help in sorting out these feelings.

Adult Children are entitled to have a separate relationship with each parent. It is difficult for children when an angry parent insists that their children must have only the same type of relationship with their former spouse that the angry parent has. It is important that parents understand that, even though they are divorcing each other, it does not mean that the children are also required to divorce the other parent. The former spouse is still their child's other parent. As an Adult Child, you might want to seek professional help to assist you to discover where your sense of self and your right to have a relationship with each parent are.

There are also practical considerations that affect Adult Children when the parental unit is ruptured. For a younger Adult Child who is still financially dependent on the parents, there are important questions. For example, are the parents still able and willing to help them through college? If not, will they have to leave school? If a parent is already involved with another person, will that new relationship take precedent financially and otherwise? If a parent is now in unexpected financial need, will an Adult Child with a nuclear family of her own be expected to help? How much help is necessary or obligated? Before the divorce, the boundaries (agreements) in your particular family around these issues were known. Now they may be uncertain unless there have already been conversations between you and each parent about these concerns. Without an attempt to get some clarity, it can leave you "up in the air," cause more anxiety, and even damage your relationships with your parents.

Keep in mind that boundaries are to help us take care of ourselves, not to control others. What works for one family might not sit well with another. Conversations can be helpful. Whatever the decision, the essential point is not to hold a rigid adherence to a previous decision, no matter what. Take time to ensure that whatever you decide, you do it consciously and based on how you evaluate the current situation. Clearly communicate with the people in your life who will be affected by your decision.

2. Figuring out and resolving differences between what may be good for my parents versus what is good for me and knowing how much support is too much or too little or too long or too short.

Divorce is one of the most stressful human experiences. It is understandable that during this crisis, parents can become lost in feeling insecure about their life, role, and future, especially the parents who did not initiate the divorce. Shock can be paralyzing. Some will experience the demoralizing effects of feeling shame. If a parent who is still physically and mentally capable is temporarily impaired in those ways, it seems reasonable that an Adult Child, particularly one who has established herself in the world, would be empathetic and willing to help through the transition. For people who have consistently made other people's feelings and needs more important than their own, and always taking care of their parents' emotions, there are some terms you may have heard—enabling and codependent. There are circumstances when these terms are valid. Keep in mind that not every act of compassion or generosity is a sign of codependence or enabling. Compassion for someone experiencing pain is a healthy response. Helping someone you care about and love is natural. The problems come when the person helping feels he always has to put others before himself.

Most parents going through divorce want their children to have good lives. They say that if they had to choose between their own lives being great on every level and their children suffering, or they are struggling while their children are doing great, they would choose the latter. Naturally, there are times during the pain and stress of the divorce that their behaviors do not actually match this claim, but, once it is brought to their awareness, most are willing to pull back from behaviors that are damaging their children. Sometimes they temporarily forget this in the midst of fear or anger. Reminded about what's at stake, they agree that, by definition, a loving parent cannot win at their child's expense. That would not be a win, but a significant loss.

In a family with healthy relationships and boundaries, it is likely that the hurting parent would also be concerned about his Adult Child and would want any dependency to be temporary. Both the Adult Child and the parent could have discussions about what is reasonable and doable and prevent it from becoming an ever-increasing undue burden. Again, this is different than a situation where a parent becomes increasingly dependent due to injury, disease, or the effects of aging.

In cases of divorce where the parent is in need of financial or emotional support that causes strain on the Adult Child, it can be helpful to discuss this with all other family members, perhaps including extended family, to establish what this family believes is reasonable and what is not. It is also important that the Adult Child feels free to have her thoughts and feelings, so that any decisions do not create ongoing resentments. If your family is not able to do this effectively on your own, then professional help can be a good investment.

3. Knowing what to say to other people.

Be clear about your personal boundaries. There are people with whom you feel safe in sharing your thoughts, feelings, and details about your personal life. There are also situations in which most people do not share information with everyone who asks. For example, although this is not necessarily true in every culture, in North America, most people are not comfortable telling other people the details of their financial affairs. In fact, many people would be willing to tell someone about their sex life before revealing how much money they made last year. So it is likely that you already have some experience in not automatically sharing personal information with some people simply because they ask. Not everyone can be trusted to be safe with your private feelings. And, of course, some are safe. It is worth taking some time to think ahead of time about how to respond to different groups.

Some people may ask about your parents' divorce out of genuine concern for them, for you, or both. Others may ask because they are relatively close, are aware that your family is going through a crisis and think that it is polite and caring to acknowledge their concern for you in this way. They are not trying to pry. Others may simply be intrusive.

Consider the nature of your relationship with the person you are talking to. Is this person a close friend or relative with whom you feel safe and secure sharing your feelings? For example, if someone close to you died, even casual acquaintances might naturally inquire about your well-being. Most of us recognize that a divorce is a serious event that affects people in major ways both emotionally and financially. A close friend or relative would likely be concerned about you and your family.

When answering, be mindful that you have a right to decline discussing, if that is your preference. You can say it is difficult for you to talk about it. If the person is a supportive confidant, you can decide to share. Most important is permitting yourself to share as much or as little as you want. You have that right. You can tell someone in a kind manner that you don't want to talk. Tell her you understand she was not trying to intrude and that you are just not ready to discuss it. You can also reply that you appreciate the concern, that it is your parents' business, and that you prefer not to discuss it. If the person knows one or both of your parents as well, you can suggest that they ask your parent directly.

When acquaintances ask about your parents' divorce, you can thank them for asking and say that it is your parents' business, and that it is not your place to discuss it. If the person asks how you are doing, you can reply with a generic response, such as "I'm okay. My parents are working it out." It is your choice about how little or much you want to share. It is helpful to think about it ahead of time. What are your limits, and what are your family's limits about sharing private information? You are not obligated to offer any more information than you choose.

When someone is intentionally intrusive or they have poor boundaries, decide on a generic response ahead of time for people in this category. An example would be a briefer version of the above. "Thank you for asking. It's my parents' business. They are working it out." If an intrusive person continues to press, and she also knows your parents, you can suggest that she ask your parents directly or repeat that you don't want to talk about your parents' private business.

4. Knowing how to deal with my parents' new significant others—Mom's "boyfriend," or Dad's new wife—is even more complicated when the new relationship preexisted the divorce.

It is usually difficult to accept a parent's new relationship, and especially so if that relationship was tied to the divorce. There may be a difference between how you feel about a new relationship with the parent who initiated the divorce, and about an affair the other parent did not know about. Have you usually felt closer to one parent than the other? Be honest with yourself. Do you feel betrayed? Do you feel pressured to support one parent over the other? If so, why? Remember the quote that opened this chapter: "I also understand that I cannot make other people change the way I want them to. I am only able to change myself."

Remind yourself again that boundaries are to protect ourselves, not to control others. You can consider whether or not you have a right to deny your parent a new companion. You can evaluate whether or not you view the new person to be right for your parent and why, or if you think the new person is good for you or not.

There may be inheritance considerations that your parents need to discuss.

5. Understanding the rules for occasions like weddings, graduations, and birthdays.

If your parents chose a nonadversarial divorce process, such as mediation, cooperative, or collaborative divorce, they might already recognize the value to their children and extended family of having everyone be able to show up at these functions without allowing conflicts to damage such milestones in their families' lives. Discussions about boundaries are important here as well. Behaviors that threaten children's well-being are violations. Those celebrating should have a choice about who attends these functions and be able to expect that the event will not be sabotaged. This includes Adult Children. It is not necessary that, when there are still deep feelings of hurt and betrayal, the parent who feels injured be required to stand next to the other parent, if that is too painful. Whatever is done, it should be done respectfully for the sake of the family members who are being celebrated. If a parent insists on taking a stand that, if a particular person attends, she is not coming, she can choose not to attend. Or, she can work with a therapist to help her process her anger, so her decision to be absent does not impact her Adult Children or grandchildren.

When there are extenuating circumstances, such as one parent being in a new relationship that preexisted and precipitated the divorce, it is important that those involved have clear conversations and agreements about whether or not to include the new person, and if so, how that will be done. Meeting with a professional who has helped other families solve these problems is a good idea. If one parent refuses to consider this option, the Adult Children may need to decide for themselves whether or not to allow that parent to deny them their right to choose their relationships with each parent. If it is one of the Adult Children who is unwilling to meet with a therapist to reassess the value or harm being created by insisting, for example, that they will not attend the wedding or graduation of a nephew or niece because a parent or new spouse is attending, that is also worthy of a frank discussion.

6. Handling my grandparents, aunts, and uncles, who now despise one of my parents after twenty-five years or more of everyone being family.

Feelings of loyalty and an obligation to support their child or sibling is understandable, though not necessarily a position that needs to be set in stone. If there was a particular offense, such as a recent or ongoing affair that precipitated the divorce, that could be a factor in deciding what to do. When a couple chooses to divorce, both have some responsibility for the deteriorations in their relationship that contributed to divorce. The underlying problems probably existed yet were not addressed for some time.

It is crucial that everyone understands that requiring children to take sides against their other parent is harmful to a child, including an Adult Child. When invited to join in a "bashing your other parent" conversation, be mindful that you have a right to decline to participate if that is your preference. You could tell the person who is attempting to have you join in that it is difficult for you to talk about it, and that you prefer not to discuss it. Simply give yourself permission to share as much or as little as you want. You have that right. You can also reply that you appreciate the concern, that it is your parents' business, and that you prefer not to discuss it.

7. What to say to one parent who is suffering more and who asks questions about the other and their new significant other.

This is another opportunity to set clear boundaries. It is natural to feel compassion for the parent who is suffering more. This is especially true when it seems clear that the parent who initiated the divorce did it uncaringly, causing unnecessary damage in an already painful experience. Adult Children can discuss this among themselves or perhaps with extended family, like the parent's sibling, for assistance. For some families, it is understood that their boundaries are permeable, and for others, it would be a violation. Ultimately, you can tell your parent that you are not comfortable reporting this information to either parent.

There are no one-size-fits-all answers. In many cases, one parent may have lost his ability to maintain his previous role of being a source of help for other family members. At least one parent may now feel she can't even help herself. Generally, one parent is several months or more behind the other in processing the divorce.

When a couple decides to divorce, often both partners have been unhappy. However, until one of them initiates a divorce, both had the option of divorcing or trying to work things out. Suddenly choice has been taken away from one by a unilateral decision by the other. It is usually shocking and painful. It is natural to feel stunned, helpless, and disoriented.

WHY IT IS IMPORTANT TO UNDERSTAND THIS AND KEEP IT IN MIND

Prior to making the decision and taking action to divorce, the spouse who acts seldom shares with the other that he is making definite plans. The parents still enjoy whatever practical benefits they are getting from the intact marriage, even though one is secretly preparing to leave. There may have been practical, even understandable reasons for doing that. These reasons can range from fear of a violent reaction, if that has been their history, to simply preferring to avoid conflict, or in some cases caring mainly about themselves.

Although a tremendous change is coming, their day-to-day life is not yet so severely disrupted. Often the person named the "leaver" is now ready to move on, and after taking the action of initiating a divorce, no longer wants to talk to the other spouse about problems, let alone try to resolve them. The leaver intends to move on with his life and frequently wants the other person, the "leavee," to stop asking questions, or trying to reconcile. The leaver often has an unrealistic expectation that the leavee should simply get over it. The leavee often feels like someone who is holding a frayed cord with no ability to get satisfactory explanations about what happened and why now?

We are not suggesting that Adult Children or anyone else take sides. That is exactly what we do not recommend. It's simply important to understand this common dynamic, and follow the suggestions recommended throughout this book. Be kind to each other, including yourself. Everyone in your family is dealing with a new situation. This new reality is impacting everyone, and it is likely that no one has been through this before. Understanding and being kind will probably help. Taking sides will create more problems for you and your family, now and in the future.

Suddenly, all family members are in situations in which the old rules, spoken and unspoken, about the ways the family functions are not dependable. It's like waking up inside a dream, and discovering you are living on another planet. When the existing social order is shattered, there is no clear understanding of boundaries. It may be that some commitments and understandings remain, but it is unclear which ones. The new agreements have not yet emerged. Until they do, what is everyone supposed to do?

Families have their practices about emotional boundaries. Those boundaries create an understanding within the family about where "I" begin, and "You" end. Some families have very firm boundaries. Some place emphasis on personal privacy and personal space. They may carefully guard personal information about feelings. Those families often consider personal questions to be impolite or maybe even violations. They value and enforce ideas of personal property. On the other end of the spectrum, boundaries can be permeable, and in some cases almost nonexistent, with no clear agreement or common understanding of how far to intrude into others' lives, and how far they will allow others into theirs.

Many families fall somewhere in between. Some families understand and respect personal property, while at the same time, family members have understandings about the casual sharing between siblings of personal things, such as clothes, sports equipment, or a shared vehicle. They may or may not share feelings. Everyone has permission to share or not share, depending on with which family members and on what topics. There are likely clear divisions between parents and children, and how that plays out, changes and expands, or contracts as the children grow. These family rules and agreements are often unspoken, and yet everyone knows what is expected.

On the extreme end, in families who have suffered the effects of trauma, such as substance abuse, the death of a parent or a child, extreme poverty, severe abuse, or similar situations, parents' ability to maintain a healthy hierarchy of responsibilities can be impaired. The boundaries in these families can be extremely permeable, and family members expect children to take on responsibilities beyond their capacity. Young children can become parentified, wherein some parent–child roles become reversed, so that the children feel responsible for taking care of their parents emotionally, physically, and financially. When such role reversals have been the norm, it can create problems for the children when they are grown and trying to establish healthy adult relationships. It is a very different situation than when parents temporarily or permanently lose their ability to cope, and Adult Children, who were well taken care of when they were growing up, now step in to help the parent through a difficult situation.

It is both reasonable and understandable that a compassionate Adult Child from a healthy family would decide to step in to help a suddenly needy parent. Nonetheless, this does not mean that it won't have a negative effect on the Adult Child. Conflicting feelings of family loyalty and of being imposed upon and trapped by parental decisions over which they have no say are reasonable reactions. Because their parents are divorcing, these Adult Children now find themselves dragged into situations they did not expect. Before the divorce, there were more or less clear family agreements along with unspoken family rules. Various roles that develop in family systems were in place. These commonly understood agreements within this particular family dictated who was responsible for what, and who was entitled to the benefits of family resources, if any. When there were problems, there were general understandings about who in the family was expected to solve them.

Parents initially set interpersonal boundaries and the nature of family relationships. When parents divorce, the understandings and agreements that the children knew their entire lives can rupture, become weakened, abandoned, or even inverted. This can last until the parents can regain their emotional stability. It can take longer for one parent than the other and will likely be disruptive for all family members. A professional can help in these situations, yet it may be difficult for some families to accept outside help for private matters.

Daniel's parents in chapter 2 were denigrating each other, which crosses a parent–child boundary and creates loyalty conflicts for the Adult Child—which parent should I believe and support? When one or both parents use their Adult Child as a confidant, it crosses another boundary. Adult Children say they feel especially uncomfortable when a parent reveals intimate marital details, and that when a parent or other family member interferes with them keeping relationships with another family member, they feel conflicted, trapped, and lost because they don't know how to resolve the conflicts.

Clear understandings and agreements about boundaries make life less complicated and prevent or decrease conflicts. Often different families have different ideas about what is normal, okay, and acceptable. Parents may favor one parenting style or a blend of parenting styles. Family boundaries reflect parenting styles and intergenerational family histories.

The Adult Children in this book demonstrate that culturally accepted norms are applicable in some but not all families. Keep in mind that rules about boundaries can be different for families without being wrong or pathological. Cultural differences and individual family histories are relevant in evaluating what would be considered useful and healthy boundaries. Some families are very private. Rigid boundaries that are important for them might seem cold and indifferent to others. Other families have a history of more involvement with each other that would seem intrusive to others but provide a sense of belonging to those families.

When defining boundaries as healthy or unhealthy, it is crucial to avoid cultural bias. In some North American families, when parents rely solely on their Adult Children for emotional support during stressful periods, it can be intrusive or otherwise unhealthy. Conversely, in some cultures where much more extended family cohesion and intergenerational obligations and relationships create a different sense of "normal and healthy," the same behaviors and attitudes can be considered natural, and too much distancing can be regarded as problematic. Similarly, in some immigrant families, sharing family problems with outsiders is not the norm, and seeking professional help can be seen as abnormal.

There are some commonalities that many cultures and families would agree are boundary violations. The key is clear understanding that parents initially establish family boundaries. Healthy boundaries focus on children's benefit and well-being. Behaviors that threaten children's well-being are violations. This is equally true when the child becomes an adult. If there are significant gray areas or outright confusion, the key to minimizing harm is for Adult Children to discuss with immediate and extended family members, when necessary, what is acceptable and what is not. The responsibility for having these conversations may typically be the province of the parents. When parents and Adult Children discuss boundary setting, they will have to rely on what has been acceptable in their particular family until now to guide them how to proceed. It might be up to the Adult Children to decide for themselves what steps they want to take to preserve these existing relationships while staying true to their needs. If parents and Adult Children want to minimize present and future conflicts with extended family and friends as much as is possible, they may have to risk being vulnerable in order to be clear.

If you were raised in a home where you had to take care of the emotions of a parent who was supposed to be your caregiver, you might have absorbed the idea that it was your responsibility to fix other people's problems and troubling emotions. In this case, it would be helpful for you to think about boundaries and how much of yourself you want to give. Children raised in families that experienced trauma often become parentified when the parents were consistently overwhelmed an unable to cope. As a result, it is common for them to automatically believe that other people's needs are always more important than their own.[2] You may be a person who automatically extends those feelings of excessive obligation and self-sacrificing responsibility for situations and consequences beyond your control.

WHEN HELPING, YOUR WELFARE IS ALSO IMPORTANT

Being empathetic toward another person's difficulties is healthy and even commendable. Wanting to be helpful is a good value. It becomes a problem if your welfare is ignored. When other people, including the people close to you, such as parents, siblings, and friends, expect that you will consistently put their welfare ahead of your own, it is worth examining those expectations. Of course, there are times when it is both commendable and healthy to go above and beyond what other people might think is reasonable, but when you do make such a decision it is also reasonable and healthy to take a moment to examine those choices, especially when it is a constantly repeated pattern.

This Is an Important Boundary Issue

If you find that you are becoming resentful, it will come out in ways that harm you or other family members. Notice whether or not you find yourself continually resenting your decisions to help, and being angry that others do not reciprocate. The key here is being aware so that deciding to give assistance is a conscious decision and not just an automatic reaction.

Requiring children to take sides against their other parent is harmful to Adult Children. It is one thing for a divorcing parent to talk about his sadness or loneliness to an Adult Child if he is not trying to enroll them in blaming, hating, or ostracizing the other parent. If the parent is looking for allies, it might be the right time for him to accept professional help.

> *Three things in human life are important. The first is to be kind. The second is to be kind. And the third is to be kind.*
> —Henry James, American-British author

8

CHANGING FAMILY ROLES AND RULES

The beliefs inside your head are not written in stone, but rather in neurons which are definitely mutable.
—Author Unknown

For divorcing parents and their Adult Children almost everything has now changed in unanticipated ways. Everyday life can feel unfamiliar and surreal. None of them have gone through an event like this before and probably don't know what to do or where to start. These parents had been sources of guidance for their Adult Children. Now, the parents may be confused, angry, hurt, emotionally needy, and distant. Some parents may have been providing financial support for younger Adult Children attending college or otherwise starting out in adult life. Suddenly, there are role reversals, and instead of giving support, the parents need emotional support, maybe even financial support.

Siblings might have different ideas about who is to blame, how much to help the parents, and whether to help them at all emotionally or financially. Siblings who were close might now be angry with one parent or the other and resent the other sibling(s) for keeping contact with the parent they consider the designated "bad guy." In this time of upheaval so much is happening. There are rapid changes in family roles and routines. There are alarming questions such as where are your parents now living, or is one or both of them living with another significant love, or even with a new family? Basic life arrangements that were never questioned are now being reconfigured in ways that were never expected.

Education can provide tools to help you reclaim your emotional balance as you are forced to move into and through this new reality. Exploring how other people have experienced situations similar to yours can help you recognize that your feelings about the multiple losses you are experiencing are normal. It can also give you ideas that you can adapt, so that your family can minimize or avoid mistakes, and contribute to your eventual healing. For instance, by keeping yourself informed about how the strains tearing at your family can damage parent and Adult Child relationships, and by knowing that the father and Adult Child relationship is the most at risk, you will be better prepared to avoid the worst mistakes.

INFORMATION YOU AND YOUR PARENTS NEED TO KNOW

Research indicates that "parent–Adult Child relationship dynamics change following parental divorce. Divorced older adults no longer have a spouse on whom to rely and often turn to their Adult Children for emotional, social, and financial support. Adult Children may find themselves in the role of caregiver. The strain of such intense obligations may weaken intergenerational ties. Limited research suggests that parent–Adult Child relationships suffer following parental divorce, as indicated by decreased interaction and quality, especially among divorced fathers and their adult children."[1]

Kathy McCoy, PhD, writes, "Divorce is tough on kids of any age and can negatively impact parent and adult child relationships. One study found, for example, that adult daughters may tend to blame fathers for a gray divorce, and that changing family dynamics—like newly divorced mothers becoming more dependent on their children—also can negatively impact parent and adult child relationships."[2]

Bruce writes:

Sheryl, a thirty-eight-year-old woman whose parents divorced two years earlier, said, "I knew my parents weren't that well suited for each other, but I guess I thought that after all those years, they would always be together. I guess it's something you count on. I mean, I never ever thought they would divorce. Why after all of these years? They were married for forty years! It has been really hard. My kids love their grandma and grandpa. They are closer to my parents than to my husband Ron's, because his parents live in Ohio. So many of our family get-togethers are harder now. There is so much tension, and my kids don't understand why Grandma and Grandpa don't live together anymore. Angela, my eight-year-old, asked if Daddy and I would ever move away. It was the day after Christmas, the first Christmas after my dad had moved out."

FAMILIES AS SYSTEMS

The formal study of psychology started as an effort to understand how to help people suffering great emotional pain. In order to help someone who is suffering, especially someone whose pain and despair seem to originate from self-inflicted problems brought on by unseen, unknown causes, it is necessary to have some basic ideas about why people do what they do. The first focus of psychiatry and psychology was on the individual and individual personality development and behaviors. Later, the concept of family roles was developed by therapists, influenced by ideas drawn from system theories that went beyond considering only individual minds. Early pioneers began to be aware of family influences as a system. Mental health professionals dealing with clients suffering from substance abuse identified certain patterns. Addictions often create extreme behaviors. Therapists and theoreticians working with families impacted by addictions were able to see the inner workings of family dynamics, because the connections and family roles were so extreme that they jumped out in bold relief.

FAMILY MEMBERS AS ROLE PLAYERS

Family therapy pioneer Virginia Satir developed a useful description of some of these roles. Later, Claudia Black and Sharon Wegscheider-Cruse [3] expanded on these concepts when writing about their work with Adult Children of alcoholics. It is not an exhaustive list of possible roles, simply common ones that they observed. Also, some family members fill more than one role, and others change roles as they grow older and significant changes occur in the family.

These descriptions can be a useful tool for understanding your and your siblings' ways of dealing with your family crisis. The role each person plays can be affected by birth order, individual personality, and gender. Later, we will provide understanding how individual personality differences and gender programming can influence your family members' perspectives, beliefs, and behaviors.

Bruce writes:

Once, while flying over Los Angeles, California, on my way home, I was looking down over the homes of millions of people. I had one of those moments, when something I already understood intellectually, I suddenly understood more profoundly emotionally. I could imagine that, under all of those roofs, wherever there were small children, whatever was going on in that home, was for them, their entire universe. The rules, customs, behaviors, and normal day-to-day routines were the basic template for what life was all about.

As we grow up, we learn to fulfill the various roles needed to make our particular family system work. The roles available to us as a small child living in the universe of our home depended on how healthy our family was. Below is a summary of the types of roles identified by Satir, Black, and Wegscheider-Cruse.

- *The Family Hero*: Some children get designated as the one who will carry the family banner to new heights. Everyone in the family knows that this person has been chosen as most likely to succeed. Most of the family's resources will be invested in this child. For example, he or she may be the one encouraged to get more education or be groomed to take over the family business.
- *The Responsible One*: This family member's job is to do the right thing and also be capable and willing to take care of holding the family together. This person is often identified as the one who writes and calls all the other family members to keep everyone connected. The Hero and the Responsible One may be the same person. It is common for family members to fill more than one role.
- *The Beautiful Loser*: This person always looks good coming in second. They often appear to have all of the necessary talents for success, but somehow never quite get to be the big winner. In some families, they are also the Responsible One, but Family Hero has been given to another member. They are expected to ignore their own needs in the service of other family members. Deep inside, they may have learned to believe they do not deserve to be a big winner. They may do all right, but to use an American football metaphor, they spend their lives settling for field goals instead of touchdowns.
- *The Placator*: This family member is the peacemaker, even if making peace means always being the person who gives in. He is an important factor in keeping warring families from breaking apart. This person has learned to avoid most conflicts and is expected to referee conflicts between those family members who are not required to regulate their anger on their own.
- *The Adaptor*: Also named the "*Lost Child*," this is often a middle child and common in families with severe problems. For example, this can occur when alcohol or other traumas affect a family, and parental skills deteriorate over time. This child's solution is to adapt to almost anything that comes up.

The unspoken agreement is, "I won't expect much from you, and in return, you won't expect much from me."
- *The Scapegoat*: This person is seen as the source of all the family's problems. "Everyone" knows that if it weren't for this person's addictions, or other irresponsible behaviors, everyone else in the family would be much better off. She often causes financial problems for herself, and then the expectation is that the Family Hero or the Responsible One will clean up the mess. Scapegoats often feel valueless and see themselves as losers.
- *The Survivor*: Children who survive growing up in an environment filled with trauma and uncertainty develop certain skills. They may have the skill of the Adaptor, who can shut down awareness of their environment and get by, or even somewhat survive on very little. Their comfort zone is trauma, drama, and last-minute solutions. A therapist I know once described it this way, "My best skill was surviving impossible messes, so I had to keep creating more of them, so I could show off my best skill."

These are some of the more common family roles, although not all of them. Also, keep in mind this is not an exact model because people are much more complicated than this. Like all models, however, if you understand them the same way you understand a map, although the map is not the territory, it does help you to get around.

Of course, all of these roles are directly governed by the person's underlying beliefs about themselves, about life, and the often unspoken agreements by family members. We know that most of our beliefs about our lives and ourselves originally came about from our interpretations of the events that happened to us when very young. Parents, siblings, and extended family members aid in the development of these interpretations, and individual personality styles also have an influence.

Established family roles and relationships often get disrupted and distorted when the divorcing parents divulge more detailed, deeply personal, or hidden, negative information about the other parent, or about the split to their Adult Children. This often creates stress and boundary issues. Adult Children can become reluctant confidants. In some cases, they can become the main emotional support and even a source of financial support to a parent, who may or may not have been particularly good at supporting the Adult Child when she was younger. Adult Children commonly report, "I thought that I did not have to worry about my parents."

Bruce writes:

Gwen, whom you met in chapter 7, felt that way before her parents decided to divorce. She said to me, "They were still healthy, they had been together for years, and I thought that they could handle their own lives. I am twenty-three, and, as you know, I already have my own problems. I guess as an adult, the world expects me to be involved and know more, but I would have preferred not to know the details of why my parents are divorcing. Maybe I would have wondered and had questions, but I don't need to hear their intimate details and all the bad things they say about the other. I can't fix this for them. If it was up to me, they wouldn't be divorcing, but I don't have any say in it."

Adult Children often hear many comments that discount their experiences about their parents' divorce, like how fortunate they are that their parents waited until they were grown, or that they don't need to worry about it. Many begin to think there is something wrong with them for feeling what they are feeling. Often, they do not seek help right away, or ever. They have never been through this before, and don't have any way to know that their experiences are valid. They say that they try to hide their feelings because others find them odd.

Adult Children sometimes wonder if they are just being selfish. These feelings of inadequacy add more stress that can impact their performance at work or school. It can cause strain in their other relationships. Meanwhile, they continue to think they are overreacting. All of this piles up. Relationships with family and friends can deteriorate. It is no wonder that some become depressed. The tendency in our culture is to minimize the impact of divorce on Adult Children. It is so pervasive that some report that when they have reached out for help, they found even their therapist was unsympathetic. That is one of the reasons that we only refer to therapists who have proper training and experience working with divorce.

We all have emotional defenses that we developed early in life to cope with whatever emotional upheavals we encountered and threats we perceived. For those who are not familiar with the concept of psychological defenses, here are some typical examples: denial, withdrawing, sudden anger, rejecting, avoiding, and excessive controlling. Divorce can inflict trauma on families. Trauma can trigger extreme versions of our unique emotional defenses. It is helpful to keep this in mind, monitor ourselves, and go easy on each other.

WHY THIS IS IMPORTANT TO UNDERSTAND

During this time of change, uncertainty, and confusion for your family, the unfamiliar rules, roles, and boundaries create emotional pain for some, if not all, family members. It is then that you may experience defensive behavior from them. And they will experience you at less than your best. Our defenses are symptoms that something is going wrong.

Emotional defenses provide ways to avoid pain. Often, they are facets of personality that others experience as negative. Be on the lookout for your defensive behaviors and those of your family members. Consciously recognize these defenses for what they are—improvised efforts to avoid pain, created when you or the other person was very young. Understanding this will help you shift your focus, so you can respond thoughtfully, instead of automatically reacting to your emotional triggers.

OUR CULTURAL ROLES INFLUENCE HOW DIVORCE AFFECTS WOMEN AND MEN DIFFERENTLY

Journalist Andy Hinds writes that in a conversation with researcher Brené Brown she shared that she "discovered in the course of her research that, contrary to her early assumptions, men's shame is not primarily inflicted by other men. Instead, it is the women in their lives who tend to be repelled when men show the chinks in their armor."[4] He writes that Brown said, "Most women pledge allegiance to this idea that women can explore their emotions, break down, fall apart—and it's healthy. . . . But guys are not allowed to fall apart. . . . Men are often pressured to open up and talk about their feelings and are criticized for being emotionally walled-off; but if they get too real, they are met with revulsion." She recalled the first time she realized she had been complicit in the shaming: "Holy Shit! I am the patriarchy!"[5]

In families where the mother was the children's primary caregiver, it is common for the children to be closer to their mothers than their fathers. Thus, when the children were growing up, they learned to see their father through "their mother's eyes." In chapter 2, for example, we met Daniel, who expressed his distress over his parents' divorce. His sister, Sue, had sided with her mother and resented that Daniel still talked with his father. That is a predictable outcome of what used to be portrayed as traditional marriage, in which the father worked outside of the home and the mother, at least in the early years, stayed home to raise the children. That typically created a closer child–maternal bond. This is one factor that contributes to the findings that Adult Children's relationships with their fathers are more at risk of deteriorating than their relationships with their mothers.

GENDER DIFFERENCES IN MARRIAGE

In our culture, women more than men are raised to think about and plan for a wedding. Most men never think about their wedding day.

For that reason, the wedding industry primarily targets women. As Bruce said earlier, he was surprised to learn how much thought, daydreaming, and planning went into this for many women when they were girls. "The global wedding industry was estimated to be worth over 300 billion dollars in 2016 and growing bigger every day. While businesses around the world were witnessing a decline in consumer spending amid tough economic conditions, the splurging on weddings trend seems to only go up."[6] "The US wedding industry hit $72 billion in revenue in 2016."[7]

These are points worth remembering when dealing with people of different genders, whose families are going through divorce. Taking all this into account, it is not surprising that women often assume more ownership of the marriage and feel more shame about the failure of marriage than men do.

It is not that men don't hurt and suffer from a divorce, although they more frequently report feeling shame over financial failure. During the divorce process, when they must reveal and discuss with strangers any past or present financial failures or difficulties, they often say that they feel personal shame. In most or perhaps in all cultures, shame is gender specific.[8]

Thus, women are more likely to experience the failure of their marriage as a personal failure and may internalize personal shame from culturally imposed expectations, just as men internalize personal shame from culturally imposed expectations that they be good providers.

It is important for divorce professionals, as well as Adult Children and their parents, to keep these gender differences in mind. It is not that men don't feel shock, sadness, and depression when their marriage fails, or that women don't feel similar emotions about financial losses. However, shame is a different emotion. Extreme shame is toxic to our mental health and can distort communication. There are also physical consequences. Shame carries the added risk of creating inflammation in our bodies,[9] and excessive inflammation carries negative consequences to our physical health.

9

RELATIONSHIPS WITH SIBLINGS, EXTENDED FAMILY, FRIENDS, AND COMMUNITY

> *Divorce has many witnesses, many victims. It is a lurid duet that entices observers to the dance; the pas de deux expands, flowers into a monstrous choreography and draws in friends, children and relatives. . . . Two people declare war on each other, and their screams and tears and days of withdrawal infect their entire world with the bacilli of their pain. There are no clean divorces. Divorces should be conducted in abattoirs, surgical wards, blood banks or funeral homes. The greatest fury comes from the wound where love once issued forth.*
>
> —Pat Conroy, American novelist

Michael and Jennifer are Adult Children whose parents are divorcing. Through their eyes, we experience how the dynamics of sibling relationships can negatively or positively impact all family members, and how overall family dynamics influence relationships between siblings. This information will help you understand yourself and your siblings, so you can more effectively negotiate sibling relationships.

As you listen in, you will hear about the challenges these Adult Children experience as they communicate about their parents' divorce with family and friends. They discover how their own struggles are affected by interpersonal family dynamics, and how the interplay between their unique family history, each person's stage of life, and personal history impacts the way the family communicates.

Michael and Jennifer are siblings, so they share some typical relationship considerations that Daniel faced in chapter 2. Those experiences are different from what Maria in chapter 2 is dealing with as an only child.

SOME CHALLENGES THAT SIBLINGS OFTEN ENCOUNTER

- How close are the siblings to their parents?
- Are any siblings historically closer to one parent?
- Are all the siblings closer to one parent or are there differences?
- How close are the siblings to each other?
- Can the siblings support each other, or is there already preexisting distance that is now exacerbated?
- Do the siblings take sides with a different parent during the divorce?
- Does geographical distance affect the sibling relationship?

In some families of Adult Children whose parents are divorcing, the siblings provide a safe space for each other. They are the only ones who know what it was like to grow up in this particular family. They share intimate family memories and perspectives that outsiders do not know. In very personal ways, they can help each other get through the now distorted version of their lives that they are all experiencing.

Unfortunately, it does not always work out that way. In some families, divorce can severely disrupt relationships between brothers and sisters. It can happen even when their relationships had been supportive and close before their parents' divorce. There are families in which one or more siblings take the side of a parent. Sometimes different siblings side with a different parent. Depending on the family history and individual personalities, Adult Children can take the attitude that "if you are not for us, you are against us." That was the case for Michael, age thirty-eight, and his sister Jennifer, thirty-six.

MICHAEL AND JENNIFER

Bruce writes:

Michael arrived early for his first appointment. When I went to greet him in the waiting room, he was sitting on a sofa looking at his phone. He was dressed casually in a maroon T-shirt and denim jeans. As I entered from his right, he was facing slightly to his left with his eyes down toward his phone.

"Hello, are you Michael?" I asked while extending my hand.

He confirmed he was, and I introduced myself. He stood up quickly, smiled pleasantly, and extended his hand in greeting. As we shook hands, I pointed out some essentials, as I always do with a new client. I advised him where to find the restroom key, asked if he wanted some water, herbal tea, or coffee, and otherwise helped him orient himself to the surroundings.

Handing me the intake paperwork I had sent him, he asked in a hesitant voice, "Do you want these now?"

I took the papers and invited him into my office. When I suggested that he could sit anywhere, he smiled and asked jokingly, "Is this a test?" He quickly added, "I have never been to a therapist before."

He chose a high-backed upholstered chair, facing away from a wall of windows, and immediately started, "I don't know where to begin," in a now even-toned voice. "My wife's friend recommended you. My parents are getting divorced. I worry about both of them. Ever since they started the divorce, my sister and I are not getting along. It's also affecting my kids because they love my parents, and they are also close to their cousins, my sister's kids. My wife thinks I'm getting too involved and stressed out."

"That's a lot to deal with," I agreed.

Michael became quiet for a bit. I waited until he was ready, and he started again, this time speaking more quickly.

"My life was going pretty good," he said. "Jennifer, my sister, and I have always been close. She's a year and a half younger. We have always gotten along. Now, she is mad at Dad, and she is mad at me because I still talk to him. Mom says she found out that he had an affair about seventeen years ago after we had both moved out. I guess Mom recently started seeing someone and now wants a divorce. Mom says it's Dad's fault. When she told Jennifer that Dad had an affair, it came out of the blue. Jennifer immediately sided with Mom and even blamed Dad for Mom having an affair. Jennifer also says she is tired of how Dad treats Mom."

He stopped, then added, "Now that I think about it, I do remember Dad yelling at Mom as we were growing up. So I get why Jennifer says she is tired of the way Dad treats Mom. Anyhow, now she won't talk to him or see him. If Dad comes to visit any other family member, she leaves when he arrives, and takes her kids and her husband Tom with her. If she knows ahead of time he was invited, she won't come. She wouldn't let her kids come to my son Jason's birthday party last week, because she knew he was going to be there. My daughter Brittany turned twelve last month. My parents showed up at different times. It was hard. When Jennifer got there with her kids and Tom, it was okay until Dad came, and then it was a real mess."

He paused briefly, then asked, "How can I not invite my kids' grandpa and grandma to their birthday?"

Continuing, he didn't wait for me to reply. "And then if I do, their cousins can't come. Either Dad is left out of any family events, or Jennifer won't come." I could see the pain in his eyes as he described the rift in his family.

"I know this is very painful," I offered, reflecting to him what I sensed.

He closed his eyes and inhaled a slow, deep breath, as though breathing in what I had said. Just as slowly, he exhaled.

"You got that right! This all hurts so much!"

He paused and became quiet. Silence can be powerful, as people are reflecting. I remained quiet, joining him in the silence.

After several moments, he continued, though pacing his words more slowly. "Tom and I are friends, and our kids are close to the same age. Until the divorce, our kids have always spent a lot of time together. My wife Debbie gets along okay with both of my parents, and she and Jennifer have gotten along okay. Debbie and I have usually gone home to my parents for Thanksgiving and Christmas. Debbie's parents live in the Bay Area near San Francisco. Two years ago, we went up there, but it has usually been at my parents'. I don't know what to do about this. Dad seems stunned, and he is also angry. I worry about him. I worry about Mom too. My wife fears that we might get stuck helping one or both of them financially. As I said, she gets along with them okay, but for her it's different. They are not her parents, and she wants to make sure that our kids and family come first. But I can't just stand by and watch us all self-destruct."

For most of the session Michael continued filling in the background. While sometimes I have to prompt a client to begin or to clarify, Michael seemed to need to get it all out. He alternated between rapid reporting and moments of silence while he thought.

I learned that growing up, Michael and his sister had a close, friendly, older brother–younger sister relationship. They shared a similar family experience through childhood, adolescence, and early adulthood, and always got along well, unlike the way it was for some of their friends with their brothers and sisters. During the transition from child to young adult, both attended the same local university. Their relationship was always easy and mutually supportive. Even as young adults, each had no hesitation about dropping over to the other's apartment without any prior notice or invitation. It continued that way after both graduated from college and started their careers. Their personalities are markedly different, but at the same time, the bond they shared was strong. Although each had their own set of friends, Michael and Jennifer had stayed as close as when they were growing up and living in the same home.

"About two weeks ago, Jennifer called me. She told me that she was really angry because I visited Dad, and still talked to him regularly. It feels like she is blaming me and treating me like an enemy."

Michael is feeling abandoned and blamed by his sister. Swept up in this unrest, he remembers the relationship they had before either of them were married and is now overcome by a deep sense of loneliness. Michael is angry, confused, and worried. He is also feeling victimized. He has questions.

One question came out as an angry complaint. "Should my sister have the right to tell me I can't see my own father?"

He then quickly followed up. "Do I have the right to insist that she continue to see him?" he asked.

I provided Michael with information about personal boundaries and suggested that these are family member boundary issues that he and Jennifer need to talk about and get some clarity.

As he talked about how close he and Jennifer had been, Michael suddenly remembered another moment when he felt a similar loss. It happened shortly after Jennifer was married. It was the natural change that siblings experience when one of them marries. Because his sister's life had merged with another who was not part of their family of origin, he had to take another person's values, feelings, expectations, and concerns into account in the way he interacted with Jennifer. Soon, many things that were done automatically as a matter of course suddenly became self-conscious, self-monitored, restrained, and some were discontinued all together. When Michael got married about eighteen months later, Jennifer made similar healthy boundary adjustments based on mutual understanding and agreement. He described it this way.

"It was kind of minor, but it was one of those sudden realizations that life has changed. It was a few weeks after Jennifer got married. I was in the neighborhood of her new home and had an automatic instinct to drop in and see how she was doing. I didn't do it because I also realized she had her new life, and I knew I had to adjust to new rules and expectations in our relationship. It wasn't that I didn't understand. I understood it perfectly, but I felt a little strange because . . ." He paused.

"Well, like something was gone. It was just a split second, and I remembered that I couldn't just pop in, because she was living with Tom, and I couldn't just drop in on him. It was different before because Jennifer and I grew up together. I know it sounds obvious and silly, but I felt different somehow."

He said that after his call with his sister, he feels the same way he felt then, only worse. At the time she called, he did not see any connection between that memory and what he experienced in the moment of Jennifer's call. I understood that Michael was experiencing what therapists call relationship uncertainty. In this instance, it occurred because Jennifer had erected unfamiliar boundaries, altering their long-established relationship and familiar customs and expectations.

Michael reported more background information. He described Jennifer and their mother as having similar personalities.

"They both tend to see the world in terms of black and white. Jennifer has always been closer to Mom than Dad. I think her attitude and loyalty are because both are female, and also because they are similar personalities."

As he spoke, I noted another factor. He described a family structure that was like many families of previous generations. Their mother was more involved than their father in raising both children. As a result of their mother being the primary caregiver during their early years while growing up, both he and his sister tended to see their father "through their mother's eyes."

Michael is unsure about where the truth lies in his parents' stories about the other. His personality style is different from both of his parents. However, because his mother was able to be a stay-at-home mom during their early years, he was closer to their mother, like his sister was. He knows his father is not a good communicator and is moody. He also thinks that his mother can be very unreasonable and rigid at times. On the other hand, his mother says his father was having an affair. He secretly wonders if she is exaggerating to justify her behavior. He feels torn between both parents and unable to count on his sister to help him figure out what to do. He cannot turn to his parents to help him get perspective, which further adds to his dilemma.

He explained, “There is no ‘them’ anymore.”

Both Michael and Jennifer have two children, similar in age. They all get along well and are close. Now, tension dominates any attempt at a family gathering. Jennifer won’t attend any event where her father is present. Their mother tries to avoid being anywhere he might show up, and insists that they inform her if there is any chance he might show up, so she can decline attending. As a result, the cousins see less of each other. Michael looks to future major traditional family holidays and celebrations with a sense of despair. He is also apprehensive about what to do if his mother brings the man she is dating to any function. He said, “I don’t know what to call him. Her ‘boyfriend’? What? I also worry that he might show up when I visit to see how Mom is doing. People don’t know how hard all of this is.”

Jennifer has jumped into rescue mode with her mother and has chosen sides. She cannot understand how Michael could act the way he does. For her, the situation is clear. Her father, an aerospace engineer who was always emotionally distant, was never very good with personal relationships and will never change. She always struggled to get his notice and approval. In Jennifer’s experience, he always expected their mother to take care of the house, and that included the children.

Their mother is a nurse and resumed working part-time when Jennifer and Michael reached middle school. She recently told them that after they married, their father abused alcohol, but got it under control before they were born. He then became preoccupied with rock climbing with his friends on weekends. Sometimes he took Michael along. Michael reported that, according to Jennifer, all of his friends were men, and most were “just like Dad,” so she did not go with them. By the time she was ready to go to college, she had given up trying to be close. On the other hand, through outdoor activities or watching sports on television, Michael was able to form somewhat of a bonded relationship with their father.

Jennifer is feeling that Michael has let her down. She has to deal with her mom's anger all by herself. Her kids see Grandma but can't see their cousins, because her mom won't be any place where their father is, and Michael continues to talk with their father and help him. Jennifer's husband Tom thinks that she should let her parents deal with all of this, but wants to be supportive, so he is also angry with Michael. When Jennifer mentions the problems she is having to her friends or other relatives, they say things like "at least you are already grown so their divorce won't affect you that much. You're already out of the house and have your own family."

Michael hears similar things from friends and relatives. He said, "I wonder if there is something wrong with me. After all, almost everyone I talk to seems to think I should just get over it. Sure, they say that it's too bad, but then act as if I should just move on and be thankful that it didn't happen until I was grown and out of the house. None of my friends have a grasp of how much this is impacting me and my family. The ones who know Jennifer think she'll get over it."

He continued, "My wife is understanding, but she doesn't like how this is affecting our children. She expects Jennifer to be more flexible when it involves all of the children, and for me to find a way to deal with all of this without it hurting our kids. She is also concerned about how this could affect us financially if we are expected to help Mom. I never expected that I would have to be taking care of my parents like this. Sure, I had imagined some time far in the future they would get old, and I would have to help, but I never thought it would be this. Nobody gets how I feel. And, I told you I don't know what to do or say if I ever have to meet the man Mom is dating. Can I just refuse?"

On top of all that distress, both Michael and Jennifer have to deal with their aunts, uncles, and their parents' family friends. Many of them have chosen sides, particularly her mother's family, most of whom encourage her to "really stick it to him" in the divorce. Michael feels he has to carry this burden alone. When he expresses any concern for his father, his maternal relatives criticize him or minimize his concerns.

Michael decided to get professional support. He realized that he had never been through anything like this before, and he needed to speak with someone who understood what was happening to his family. One of the decisions he made as a result of our meetings was to do his best to understand each parent's emotional state, and to be as empathetic as possible. He reported that it has been helpful. He has thought about how hurt, confused, and possibly angry he would feel if he was suddenly faced with being in a divorce with his wife. At the same time, he also needs support in dealing with his own emotions. He reminds himself that no one in his family has ever been in this exact situation before. It's so fresh, and this applies to dealing with his sister too. All of them are devastated. Michael has discovered that it is tough for him and all of his family members to be empathetic with each other while in the midst of their own emotions.

For most people, parental divorce qualifies as a traumatic experience. Whether an Adult Child or still a minor, it can hit hard. Our reactions to trauma can easily bring out the worst in us. Whether you are an Adult Child or a divorcing parent, it is helpful to monitor your triggers and moods, so you can pull yourselves back from behaviors you may regret when you are not angry or in despair.

A REMINDER ABOUT GENDER AND PERSONALITY DIFFERENCES

When dealing with your siblings, parents, or other extended family members, also consider gender and personality-style differences. The descriptions outlined below may describe some members of your family.

Even in good times, the person whose personality is diametrically opposite of yours can be difficult to understand. As your families move to a postdivorce stage, you may want to avoid common problems that can damage your ongoing relationships with your siblings. For example, siblings who are more concrete and tend to see things in terms of black or white with no gray areas may have a harder time after the parental divorce making peace with the parent they deemed the "designated bad person." They can perceive a sibling who takes a gentler view and expresses concern for the "designated bad" parent as betraying the other family members. Or, siblings can become judgmental and presume the right to decide what type of relationship their siblings are allowed to have with each parent. When all of you are under stress, this can amplify. In most cases, taking sides against either parent can put ongoing relationships with your siblings at risk. It is generally better to recognize that your parents' relationship with each other is different than your relationship with either parent. Their relationship is their business, and they established the terms before you were born. If you and your siblings keep this is in mind, you may have an easier time understanding each other and your parents.

People often attribute to gender differences what are actually personality and character differences. For example, consider people who are the impulsive, go-getter, go-for-it, gun-slinger, shoot-from-the-hip-type of person. She might be called a leader, a potential entrepreneur, or a heroic daredevil if she were a man. A Man's Man! However, women who have that personality tend to be called ugly names, especially if they act out sexually, speak too loudly, or are "too wild or pushy." You can fill in the blanks with other labels.

It is not only men who call women who have a more flamboyant or competitive personality derogatory names. Women do so as well because they are trained just like men to ascribe gender differences to inherent personality differences. Girls and women who fit this personality are also out of step with gender stereotypes. When they rise to leadership positions, others may criticize them for being too bossy, whereas they might praise a boy for the same behavior. On the other hand, boys and men who are concerned with relationships, creativity, and cooperation versus aggression and competition are seen as going against the norm of male culture standards. They often report feeling they do not fit in, like "strangers in a strange land" while growing up and in adulthood.

Emotionally surviving the early years in school can be difficult for girls and boys, who do not fit cultural gender expectations. Some boys become overly competitive in an attempt to fit in. When girls assert themselves forcefully, often their peers label them "bossy," and they learn to downplay personal excellence in order to fit in.[1]

FAMILIES WITH BOTH ADULT AND MINOR CHILDREN

Some families have a mix of Adult Children and minor children. Their Adult Children may be out of the family home, in college or specialized training, working in their established careers, single or married, with or without children of their own. The minor children live in the family home and are still dependent on their parents. In those cases, while the older children might prefer to avoid dealing with their parents' divorce, it becomes clear that it is not possible for younger siblings still at home to do so. The older siblings, who experienced the advantages of being raised in an intact family but are now entangled in their own problems generated by their parents' divorce, might overlook the problems their younger siblings are experiencing.

When working with families with both minor and Adult Children, we coach the older siblings to go out of their way to stay connected to their younger siblings, who are losing those advantages and will never get them back. We tell them that they can help their younger siblings a great deal by showing them that, despite their parents' divorce, they are all still family.

THE SMYTHES

Bruce writes:

Brent and Phyllis Smythe were married for twenty-nine years. Their financial advisor referred them to me. She had encouraged them to use a nonadversarial divorce process, such as collaborative divorce or mediation. She was a family friend who had seen contentious divorces damage families. As a result, she had become a strong advocate for more peaceful approaches for friends and clients who are divorcing.

The Smythes chose a collaborative divorce process using a multidisciplinary team of divorce professionals, comprised of legal, financial, and mental health professionals experienced in nonadversarial divorce practices. Their team consisted of two collaborative family law attorneys (one attorney for each spouse), two divorce coaches (each a licensed therapist), one neutral financial specialist, and one neutral child specialist (NCS) (also a licensed therapist). The neutral child specialist serves as the voice of the children, both minor and Adult. The focus is to help the coparents keep their children at the center instead of in the middle of the parents' divorce.

The couple scheduled an appointment to meet and see if it was a good fit for me to serve their family as their NCS during their divorce. In that meeting I learned that they had been married twenty-eight years and had four children: Robert, twenty-six years old, attending law school; Sandra, twenty-four years old, starting medical school; James, nineteen years old, attending his first year of college; and, Richard, seventeen years old, in his senior year of high school.

I briefly described my role as the NCS. "The neutral child specialist is a licensed mental health professional with specialized training in mediation and collaborative divorce and has expertise and experience working with minor and Adult Children, and parents going through divorce. The NCS brings the voice of your minor and Adult Children into the process and serves on the team as a neutral representative of your children's needs and preferences."

I explained, "At the full team meetings when you cocreate your agreements, what you might call the business meetings, the NCS 'holds the space' for all of your children, as though they are present in the meetings. I want it to be clear that your children have a voice not a choice, because it is you, their parents, who are divorcing, and who will be making the decisions, some of which will affect all of your children."

As I always do, I expanded my explanation *to make it clear* that, as their family's NCS, I am not serving as a custody evaluator, nor do I provide a written report or recommendations, as a custody evaluator would. I described how, along with their collaborative divorce coaches, I would assist them to make better coparenting decisions for their family, and that as part of that process, their coaches and I would help them improve their communication. I also reminded them that ultimately, their spouse is always going to be their children's other parent, and that it is in their children's best interests for both of them to keep that in mind when interacting with each other.

Phyllis asked some questions about how I go about this role. I described my typical process and supplemented it with several informational handouts, including a detailed description explaining how I work in my role as the NCS. I explained that I gather information by speaking with their children, including their Adult Children, because their divorce is also affecting their Adult Children's lives. I meet with minor children in person and include the parents in the first meeting, so their children will know that their parents are unified in wanting them to work with me.

I know that children, and especially teenagers, are "checking me out" in a first meeting and deciding whether or not they trust me enough to share any information that could help me help them and their parents. To this end, I explain to the coparents and the children that I will not quote the children directly about any matters that they want to keep confidential. Sometimes children want to tell their parents what they want them to know, sometimes not. If they do not want to share something with their parents and think I would pass it on to their parents, they are reluctant to tell me. I remind everyone of the limits of confidentiality and review what I am mandated to report, such as elder abuse or child abuse. I also assure the coparents that, if I learn about something dangerous to a minor child, I would discuss it with the child and work out a way for the child or me to inform them.

I noted, "Often Adult Children are reluctant participants in their parents' divorce and prefer to keep some distance. In this case, since all of your children live within easy driving distance, it could benefit your two younger children if their older brother and sister participated in a joint in-person meeting with the younger ones and me."

A few days later, Brent and Phyllis informed me that they had chosen me to be the NCS. I told them I was honored to serve their family in this role and sent them the "Child Information Questionnaire." I requested that each coparent complete a questionnaire about each child, including the Adult Children. We scheduled the first meeting with all four children.

On a cool Saturday morning, the four children and I met in my office. The family had decided that the coparents would not attend, so the siblings could feel free to talk openly. The children all spoke positively about their parents. As they described their parents, all four agreed about each parent's strengths and weaknesses. I explained that, if they are willing, in this first meeting I would like to know what they need from their parents as they go through their divorce, and what they want their parents to know and consider.

Robert and Sandra, the two oldest, began. Sandra said, "I guess it wasn't really a surprise that they are divorcing, although I guess it was still a shock. Robert and I have been out of the house for years now. My parents helped both of us financially through school. I don't know how much they want to help me through graduate school. That's up to them. I would like to know what they intend so that I can make plans. I don't feel entitled to it, but I do want to know."

Robert added, "Dad is moving out. Mom is the one who wants the divorce. They haven't told me much. James and Richard still live at home and probably have heard more than Sandra and I. Like Sandra said, I don't expect them to keep helping with graduate school but would like to know what to expect. I think they will still help James and Richard. James just started college, and Richard still has a year to go in high school. My parents want them to go to college. Mom is already going back to school. She wants to become a CPA."

Like their older siblings, James and Richard were polite. They all seemed comfortable together, but they allowed their older siblings to lead the way. They did contribute to the discussion when prompted. Both older siblings expressed concern about James and Richard and acknowledged that they had benefited from reaching adulthood with the family intact. Both readily stated their intention to make an effort to maintain closer communication with the younger brothers, and Richard and James said they appreciated that.

In future meetings with the coparents, I noted how warm their children were toward each other. I introduced the idea that the children are the real wealth of the family. Both Brent and Phyllis readily agreed to this framing. This concept was useful later in the divorce process when it came time for them to make financial, coparenting, and other decisions. There were times when they appeared to be stuck in impasse. When their collaborative professionals refocused them on their previously stated intentions to cocreate agreements that would benefit *all* the family members, they chose to set aside their hurts and anger and cocreate agreements that worked for all family members.

While academic research has virtually ignored the effect of late-life parental divorce on adult sibling relationships, Dr. Joleen Greenwood's study found themes that the Adult Children in this chapter have been experiencing. The majority of Adult Children in her study reported that their adult sibling relationships were not negatively affected by their parents' divorce. Some turned to each other for support and became closer. Others overcame geographical distance and remained close. Those who took a different parent's side during the divorce, thus pitting themselves against one another, reported that their relationships were negatively affected, although their relationships improved over time. The siblings who took the same side were more likely to support one another and reported that it strengthened their relationship.[2] Even though only a minority of Adult Children in this study reported that parental divorce negatively affected their sibling relationships, the findings indicate that taking different parent's sides during the divorce harms the adult sibling relationships and interferes with siblings being able to provide support for one another during painful transitions in their families.

As you read this final quotation, remember that taking sides during your parents' divorce may cause you more problems. You can be supportive of your parents without allowing yourself to take sides in their disputes. Your relationship with each parent is different from the one each parent has with the other.

> *Sibling relationships . . . outlast marriages, survive the death of parents, resurface after quarrels that would sink any friendship. They flourish in a thousand incarnations of closeness and distance, warmth, loyalty and distrust.*
> —Erica E. Goode, American journalist

10

FAMILY TRADITIONS AND RITUALS

The bond that links your true family is not one of blood, but of respect and joy in each other's life.
—Richard Bach, American writer

Family traditions and rituals are frequently connected to holidays, religious observances, vacations, celebrations such as birthdays, and other reoccurring significant events. Adult Children of gray divorce, whether married or not, or have children or not, usually have concerns about how to effectively manage these emotionally filled occasions. In addition to losing your parents as a unified family parental unit, there are common disruptions. Examples include the loss of sharing family holidays, the loss of being able to just casually drop in on your parents for an unplanned visit if they are involved with new significant others, additional stress when your parents insist that you include their new significant others in all family get-togethers that causes the focus to swing to the parents instead of the reason for the event, and adjusting to the reality that your parent's goals and interests in life do not necessarily include the best interests of your other parent. In fact, for many of you, the hurt and hostility one or both parents feel means that their goals in life might intentionally exclude caring about the other.

In this new normal, events that were intended to be joyful celebrations can turn into tension-filled affairs. Even with thoughtful preparation ahead of time, an Adult Child might feel stressed just from knowing that nonfamily members will be involved in the decisions. For example, what to do when a parent refuses to attend a grandchild's birthday celebration unless she can bring the person with whom she had the affair that triggered the parents' divorce?

Through the information gathered from academic research, public news stories, and the experiences of two new characters, Sheila, an Adult Child of gray divorce, and her husband Don, you will discover tools and skills to help during such emotion-packed occasions. Seeing how Sheila and Don encounter typical problems can help you blend existing and new traditions.

Maureen Culkin Rhyne, PhD, noted, "Family traditions and rituals serve as a source of security and continuity over the years. The celebrations and observation of holidays and life marker events, like graduations, weddings, and birthdays, provide a structure for shared observation and acknowledgement of being connected to a family. The disruption of these patterns when parents divorce may create concern about family continuity."[1]

As one of life's major stressful events, divorce has been compared to death. However, generally established rites and rituals that offer guidance for the behavior of friends, extended family, and acquaintances acknowledge one's passing. The same is not so for most divorces. Even though almost everyone knows a family who has experienced divorce, there are few common ground rules. This is especially true for Adult Children. As a result, often friends, family, and acquaintances do not know what is appropriate to say or do. This is one reason why the Adult Children often hear comments such as "At least you're lucky it didn't happen when you were younger."

Austin, Texas family-law attorney Janice Green remarks, "A lot of parents who are in my office seeking a later-in-life divorce haven't really done a lot of thinking about how it's going to impact their kids. . . . But adult kids have longer-established family rituals and home memories than the younger ones, so in some sense the divorce can cause more of an impact."[2] Rhyne also noted that there are studies showing that the mother–Adult Child bond is usually stronger than the father–Adult Child bond,[3] and "in many traditional families, men have been groomed to be breadwinners and women caregivers. Fathers often feel misunderstood. They have been working hard to support their families and feel they have been prioritizing family needs above their own. The children, instead of sharing that feeling, experienced their fathers as being absent and someone who just took care of work."[4] We have found this to be true in our work with families. Rhyne added that "as more women entered the workforce, many woman having been raised to be nurturers more than many men, are more aware of parenting responsibilities . . . we socialize women to be the nurturers and it is so insidious that it may take on the guise of a genetic nature. . . . When parents divorce at mid-life, we continue to see that the relationships between fathers and Adult Children tend to deteriorate more than do the mother–Adult Child relationships."[5]

Another research article stated, "It is not too surprising to find that in families with high conflict divorce the Adult Children reported high stress and feelings of being highly pressured to take sides in their parents' divorce. This was especially true for women."[6]

We have already described how the disruptive effects of divorce continue for years, including how it can affect Adult Children whose parents had a long marriage. There are special considerations for how it affects younger Adult Children, because the transition from child to young adult to full adulthood is complex. The continued existence of long-held family traditions and celebrations are suddenly at risk. Even when there is no divorce, usually Adult Children face decisions about which traditions to abandon or maintain.[7]

For Adult Children, the divorce of their older parents is not a single, one-off life event. It's a process. There are ever-changing agreements and disappointments that require rethinking and renegotiating boundaries. Often this is the first time that family members must consciously discuss boundaries that they had always known without any specific conversations. Some traditions are maintained, some change, and some fade. Sometimes parents and extended family members stop participating. Celebrations and holiday traditions often split into two events. For many, when a parent becomes involved with a new person or remarries, it can become even more complicated and often painful.

SHEILA

Bruce writes:

In October, I began seeing eleven-year-old Jonathan, who was experiencing severe anxiety. He was just starting middle school. It was three weeks before Thanksgiving, and Jonathan was making rapid progress. I had scheduled a family meeting to update his parents. I met with his parents, Sheila, a thirty-eight-year-old real estate agent, and Don, a forty-two-year-old high-school assistant principal, immediately after meeting with Jonathan. While I met with his parents, he remained in the waiting room working on his homework.

Sheila and Don chose to sit together on a small sofa immediately across from the windows on one side of my office. I chose a seat facing them. Before I could begin to discuss Jonathan, Sheila said she wanted to get my opinion on something else first. She then immediately began to talk about how difficult the holidays had become since her parents' divorce two years ago.

She began, "Growing up, I used to love the holidays. When Don and I got married, we decided to try to go to each of our parents' homes for Thanksgiving, and alternate Christmas Eve and Christmas Day in different years. It worked out pretty well for a couple of years, but realistically, my mom was much more into the holidays than Don's. We always had my grandparents, aunts, uncles, and cousins over. My parents' house had become the new Holiday Central when my mom took over for my grandmother. My brother Jack also came every year, with his wife, and my nephews. Don's parents came some years too. But now . . ." She made a muffled noise and paused.

"Now it is so hard. My mom is living in a small place with a tiny kitchen. She doesn't want to do any of that anymore. I am like my grandmother and my mom, so I have tried to keep it together. But I can't have both of my parents. My mom is the one who asked for a divorce. But it is my dad who met someone and now lives with her. They always argued a lot. I guess Jack, he's my brother, and I got used to it growing up, but we never thought they would divorce. They have been married more than forty years. I mean, who does that? And my dad moved into another family."

Her voice lowered as she added plaintively, "Who does THAT?"

I nodded to show empathy and that I was following her as she continued.

"The first time, two years ago, I agreed to host the holidays, but then I had to figure out how to have my parents together. I only wanted Dad without the woman he is living with, Louise, so it wouldn't trigger Mom, but then Dad felt it would be easier to skip it, to avoid slighting Louise. It was all tense and strange. Grandma and Grandpa, my mom's parents, were willing to come. My other grandpa, my dad's father, died a few years ago. My dad's mom, my other grandma, came, but when my dad didn't, it was awkward for her. And my kids didn't have their grandpa, and they won't have their cousins this year. My brother Jack's wife decided that this year she wants their family to go to her brother's place. They have a smaller family, it's just her mom and her brother's family, and now she and Jack and his kids will be going there from now on probably."

"That sounds very difficult for all of you," I said while making a mental note about how this was likely to affect Jonathan. I was aware of the general situation from the questionnaires his parents had completed when I first started to see Jonathan. Now Sheila was providing a more detailed picture. As clients become more comfortable with our relationship, it is not unusual for them to reveal that the original concerns are more complex than they first presented.

Sheila continued, "Last summer was even worse. Up until the divorce, we would all go to my mom and dad's second home for a week. It's up by Lake Tahoe. But now we need to find out if Dad and his new family will be there. My mom will only go if Jack or I take her because it's such a long drive. And figuring out Christmas! I always thought Jonathan would get the fun of family. All the younger cousins get along but . . . I never expected this. I think Jack expects me to take care of Mom, and he gets out of it. I don't know how to handle all this. What do you think? I know other people whose parents divorced, but they were kids then. I never expected or thought about all of this. How do other people handle this?"

When Sheila paused, I shared that I have heard similar stories from other people whose parents divorced when they were already grown and out of the house. I was aware that overall most people don't get enough understanding, empathy, or support when this happens. I validated her feelings. I told her that while there is not a large body of research about how divorce affects people who are already grown when their parents divorce, from what I have read and seen, her experience is more or less the norm. People, in general, don't really think about how much this impacts the whole extended family unless someone points it out, or it happens to their family.

Don added, "I worry about how this affects Jonathan. He used to enjoy that everyone got together on the holidays. He still has my mom and dad, but I know he loves his other grandparents. This is stressing Sheila so much, trying to make it all work, and I think she is taking on too much." He turned to Sheila and offered, "Why don't you let Jack handle more of this? I don't think it is worth all this strain."

Sheila looked hurt momentarily and then replied angrily, "It's not your family that's falling apart. You know how much we used to love Thanksgiving and Christmas."

Turning to me, she said, "And I don't really like my dad's new wife or whatever he calls her. It just makes everything more difficult. It seems like he has left us and is all into his other family now."

I shared with Sheila and Don that holidays are difficult for many people. I said, "People drive around and see billboards with a happy family getting ready to eat turkey, and everyone is smiling. It's in magazines, movies, and television. We all grew up seeing these magazine and billboard versions of the perfect, happy family at Christmas and Thanksgiving. At the same time, people then reflect that their family does not live up to or even resemble this depicted ideal. For many people, uncomfortable memories and feelings accompany the holidays."

Sheila interjected, "That's me now. But it didn't used to be. The holidays have gone from being something to look forward to something I dread."

I said, "I've seen people, usually women, because you are the main kinship keepers for families, but not just women, who keep trying to place that fantasy template from billboards and made-for-TV movies over their own family during holidays, and they end up making it worse for themselves. They keep trying to make that unrealistic template fit. Of course, it doesn't, so they have a miserable time. I often think that if instead of trying for a larger-than-life experience, they decided to focus on appreciating whatever is good, or even just okay about the real people who are actually present, they could have a human-scale, enjoyable event. Since you asked for my ideas, maybe you could scale down your expectations and remind yourself that you can't bring back your past. Don't rob yourself of your present opportunity to enrich your family's memories. You could start by inviting the people you want to have there. If you feel obligated to have other people and can do it without feeling resentful, go ahead and invite them too. You can start to create a new version of *your* family traditions. Above all, when you are trying to do this, be kind and gentle with yourself. This is new territory, and it may take a few tries to get it the way you want."

SOME FAMILIES HAVE BEEN ABLE TO CREATE BETTER OPTIONS

There are some exceptions. Some marital therapists create a divorce ceremony. Just as their wedding provided a ritual for the couple, family, and friends that honored the beginning of the marriage, the divorce ceremony creates a ritual to mark the end of a marriage in a peaceful, dignified manner that honors the marriage they had, and adds closure.

In some instances, a divorcing couple will create their own divorce ceremony. Here is how BuzzFeedNews.com reported about one on December 19, 2016. The article, about a divorcing couple in California who had been married for twenty-four years and had Adult Children, reported that the couple threw a "'Divorce Party' to Make Their Split Less Awkward. . . . On the day their divorce was finalized, the California-based pair threw a party with catered food, drinking, and dancing. . . . They organized the bash, in part, to dispel potential discomfort for family and friends." The couple said that they did it "to help them understand we are the same people, that there should be no awkwardness. We wanted to divide what we had built together fairly and to keep family first. We felt that we did that, and we felt that was a reason to celebrate."[8]

If you are a divorcing parent with minor or Adult Children, you might consider adapting these options to help your family. If you are an Adult Child whose parents are in the process of divorcing, perhaps you can share the information in this book with them. Knowledge offers options. Yet for many families, it may be too soon to make these adjustments.

11

PARENTAL DATING, REPARTNERING, AND REMARRIAGE

Change, like healing, takes time.
—Veronica Roth, American writer

Divorce ruptures the attachment bonds that bind family members to each other individually and as a family. The pain and loss experienced by Adult Children of gray divorce that ensues from this rupture can last for years. Grieving is the expression of pain and loss. Grieving has no specific timeline. The loss of the intact family is always a loss.

When parents are moving on with their lives by dating, repartnering, and remarrying, it is helpful for Adult Children to revisit the concept of revocable and irrevocable loss described in Emery's Divorce Grief Theory in chapter 4. Death is an irrevocable loss that cannot be reversed. Divorce is a revocable loss that *could* be reversed. One day Mom and Dad *could* reconcile. No matter what the facts of the divorce are, the revocability of Dad and Mom's divorce protracts the grief process for Adult Children of gray divorce. As long as both parents are still living, the revocability is never final. The possibility of reconciliation can remain for (minor and) Adult Children and for the couple as well. Even though Adult Children can understand intellectually that it is unlikely that their parents will reconcile, at the emotional level, their hopes and fantasies of the family becoming as it *was in the past* can live on. Parents moving on can dash these hopes and fantasies. Adult Children must then confront this additional loss. In fact, recent research indicates that Adult Children often experience their parents' new relationships as a loss.[1] While Adult Children can be capable of understanding that their parents want to move on with their lives, they may not yet be ready to accept it emotionally, because they may still be grieving their losses from their parents' divorce. The intellectual processing and emotional processing of revocable loss work on different schedules.

It often occurs that parents who are dating and their Adult Children, who are still grieving, are on different timelines. While their parents are moving through their developmental stages of divorce, Adult Children of gray divorce are simultaneously navigating two stages of adult development—the developmental stages regarding their parents' divorce and their personal adult developmental stages that we discussed in chapter 5. For example, some divorced parents are looking forward to a new start in their lives and can be excited that someone new wants to be with them. Adult Children of gray divorce never knew their parents when they were dating each other, so their parents' dating behavior is unfamiliar and can seem "un-mother-like" or "un-father-like." The parent may be ready to begin a new life by dating before the Adult Child is ready to see the parent as a dating, sexual, me-focused human being separate from being just "Mom" or "Dad." Anger, sadness, and withdrawal, common components of grieving, can overcome the Adult Child.

Carol writes:

Elvira was a thirty-year-old Adult Child of gray divorce. She had sunk into the far corner of the loveseat across from me and was sitting statue-still as the minutes ticked away. Her shoulders were slumped. Her forearms and hands rested on her lap. She stared intensely at a tissue that was in her hands, while her fingers folded and unfolded it over and over, this way and that as if it were a puzzle that would reveal the answer she was seeking if only she could find the right combinations of folds. Tears slowly spilled from her eyes down both sides of her face. Minutes ticked away until I broke the silence and said, "You know, Elvira, we have discussed before that Adult Children of gray divorce are grieving many losses."

Suddenly Elvira's face reddened, and her teeth clenched so tightly that her jawbone muscles bulged, threatening to erupt through her skin. She spewed, "When I saw that Dad was dating, I screamed at him, 'Why don't you act your age! I see you looking at yourself in the mirror, checking out your body, your clothes, your teeth, and your hairline! You've even dyed your hair! You are fifty-five years old, and you're acting like a giddy teenager! You should not be wearing clothes that a guy *I* am dating would wear! You are embarrassing yourself and me!'" She had angrily lashed out at him for not being "parent-like." She saw a "giddy teenager," and the pain of losing her father torpedoed into anger. For some people, anger is one of the early stages of grieving.

Samir, a thirty-four-year-old lawyer, describes a different experience that many Adult Children also report. Sadness wrenched his face as he spoke. "You know, Mom started dating right away after she left Dad. It seemed really fast to me. Dad was struggling with depression. She asked me to meet the man she was dating. I thought, 'Well, I *am* an adult, so I should be able to handle seeing her with someone other than Dad.' I was surprised how unprepared I was to see her showing affection and concern to this man, when I never saw her show it to Dad when she and Dad were together. Maybe they did when I was younger, and I just don't remember it. I don't know. I think I feel sadder now than I did when Mom first told me she was leaving Dad. I feel like I have fallen into another layer, a deeper layer of sadness about it, you know. Sometimes I think I'm drowning in this sadness, and I don't know how to save myself."

I replied, "What you are experiencing is part of the grieving process, Samir. As children grow up, they tend to view the experiences of their parents and their family as their 'normal.' Later, when they see that the 'normal' of other couples and families looks different from what they saw in their own family, they are often overcome by a deep sadness, when they realize that their family's 'normal' wasn't the 'normal' that they now wish they had experienced. In those moments, they can actually see what they had lost all along but didn't know they had lost it. So, when you recall your family history juxtaposed to your mother's new affectionate and caring relationship, you feel the pangs of loss for something you didn't yet know you had lost until that moment."

Or, the Adult Child may channel his anger into withdrawal. Twenty-four-year-old Jason repeatedly told his mother, who was the one who filed for divorce, "It's your life. Do whatever you want. You already have anyhow. Go ahead and 'be happy' as you say you *deserve* to be. I don't want any part of your dating. I don't want to hear about it. Just pretend I don't exist, which you already do anyway. You act like I am not supposed to have any feelings about you selfishly destroying our family!"

The stories that Adult Children describe about what they often experience depict the deep pain and sadness they feel when they are forgotten and overlooked. They are expected to be "too old to hurt" because they are "adults." They are the invisible children of gray divorce.

FACTORS THAT AFFECT ADULT CHILDREN'S ACCEPTANCE OF THEIR PARENTS' DATING

Many conflicting feelings can arise in Adult Children when their parents start dating. Adult Children tend to hold on to the pictures and memories of their past lives with their family of origin. The Adult Child may view her parent's new significant other as an interloper and feel jealous of the relationship that her parent has with the new person. This is especially common when the Adult Child and parent have been close over the years. Or conversely, when the Adult Child and parent have not been close, or have been estranged, and they have begun to build a new, emotionally fulfilling relationship with each other that the Adult Child never experienced.

Loyalty issues may develop. He may feel disloyal to his mother and think he should keep secret that his father is dating. Not wanting to hurt his mother or receive an angry blast from her if he tells her that his father is dating, he can feel conflicted whether to lie or tell her the truth when asked, "Have you talked with your dad lately? What's new with him?" Or, his mother may specifically ask if his father is dating. If your parent asks you such questions about your other parent, you can simply say that you love both of them, are uncomfortable talking about your other parent, and prefer not to be a messenger.

Sometimes parents will ask their Adult Children to keep a secret. If your parent asks you not to tell the other parent he is dating, you can say, "You are my parents. I love both of you, and I value my relationship with both of you, so I am unwilling to keep secrets."

If the Adult Child and parent have been estranged, the Adult Child may not be as affected by the parent dating. Perhaps they were not that close during the Adult Child's childhood and adolescence, and she may have already grieved this parent as lost to her.

Sometimes an Adult Child is relieved and even happy that the parents divorced because he knows that one or both parents were unhappy during the marriage. Or, if the marriage was a high-conflict one, filled with arguing; mental, emotional, or physical spousal abuse; infidelity; financial impropriety by one parent; substance abuse; or addiction, he may feel happy that his parents are divorcing and that the parent who was abused is beginning to rebuild her life. He may also simultaneously feel guilty for feeling happy. Such conflicting feelings can cause him to reject the idea of his other parent being with a new person.

However, if the parents' divorce was bitterly fought, and they dragged their Adult Child into the middle, or if one or both parents continuously denigrated the other to the Adult Child, it can impede the Adult Child's grieving process. She will likely not be ready or able to accept that her parent appears to be happy and moving on with his life. As child psychologist Haim Ginnott instructed, "Children are like wet cement. Whatever falls on them leaves an impression." In situations like the above, the Adult Child is likely not as far along in her grieving process as her parent, who appears to be happily moving forward in his life.

Since grieving pain and loss takes time, generally, the more time that has passed since the parents' divorce, the farther along the Adult Child will be in his healing from the losses he experienced during and after his parents' divorce, and the more likely he will be able to accept his parent dating. If there has been an adequate passage of time for grieving, the Adult Child can be relieved, and even happy that the parent is beginning to rebuild his life. He may even be hopeful that his parent will have someone to share the rest of his life with, and someone to help take care of the parent in his aging years, so the parent is less of a burden and responsibility to the Adult Child.

Seeking assistance from a professional, such as a member of the clergy or a therapist who is experienced in the stages of Adult Children's development during and after parental divorce, can facilitate the Adult Child's grieving process and help him understand the changing family dynamics, roles, and traditions that occur when parents begin dating, repartnering, and remarrying.

UNFAMILIAR ROLES

When Elvira screamed at her dad to act his age, he replied, "Why can't you be happy for me that I am finding love?" Adult Children report that this feels like a role reversal to them and they wonder, "Isn't the *parent* the one who is supposed to be happy that *I* have found love, not the reverse?" Elvira shared, "Being in such an unfamiliar role is uncomfortable and feels surreal to me. It's weird! He's my parent, but he is acting younger than I am!"

Some parents treat their Adult Children as peers and want to share dating stories with them. The "Child" part of the "Adult Child" resists this. The roles have changed. Adult Children often report not knowing what to do or say when this happens, feeling confused and sometimes even disgusted. Often the parent questions herself when this occurs, thinking that she must have been a bad parent when her child was growing up because her daughter is struggling so much with something that the parent wants her daughter to be happy about. These parents don't understand what their Adult Children are experiencing.

Sometimes Adult Children are concerned about their parents' safety and welfare. If the parent struggles with depression during and after the divorce, the Adult Child may fear the parent may become so again if the dating doesn't work out. What will the Adult Child do if that happens? This is a role reversal for the Adult Child, and many don't know how to handle it. How will she convince her parent to seek professional help? What if the parent becomes suicidal? Again, seeking counsel from a professional who has the expertise to assist the Adult Child to navigate these new experiences is helpful.

Adult Children often have valid concerns about their parents when they are dating and repartnering. Conversely, some Adult Children report that they think that their parents are adults and can do whatever they want. Experiencing newfound freedom from what they felt were the shackles of their marriage, parents may become promiscuous. They may be naïve and easily targeted by con men and gold-diggers. If you have these concerns, consult with elder abuse services or other professionals, such as elder abuse lawyers or therapists experienced in elder issues. If you fear that your parent could fall prey to con artists, discuss your concerns with your parent. You can ask her to commit that she will refrain from giving expensive gifts to a new partner and will obtain a Prenuptial Agreement if the relationship is leading toward marriage. Enlist your siblings so that you can decide how to deal with your parents in a united way. Practice using with your parents and siblings the effective communication skills you've been learning in this book. Effective communication can diffuse family conflict and avoid alliances from forming, pitting family members against each other.

ADULT CHILDREN OFTEN WORRY ABOUT HOW PARENTAL DATING WILL AFFECT THEIR PARENTS' RELATIONSHIP WITH THEM AND THEIR CHILDREN

Sometimes for years, an Adult Child has longed to be closer to his parent, and since the divorce, they have indeed been so. When his parent starts dating, he may feel that he was needed until the new person came along, then cast aside and rejected, just as he felt growing up—more pain and loss for him. He may fear that he will not be able to handle future rejection and that being ignored or rejected again by his parent will affect him in his future relationships.

Perhaps the Adult Child felt second to the parent's work, friends, hobbies, or volunteer activities. The dating partner can represent a new threat of such rejection again. She begins to wonder, "What will holidays and gatherings be like? Will this new person pull Mom into *his* family gatherings and away from me? Will Mom abandon my children, her grandchildren? Will my children lose their grandmother and all of those holiday memories? What if Dad becomes a serial dater? What kind of role model will that be for my kids?"

OFTEN ADULT CHILDREN, WHETHER DATING OR MARRIED, BEGIN QUESTIONING THEIR ABILITY TO MAINTAIN A HEALTHY, COMMITTED RELATIONSHIP

Many Adult Children are still attempting to navigate their own love relationships, and evaluating themselves as romantic partners, while at the same time reevaluating their divorcing parents as role models of romantic and marriage partners.

They may already be married and begin to reevaluate themselves as marriage partners in light of their parents' failed marriage. They often wonder if their marriages are destined to end in divorce too. This can be happening at the same time that their parents want their Adult Children to be happy for them as their parents move into the next stage of their lives. A parent dating may trigger anger at the parent, especially if this is the parent who left the marriage. The juxtaposition of the Adult Child questioning her relationship capability and her parent dating can create conflicting feelings for the Adult Child.

After several sessions, Maria reflected, "I am happy for Dad and sad for myself. I wouldn't have to be sad if the divorce hadn't happened. I am the one paying for the divorce, and Dad is beginning a new, possibly happy life! It's unjust! I didn't ask for this! It's *their* divorce yet it is impacting *me* in so many ways. And he just moves on! What kind of role model is he for me? I always thought they were happily married. What if I have learned from them how to have a failed marriage too!"

OTHER FACTORS THAT MAKE PARENTAL DATING, REPARTNERING, AND REMARRIAGE DIFFICULT FOR ADULT CHILDREN

The Adult Child's acceptance of his parent dating, repartnering, or marrying the significant other can become more difficult if the significant other has been associated with the Adult Child's family in some way, for example, as a friend of the family, the Adult Child's teacher or athletic coach, a parent of a friend of the Adult Child, or a peer of the Adult Child.

Or sometimes the significant other "comes on too strong," tries to be too friendly, wants to rewrite the family history, doesn't allow reminiscing about "before the divorce" times, doesn't allow the Adult Child to have one-on-one time with the parent, and tries to establish new family traditions too quickly. Often Adult Children don't want to let go of the old traditions. It is a loss, and it is sad to remember them, while at the same time being involved in new traditions.

If the significant other has children and grandchildren, the "blended family" issues often delay the families integrating, if ever. These familial relationships can be complicated and bring distress to all family members. There is more information about this for your parents and you in chapter 12.

Your coparents' relationship can also affect your other family relationships. Research that followed the lives of divorced families for twenty years found that children who reported that their parents were cooperative also reported better relationships with their parents, grandparents, stepparents, and siblings;[2] the ability of divorced parents to establish a supportive, low-conflict parental unit reverberates throughout the family even twenty years later;[3] and that when divorced spouses remain at war with each other, it can affect children's kinship relationships.[4]

Eventually, accepting change, building new connectedness, and celebrating life's events with your family members can facilitate healing. The following chapters provide more tools for this.

DISCUSS IMPORTANT TOPICS WITH YOUR PARENTS

Attempt to discuss with your parents what you are feeling. For example, share with them your grief, pain, loss, depression, shame, fear, and anger, and where you are in your grieving process. You and your parents are likely in different stages of grieving. Invite a trusted friend or family member of your parent to be present and involved when you have these conversations. Ask your parents to attend counseling with you so that you both have a safe environment for having what are often difficult discussions.

It's appropriate for you to attempt to educate your parents about your grieving and loss. However, be aware if you are trying to prevent your parent from moving on with her own life because it is too painful for you. That would not be appropriate. It's also a good idea to discuss your feelings with someone other than your parent first—a friend, relative, or professional experienced in the issues of Adult Children of gray divorce.

Listen to and acknowledge your parents' desires and concerns as well. Expect that you and your parents are likely having different feelings and may have different values. Accept this and avoid attempting to convince them to have your same values. You are on different life paths. You may still be looking backward at the family that was, and your parent may be looking forward to building a new life.

You may have valid concerns for your parent's safety and welfare. Perhaps your parent has become promiscuous and is naïve. If your parent has now abandoned the values that he instilled in you growing up, it can create conflicted feelings for you. For example, if he raised you to value monogamy, and you now know he had extramarital affairs and is currently dating multiple people, you may wonder, "Which parent should I trust, the former one or the current one? And which values should I have now?" Sometimes Adult Children in this situation model after their parent and begin being promiscuous themselves.

Remember that you are always your parent's child, even though you are in an adult body. You may have strong feelings about your parent dating. If your parent expects you to adjust and accept his dating immediately or makes your parent–child relationship contingent upon you accepting his significant other, discuss with him that you still want one-on-one time with him, and that you need some time to adjust, just as a younger child would. Adult Children often view their parents as a unit. Spending time with each parent individually can help both of you evolve your relationship into a more fulfilling one for both of you. Your formative years and identity are enwrapped in all of the years your family was together. Many Adult Children report that the rupture of the familial bonds that ensue from their parents' divorce shakes their identity to the core.

Know that to avoid conflicting feelings, many Adult Children withdraw and ignore their parent who is dating. You may express anger at your parent or her new significant other. This can spring from your frustration that it seems to you that your parent has discarded your past life together, while you are still grieving all the losses.

Remember that your parents divorced each other. They did not divorce you. They may need reminding about this. They will always be the parents and you their child. Ask them to acknowledge and honor this relationship.

Be aware and acknowledge that one of your parents may need more help from you and discuss this with your other parent if she seems jealous of this or guilt-trips you about it.

Often the parent who has decided to move on to his new life has the unrealistic expectation that "everyone will get along and be one happy family." This ignores your grief process and your timeline for accepting and integrating this major life change. Often Adult Children don't want to be part of a new family. Your parent and your ideas of happiness may be in direct conflict. Discuss this with your parents. Invite them to discuss these difficult topics with you. The assistance of a professional is often helpful.[5]

Seeing your parents in unfamiliar roles with new partners; being more vulnerable to depression, con people, and gold-diggers; being less reliable, less available, less parent-like; and being happier than you ever recall seeing them can engender conflicted feelings in you, even if you are happy for them. If you have been unsuccessful resolving your negative feelings toward a parent, of if your relationship with him is fractured, ask him to go to counseling with you, so a professional can help you hear each other.

DISCUSSIONS ABOUT MONEY ARE IMPORTANT

This is also a common concern of Adult Children. Often a parent will change the estate plan to include the new partner, leaving the biological children second to the new partner, or equal to biological children they have together. Research has found that later-life marriages are associated with a decreased likelihood of parents providing a financial transfer to an Adult Child,[6] so this is a valid concern.

Divorce is a family event that affects everyone in the family. All the family members are transitioning to a "new normal." In the next chapter we explore what your parents can do to help you through the changes you and your family are experiencing.

The family—that dear octopus from whose tentacles we never quite escape, nor, in our innermost hearts, never quite wish to.
—Dodie Smith, English children's author and playwright

12

HOW PARENTS OF GRAY DIVORCE CAN HELP THEIR ADULT CHILDREN

> *But in the real world, you couldn't really just split a family down the middle, mom on one side, dad the other, with the child equally divided between. It was like when you ripped a piece of paper into two: no matter how you tried, the seams never fit exactly right again. It was what you couldn't see, those tiniest of pieces, that were lost in the severing, and their absence kept everything from being complete.*
>
> —Sarah Dessen, author of *What Happened to Goodbye*

Gray divorce is burgeoning in the United States and abroad.[1] The prevailing myth is that because Adult Children are adults when their parents divorce, they won't be affected. Yet, many Adult Children report that the rupture of the familial bonds that ensue from their parents' divorce shakes them to their core. Marjory Campbell explains, "Divorce is a phenomenon that is forced upon the adult children with an expectation to not only survive it without scarring but to heal the wounds of their parents, a task too great to be achieved."[2] It is crucial that parents understand and remember her words.

Of course, most parents want their children to be okay, so this too makes it easy for parents and others to believe that, since Adult

Children of gray divorce are in college, or vocational training, or already working, and building "their own lives," they will simply "roll with it," "get over it," and adapt to the family crisis churning in the wake of divorce. This belief makes it easy for parents to minimize or completely overlook what their Adult Children are feeling during their parents' separation, divorce, and the ensuing years when, for the first time in their lives, their Adult Children are experiencing their parents not as the accustomed parental unit, but as single parents. Often Adult Children want to avoid hurting their parents' feelings and complicating their parents' situations, so they refrain from saying what they are feeling. Unaware that their feelings are valid, they often suffer in silence, internalizing their pain, and feeling isolated. They become the invisible children of gray divorce. How can you help your Adult Children and ensure that they do not feel invisible?

Many factors affect what Adult Children are feeling about their parents' separation and divorce. Let's explore these factors, so you can avoid making your Adult Children's struggles worse and help them during your family's major life transition and restructuring.

> *All changes involve loss just as all losses require change.*
> —K. K. Goldsworthy, Australian social worker and researcher

UNDERSTAND THAT YOUR ADULT CHILD IS GRIEVING AND BE PATIENT WITH HER

Divorce brings with it many losses. Your Adult Child and the "younger child" inside may be in pain and grieving all that is lost. As we discussed in chapter 4, the losses for your Adult Children are many—the loss of the constancy and continuity of their nuclear family; their parents' love; their intact extended family and support systems of family friends and community; decades-long family togetherness and family memories; their own identity that grew from their formative years when their family was together; their dreams about future family celebrations, traditions, and rituals, such as graduations, weddings, and births; their family home that was the family's nest, a place to bring their own children, if they have children, to share where they grew up; and their parents united as grandparents.

Younger Adult Children often lose financial support from their parents. Both younger and older Adult Children may lose emotional support from their parents, when their parents become less available to them because their parents are experiencing their own life crises, replete with pain and losses.

Many Adult Children echo what Maria bemoaned in chapter 4, "In that moment . . . in that moment when my mother told me that my father had left us, my family, my history, and my future changed forever."

Grieving takes time, often a lot of time. Realize and accept this. You and your Adult Child are undergoing different experiences. You are divorcing your spouse, or your spouse is divorcing you. In either scenario, your Adult Child's parents are divorcing. You are looking toward your future life. Or, if you are the spouse being left, you are likely swimming in your own pain of loss. At the same time, your Adult Child is dealing with all of the "*nevers*"—"I *never* imagined that my parents would divorce after being married for twenty-eight years. We will *never* be together in the home where my siblings and I grew up. . . . My parents will *never* be together at family celebrations like holidays and births, or ceremonies like graduations. My parents will *never* be together as grandparents for our children in the home where I grew up." There are so many *nevers.*

Expect and accept that, although grieving is accompanying both of you on this life journey, your Adult Child is likely experiencing a range of feelings that are different from yours. Expect that her timeline for grieving, acceptance, and healing may be on a different trajectory and last a different length of time than yours. Tell your Adult Child that you understand and respect her timeline for grieving the losses, acceptance of your divorce, and healing. Refrain from judging your Adult Child's feelings and the course of her timeline, just as you want her to refrain from judging yours.

AVOID CONFLICT AND BE AMICABLE WITH YOUR ADULT CHILD'S OTHER PARENT

In the United States and many other countries, the default divorce process is litigation, which is an adversarial process. It is a win-lose process. Yet, Adult Children, like minor children, almost unanimously proclaim that their uppermost wish is that their parents will be amicable during and after their divorce. It has long been known that ongoing parental conflict increases children's risk of psychological and social problems and that improving the relationships between parents and their children helps children cope better in the months and years following the divorce.[3] Research has found that interparental conflict is associated with feeling caught between parents in young adults aged nineteen to thirty-seven, and indicates that these feelings are linked with weak parent–child relationships and well-being, irrespective of children's ages.[4] If you choose a family-focused, out-of-court divorce process like mediation or collaborative divorce, you have the opportunity to minimize the emotional and financial costs that so often accompany litigated divorces. In fact, research indicates that mediation can be beneficial for emotional satisfaction, spousal relationships, and children's needs.[5]

You can also suggest your Adult Children attend family therapy with you before, during, or after your divorce, so that you can hear their concerns and provide a setting for you and them to begin healing from the losses you are all experiencing. The losses continue to grow for everyone—for you, your Adult Children, and your entire extended family—grandparents, aunts, uncles, cousins, and so on.

You and your Adult Child's other parent will always be *co*parents, with the emphasis on "*co*." Is your coparenting relationship a positive one or a negative one? Some Adult Children of gray divorce say that their parents have no relationship. It is not possible for parents to have *no* relationship because they are always the parents. What they mean is that their parents have a negative coparenting relationship. How would it benefit these Adult Children if their *co*parents were able to create win-win solutions for themselves that would also benefit their Adult Children and extended family members?

Carol read a similar story in Fisher and Shapiro's book *Beyond Reason: Using Emotions as You Negotiate* that inspired her to write the passage below to illustrate to coparents of children of all ages how important it is for them to have cooperative and friendly coparenting relationships.

> Ten pairs of divorcing parents were attending a coparenting training class. The facilitator instructed each pair of coparents to sit together facing each other, with their right elbows on the table. "Grasp your partner's right hand with you own right hand and don't let go. Each coparent will get one point every time the back of your coparent's right hand touches the table. The goal for each coparent is to get as many points for himself as possible during the exercise. Keep your eyes closed and be completely indifferent to how many points your other coparent gets. You will have one minute for this exercise. Ready, set, go!"
>
> For one minute, nine coparent pairs struggled as each coparent tried to physically force the back of the other's right hand down to the table. The tenth coparent pair was the lone exception. One coparent immediately remembered that her goal was to get as many points for herself as possible. Following the facilitator's directions, she kept her eyes closed and became indifferent to how many points her coparent got. Instead of trying to push her coparent's hand down to the table, she surprised him by immediately *pulling* his hand down to the table and giving him an easy point as the back of her hand touched the table. She then quickly pushed his hand to the table, taking an easy point for herself. Her coparent immediately caught on. Keeping their eyes closed and their right elbows on the table, they swung their clasped hands back and forth as many times as they could.
>
> After the conclusion of the exercise, each pair of coparents reported to the group how many points each had earned. No one had more than two points, except for the coparent pair who had cooperated. They had each earned more than ten points.
>
> Despite the directions to the coparents that they were *partners* and that they were to be indifferent to how many points

> their other coparent got, the other nine coparent pairs assumed that they were adversaries. This assumption prevented them from earning as many points as they could have earned.

Which coparenting pair in the above story do you want to be for your Adult Children and extended family? What is the legacy you want to leave them about this time their lives? What do you want to role model for them about how you resolve conflict?

UNDERSTAND THAT YOUR DIVORCE IMPACTS YOUR ADULT CHILDREN IN MANY WAYS

Adult Children often continue to view their parents as a unit. This unit is now ruptured and gone forever. The roles, family traditions, and rituals are changing. They now have to plan vacations and holidays differently. Will they need to schedule two different times to see each of you? How does your divorce impact them financially, their inheritance, the possibility of their eventual caretaking role for one or both of you? Your spousal relationship is ending, but you will always be your Adult Child's parents. If you and your Adult Child's other parent can be an amicable and supportive parental unit in your Adult Child's life, it can mitigate the pain from your Adult Child's losses.

MAKE YOUR ADULT CHILDREN'S CELEBRATORY EVENTS ABOUT THEM, NOT ABOUT YOU

Often divorcing or divorced parents who are still hurt and angry with each other ruin these celebrations for the Adult Children.

Carol writes:

Steven graduated from college two years before his parents' acrimonious divorce began. He was worried about his brother Andrew's graduation from college. He sat erect on the sofa in my office and flailed his arms like a drowning man. He was crying and shouting at the same time. "Why can't our parents just be civil this one day? But, no! They have been complaining about where each was going to sit and asking why it was necessary to have photos taken of my brother and them together. They even asked, 'Doesn't Andrew know how much we dislike each other?' Like Andrew's graduation was about *them* and not about Andrew! Why can't they put their anger and hatred aside and celebrate their son's accomplishment?"

Constance Ahrons writes that it can be a powerful intervention to ask coparents to imagine some years ahead and envision a future event like a graduation or a wedding of their child, and then to ask them how they will participate in that shared happy occasion.[6] Her research found that even twenty years after the divorce, when children were grown and many had their own children, they still wanted their parents to get along, and most wanted to share special family occasions with both parents and extended kin; when parents are still battling or denigrate each other, children are likely to withdraw from relationships with one or both parents. It's not the divorce per se, but the behavior and the quality of the coparenting relationship that continues to echo throughout the family system.[7]

Even if your separation and divorce was rancorous, remember that you once fell in love and created a family together. That family still exists, even though you are divorced. Rather than allowing tension, resentment, and anger to harden like drying cement and become the landscape of your family, set a goal to eventually attend some of the family celebrations such as graduations, birthdays, weddings, and grandchildren's performances. Dance together at your Adult Children's weddings. Sit with the other family members, so that your Adult Children can still feel a sense of family. Giving your family such a gift can go a long way toward healing.

TO GAUGE THE IMPACT OF THIS LIFE EVENT, PAY MORE ATTENTION TO THE CHILD PART OF YOUR ADULT CHILD

Although your Adult Child is in an adult body, the "younger child" is also inside, in pain and grieving all that she has lost. The Child part may have strong, uncomfortable feelings about your dating. Avoid expecting your Adult Child to adjust and accept your dating immediately. She will likely need time to adjust, just as a younger child would. Adult Children often view their parents as a unit, so it's difficult to see you with someone new. Your Adult Child's formative years and identity are enwrapped in all of the years the family was together. It often takes time for Adult Children to adjust to see you separate from your past lives together.

Remember that you will always be the parent and your Adult Child will always be your Child. You are divorcing your spouse, not your Adult Child. During and after divorce, many parents forget this. They move on with their lives oblivious to how the divorce is affecting their Adult Children. Many parents focus more on their own pain and fear, or on their happiness in their new lives, starting new relationships, and moving away. They forget to nurture their relationship with their Adult Children.

The parent–child relationship is forever. Assure your Adult Children that you still want one-on-one time with them, so that they know that you value your relationship with them. Be mindful to avoid creating a situation like the one Amelia shares. "I was twenty-four and working at my first job after college when Mom and Dad divorced. Mom left New York and moved sixty miles away, saying that she needed to start her new life and get far away from Dad and her old life here. She was completely focused on herself. I felt kicked to the curb, invisible and unimportant to her! She never even acknowledged that I still existed! I felt so alone, so isolated, being here amid the trail of wreck and ruin of their relationship. I had become part of her 'old life.' I thought, 'Great, *this* is home?' I was in shock and very sad."

RESPECT THE GENERATIONAL BOUNDARY LINES

> *When mom and dad went to war the only prisoners they took were the children.*
> —Pat Conroy, American novelist

Honor the parent–Adult Child relationship and know that your Adult Child may need you to say that you understand that you are still the parent and that your Adult Child is not your friend, your confidant, your therapist, your dating buddy, or your surrogate spouse. Maintain a firm boundary in this parent–child relationship, even if your Adult Child doesn't. Sometimes Adult Children feel guilty and think that they *should* be their parent's confidant, help-mate, or dating buddy. It may feel good to be close to your Adult Child in this way and to think that your Adult Child understands you. Nevertheless, resist allowing your Adult Child to slide into this role reversal.

Be aware and acknowledge that sometimes the other parent may need more help from your Adult Child than you do. Be accepting of this and avoid feeling jealous about their relationship. If you complain to your Adult Child that he is spending more time with his other parent than with you, you can cause your Adult Child to feel guilty about the time he is spending with his other parent. When people feel guilty, they often avoid the person who is guilt-tripping them. So, you can actually create a reaction that is the opposite of the one you want.

Adult Children report that, even if they think that they should be helping their parent, they feel caught in the middle between their parents when one parent rants about their other parent or shares the details about what went awry in their marriage, their sex life, their finances, and the legalities of their divorce process. Avoid discussing these topics with your Adult Child because it assumes a peer relationship and can cause your Adult Child to feel unease and additional loss—the loss of you as the parent. When this occurs, your Adult Child can become overwhelmed by conflicting feelings and begin to wonder, "Was everything about our family unreal, a fantasy, like a movie set that is just a façade?" He may react with anger toward you or withdraw from you.

No matter how upset you are with your spouse or hate what he has done during your marriage, avoid trying to enroll your Adult Child to align with you against her other parent. If you have conversations like these with your Adult Child, you can create loyalty issues for your Adult Child that exacerbate the loyalty issues that Adult Children naturally feel. It is human nature for Adult Children to attempt to figure out which parent is more at fault for the divorce and blame that parent while aligning with the other parent. (Minor children do this too.) Your Adult Child is part of both of you. If you attempt to "win her to your side," you put her in the uncomfortable position of knowing information about her other parent that is inappropriate.

And avoid asking your Adult Child for advice on sexual matters. Your Adult Child is not your peer. Discuss your sexual questions with a friend or professional.

If bitterness, anger, and hatred describe your divorce, a simple rule to follow is one that Adult Children often say. "Love me more than you hate my mother or father and don't put me in the middle. I want to be free to have whatever relationship I want with both of you."

Be vigilant and avoid crossing generational boundary lines. Your Adult Child will thank you.

KEEP THE LINES OF COMMUNICATION WITH YOUR ADULT CHILD OPEN

Your Adult Child may have an idealized view of you that makes it difficult for him to integrate two conflicting views. For example, some Adult Children often still maintain an idealized view of a parent as their "greater than life parent." Or, due to the circumstances surrounding your divorce such as affairs, financial impropriety, or emotional, mental, physical, or sexual abuse, he may now have a diminished view of you. Remember that the reality of divorce may engender a view that both you and his other parent are flawed.

The parent–child relationship is unique. No matter how old your Adult Child is, you are still his parent, and he is still your child. You may be operating from different viewpoints about your roles. Because your child is an adult now, you may consider him in the role of your peer, while he still sees you in the parental role. Discuss with your Adult Child the different views you may have of each other's roles in your relationship.

If your relationship with your Adult Child is fractured, be the one to reach out to him and ask him to go to counseling to improve your communication and eventually heal and restore your relationship. Understand that it is not your Adult Child's role to initiate this, though some Adult Children do. It is *your* role as the parent. Be the role model for change and healing.

> *Just like children, emotions heal when they are heard and validated.*
> —Jill Bolte Taylor

Eliminate *shoulds*: "You should be happy for me . . . You shouldn't be sad. You shouldn't be angry . . ." Feelings simply are. Likely, your Adult Children will not be as happy as you are about your new life. While your energy is focused on moving away from your past life with your Adult Child's other parent and moving toward your future, your Adult Child is looking backward at what she is losing from her past and what will always be her past, not her future. She is losing her family history, her family being together, and the future she thought she and her family would have. Expecting your Adult Child to be as happy for you in your new life is disrespectful to her feelings and her journey on grief's path.

Understand that to avoid conflicting feelings, many Adult Children withdraw and ignore their parent who is dating or repartnering. Or, she may express anger at you or your new significant other. This can arise from her frustration that it seems that you have discarded her and your past life together while she is still grieving the losses.

Know that she is grieving the loss of her intact family, the family home, a place to bring her children and share the "nest" where she grew up.

Divorce usually occurs when one parent has decided to have a new life. Understand that your Adult Child may not be as happy about your new life as you are. You are looking forward to your new life. Your Adult Child is looking backward at what he has lost and what will always be a loss. He is feeling pain and sadness while you are looking forward. You may have the unrealistic expectation that "everyone will get along and be one happy family." This ignores your Adult Child's grief process. Often Adult Children do not want to be part of a new family. Your Adult Child and your ideas of happiness may be in direct conflict.

Realize that your Adult Children are navigating their personal developmental stages, while simultaneously navigating their divorce-related developmental stages. Your Adult Child's divorce-related developmental stages are different from your divorce-related developmental stage. For example, you may be ready to begin a new life by dating while your Adult Child is still moving through his grieving process. Your Adult Child may not be ready to see you as a dating, sexual, me-focused human being, separate from "Mom" or "Dad," who is evolving into a person beyond "Dad" or "Mom." It's a timing issue.

Often, Adult Children are worried that the parent could be a victim of a con person. If this occurs, you could assure your Adult Child that you will not give expensive gifts to this new partner and that you will get a Prenuptial Agreement if the relationship is leading to marriage.

ACCEPT THAT YOU AND YOUR ADULT CHILD MAY HAVE DIFFERENT VALUES

Sometimes Adult Children have concern for their dating parents' safety and welfare, for example, if there is promiscuity, naïveté, or parental behavior that is contrary to the values with which the parent raised the child. Adult Children can have conflicted feelings about this and wonder, "Which parent should I trust, the former parent or the current one, and which values?" If your Adult Children are willing to, discuss these differences with them. Avoid trying to convince them to have your values.

UNDERSTAND HOW DATING, REPARTNERING, OR REMARRYING CAN AFFECT YOUR ADULT CHILD

Avoid making your parent–Adult Child relationship contingent upon the Adult Child accepting your new significant other. And avoid insisting that your new partner be involved in all activities with your Adult Child. Many Adult Children report that their parents never talk about their previous family lives together. Assure your Adult Child that you want to spend one-on-one time with him, and *you* be the one to reach out to *him* to schedule the one-on-one time. Reminisce about fond memories, so that he knows that you value the family that you had together and that you have not erased his entire family history with you and his other parent. If he is married, schedule time for just the three of you to be together. If he has children, schedule time for only his family and you to spend time together. You will always be the parent. Attempt to understand what he is experiencing.

If your significant other resists such time without her being present, seek professional help for understanding and guidance about "blended family" issues. A blended family is one where at least one parent has children that are not genetically related to the other spouse or partner. It often takes a long time for the new significant other to become integrated into the relationship with your Adult Children. Be patient.

If your significant other is living in the family home with you, understand that this can be very painful for the Adult Children. It is as though you have replaced their other parent and erased their family.

Resist telling your Adult Child how happy your significant other's children are for you and how accepting they are of you and your new relationship. Such comparisons will only alienate your Adult Child. She will likely feel that you do not understand what she is feeling. When Maria's father told her how supportive of their relationship his new partner's children were, she screamed at him with a fury she had never experienced, "Of course they are! You have abandoned Mom and me for your girlfriend and them! I bet they are glad to have the father *I* have lost! You don't get it at all! You have left me in this misery! Go have your happy life with all of them! I hate what you have done to me and our family."

> *Remarriage is not a neutral event for children.*
> —Claire Cartwright

Many divorced parents remarry and some form long-standing partnerships without marrying. Recent research indicates that about 22 percent of women and 37 percent of men repartnered within ten years after gray divorce, and cohabitation occurred more often than remarriage.[8] When you repartner or remarry, it is another life transition for your Adult Children and their children, if they have children, and the extended family kinship system. Perhaps your significant other also has grandchildren. Understand that there are "blended family" issues that occur in these situations. Patricia Papernow writes that the term "blended family" is a misnomer because "becoming a stepfamily is not like blending raspberries and blueberries together to make a smoothie. It is much more like creating a family out of a group of Japanese and a group of Italians, some of whom are not at all interested in sharing. This metaphor can help stepcouples to shift their energies from straining to blend, to getting to know each other, and it helps normalize the constant jolts by the differences that characterize early stepfamily life."[9] Dr. Papernow's book about stepfamily relationships provides excellent information and tools for parents and their Adult Children to navigate the often-turbulent stepfamily waters.

Often Adult Children and their children feel replaced by the children and grandchildren of a significant other. Perhaps your "new family" spends more time with you than your "first" family. Discuss with your Adult Children their concerns and let them know that you genuinely hear their concerns. Avoid telling them how they *should* feel or what they *should* do. Assuming that everyone will be one big happy family is a mistake. Your Adult Child may not be as happy as you are about your new life.

If your Adult Child lived through you and his other parent fighting or if there was abuse, chemical dependency, or other improprieties, your Adult Child may be glad that you are divorcing. Remember though, that it is likely that he may be grieving all of the losses described above.

SPECIFIC STEPS THAT PARENTS CAN TAKE TO OVERCOME SPECIFIC CONCERNS

Agree to see a therapist, clergy person, or other professional—for example, a financial advisor or estate planner—with your Adult Children to address their specific concerns.

CONSIDER LEGAL AND FINANCIAL ISSUES IMPACTING YOUR ADULT CHILDREN

Share with your Adult Children your estate-planning documents (power of attorney, advanced healthcare directives, guardian of minor children), digital assets, all bank account numbers, passwords, social media accounts and passwords, Trust, and long-term care and Prenuptial Agreements.

Families provide over 75 percent of all long-term care for older adults.[10] The 2013 US Senate Commission on Long-Term Care has projected that this need for the aging population will more than double between 2010 and 2050.[11]

ESTATE PLANNING, PRENUPTIAL AGREEMENTS, AND LONG-TERM ELDER CARE FOR DIVORCING COUPLES AND THEIR ADULT CHILDREN

Brian Don Levy, collaborative divorce attorney, mediator, and estate-planning attorney, shares his expertise: [12]*

When families restructure through a divorce process, the divorce process can provide a unique opportunity for some clients to use the same financial information gathered within a divorce process to also create an estate plan. This provides you, the divorcing spouse, with the opportunity to take responsibility for your own life decisions, and at the same time relieve your Adult Children from the burden of problem solving for you, should you lack legal capacity in the future.

The essence of a core value in estate planning is making a plan in advance, naming whom you want to receive the things you own after you die, when and how you want them to receive those things, and providing clear and legally binding instructions for solving foreseeable and potentially life-altering problems in advance, should they arise in the future. You will, of course, want this to happen within the least amount of time, while minimizing potential tax consequences and avoiding unnecessary legal fees and court costs.

Estate Planning

An estate-planning portfolio can include solutions for many of the easily foreseeable life problems that could occur, such as:

- The orderly transfer of assets after you die, without the cost and delay of probate court.
- Instructions for passing on your *values* (religion, education, hard work, etc.) in addition to your *valuables*.
- Instructions for your care if you become disabled in the future.
- Naming a guardian and/or an inheritance manager for minor children.

- Providing for family members with special needs without disrupting current or potential future government benefits.
- Providing for loved ones who might be irresponsible with money, or who may need future protection from creditors or divorce.
- Making legal decisions for you, should you become incapacitated for a temporary period of time.
- Making healthcare decisions, such as "prolong life" or "do not resuscitate."
- Providing for the support and maintenance of your pets after you die.
- Creating a gun Trust to facilitate ownership and transfer of legally obtained firearms.
- Minimizing taxes, court costs, and unnecessary legal fees.

Estate planning should be viewed as an ongoing process, not a one-time event. Your plan should be reviewed and updated as your family and financial situations (and laws) change over your lifetime.

Estate Planning Really Is for Everyone

Estate planning is not just for "retired" or "older" people, although people do tend to think about it more as they get older. Unfortunately, we can't predict how long we will live, and illness and/or accidents suddenly happen to people of all ages. Estate planning is not just for "the wealthy" either, although people who have built some wealth do often think more about how to preserve it. Good estate planning often means more to families with modest assets, because they can afford to lose the least.

Because the financial information gathered in the divorce process is assumed to be current, complete, and relevant to the estate-planning process, creating your estate-planning portfolio coming out of a divorce offers you the opportunity to become more efficient, streamlined, and for some people, the opportunity to take control of their decision making that pertains to life, death, and everything that lies in between.

Moreover, divorce symbolically represents the closing of one life chapter, and the beginning of the next life chapter. Since complete estate planning provides solutions for some of life's foreseeable problems, if or when they occur, starting the new postdivorce life chapter is an opportune time to solidify the decision making required within the context of a well-thought-out estate plan. For most, the spouse/partner you are divorcing will no longer be desired as a decision maker for you in the event your future circumstances are such that you are unable to speak for yourself. For your Adult Children, estate planning coming out of a divorce can provide them with the knowledge that their inheritance is secure, and/or provide them with the peace of mind in knowing that legal documents have been created to support the execution of your desires in the event of a life crisis in which you cannot speak for yourself.

In most jurisdictions, probate avoidance comes about because the individual retains the right to manage the Trust that owns the assets, rather than owning the assets as an individual and managing them. In California, assets owned by a Trust are not subject to probate and currently they are not subject to Medical recapture per Senate Bill #833. Be sure to consult with an experienced attorney in your jurisdiction regarding laws that are applicable to you.

If You Don't Have a Plan, Your State or Local Jurisdiction May Have One for You and You Probably Won't Like It

At disability: If your name is on the title of your assets, and you can't conduct necessary business affairs due to mental or physical incapacity, in most jurisdictions only a court appointee can sign legal documents for you. In that case, the court, and not your family, will control how your assets are used to care for you through a conservatorship or guardianship (depending on the term used in your jurisdiction). Thus, it can become unpredictable, expensive, very time consuming, and perhaps difficult or impossible to reverse, even if you recover, while at the same time being open to the public. Consult with a legal professional in your jurisdiction about laws that are applicable to you.

At your death: If you die without an intentional estate plan, your assets will be distributed according to the probate laws governing your jurisdiction. Thus, if you die without an estate plan, your jurisdiction will provide the mandatory format under which your heirs will receive what your jurisdiction deems required under applicable law. That means your loved ones may or may not receive a portion of your estate, which may be much different than your desire for your loved ones.

In Many Jurisdictions, Going Through Probate Court Is Likely to Be Expensive, Time Consuming, and Can Lead to Unintended Consequences

I expect that most legal professionals would agree with my belief that the process of going through a probate court to distribute property adds to the risk of additional financial costs, delays, and unintended consequences. I have the very same belief if your family is or recently has transitioned as a result of any divorce process. The divorce process is either governed by the laws of your local jurisdiction or the Prenuptial Agreement of the divorcing couple. Thus, I believe that getting married without a Prenuptial Agreement also adds to the risk of additional financial costs, delays, and unintended consequences.

If you get married without a Prenuptial Agreement, your local jurisdictions will have one for you. The laws in California and in many jurisdictions involve community property and separate property issues, and there are very complex and convoluted laws and rules that can be argued either way and oftentimes leads to unwanted consequences. Thus, Prenuptial Agreements are frequently used as planning tools, especially among the "gray divorce" segment of the population.

Just as a Prenuptial Agreement is intended to avoid a costly trip to your local family law court should your marriage become another "statistic," a well-planned estate-planning portfolio is intended to avoid the cost of going through probate court to transfer your assets and manage your estate, all of which is avoidable in many jurisdictions.

When considering possible planning tools for your estate, for your marriage, and/or your family, be sure to consult with an experienced lawyer in your jurisdiction regarding laws that are applicable to you.

In Many Jurisdictions an Estate Plan Begins with a Will, a Living Trust, and Usually Both

For example, in California, a Will essentially provides your instructions for the distribution of your assets after your life ends, but it *does not* avoid probate court. Rather, a Will is the road most likely to lead directly to probate court in many jurisdictions. Thus, any assets titled in your name or directed by your Will shall likely go through a probate-court process designed by your local jurisdiction before any of your assets can be distributed to your heirs. (If you own property in other states or jurisdictions, your family will probably face multiple probates, each one according to the laws in the jurisdiction where your property is located.) The process varies greatly from jurisdiction to jurisdiction and it can become expensive with legal fees, executor fees, and court costs and resultant delays in the process. It can also take from nine months to two years or longer. With rare exception, probate files are open to the public and excluded heirs are encouraged to come forward and seek a share of your estate. In short, the court system, not your family, controls the process. Be sure to consult with an experienced lawyer in your jurisdiction regarding laws that are applicable to you.

Not everything you own will go through probate. Jointly owned property in joint tenancy and assets that allow you to designate a beneficiary (for example, life insurance, IRAs, 401(k)s, annuities, etc.), are not controlled by your Will and usually will transfer to the new owner or beneficiary without probate. There are, however, many problems with jointly owned assets and debts, and avoidance of probate is not guaranteed. For example, if a valid beneficiary is not named, the assets will have to go through a costly and time-consuming probate and will be distributed along with the rest of your estate. If you name a minor as a beneficiary, the court will probably insist on a guardianship until the child legally becomes an adult. For these reasons, a revocable living Trust is preferred by many families and estate-planning professionals. It is designed to avoid probate at death (including multiple probates if you own property in other states), prevent court control of assets at incapacity, bring all of your assets (even those with beneficiary designations) together into one plan, provide maximum privacy, is valid in every state, and can be changed by you at any time during your lifetime. It can also reflect your love and values to your family and future generations.

Unlike a Will, a living Trust doesn't have to die with you. Assets can stay in your Trust, managed by the trustee you selected, until your beneficiaries reach the age you want them to inherit. Your Trust can continue longer to provide for a loved one with special needs, or to protect the assets from beneficiaries' creditors, spouses, and irresponsible spending.

A living Trust is more expensive initially than a Will but considering it can avoid court interference at incapacity and death, many people consider it to be a huge bargain and money well spent. While more expensive than a Will, it is usually much less expensive than the probate costs that are being bypassed in many jurisdictions.

So why do many estate-planning professionals recommend both a Will and a Trust in a well-thought-out estate-planning portfolio? After all, the Trust is designed to avoid probate, and a Will may very well be the pathway directly to probate court. The answer lies in the passage of time. Simply put, if you die owning an asset as an individual, rather than having your Trust as the owner, in many jurisdictions your family is automatically headed to probate court. The potential problem that a Will solves within an estate plan is the problem of failing for any reason to properly title assets within the Trust. This oftentimes takes place long after the Trust has been created. These types of Wills are generally referred to as a "pour over Will" in that any assets owned by the individual upon their death "pours over" into the Trust and is disbursed as directed in the Trust.

Would your family know where to find your financial records, asset title documents, and insurance policies if something happened to you? For many, planning your estate-planning portfolio will help you organize and maintain your records, locate titles and beneficiary designations, and find and correct errors. For those coming out of a divorce situation, at least in California, those same financial records, titles, and insurance policies were already fleshed out and made available within the divorce process.

Most people don't give much thought to the wording they put on titles and beneficiary designations. You may have had good intentions, but an innocent error can create all kinds of problems for your family and loved ones at your disability and/or death. Beneficiary designations are often out of date or otherwise deficient. Naming the wrong beneficiary on your tax-deferred plan can lead to devastating tax consequences. It is much better for you to take the time to do this correctly *now*, than for your family to pay a lawyer to try to fix things *later*. Assets transferred incident to a divorce process create the opportunity to use the divorce asset-transfer process to achieve asset transfers to a living Trust. Be sure to consult with an experienced lawyer in your jurisdiction regarding laws that are applicable to you.

Estate Planning Does Not Have to Be Expensive

If you don't think you can afford a complex estate plan now, start with what you *can* afford. Then, let your planning develop and expand as your needs change and your financial situation improves. Don't try to do this yourself to save money. An experienced attorney will be able to provide critical guidance and peace of mind that your documents are prepared properly. It has been my experience as a California lawyer that the cost of an estate plan is almost always much less than the financial cost of going to probate court, and the transfer of assets after your death is much quicker than what would occur in probate court. In California, it is not uncommon for probate court to be a two-year-long process, with multiple layers of professional fees, costs, unforeseen delays, and expenses.

The Best Benefit Is Peace of Mind

Knowing you have a properly prepared and legally enforceable plan in place—one that contains your instructions and will protect your Adult Children and other loved ones—will give you and them peace of mind. This is one of the most thoughtful and considerate things you can do for yourself and for your Adult Children. They will have a clear understanding of what your choice is in the event that you are unable to communicate your choice for any reason whatsoever. They will be able to grieve for your loss without having the burden of figuring out a puzzle that only you know the answers to, and you are not available.

Prenuptial Agreements

Published statistics show that in the United States, 50 percent of first marriages, 67 percent of second, and 74 percent of third marriages end in divorce.[13] These are eye-popping numbers. For Adult Children, it is important to have this discussion with a parent who is coming out of a divorce process and is likely to consider another try at marriage. Discussing the value of a Prenuptial Agreement with that parent has value for the Adult Child in as many ways as there are children with parents coming out of a divorce, and possibly going into a remarriage.

Parents of Adult Children can encourage their Adult Children to seek legal counsel regarding the use of Prenuptial Agreements as a planning tool. That being said, in many jurisdictions, parents can use their estate-planning portfolio to protect their children should their child unfortunately become another divorce statistic. Be sure to consult with an experienced lawyer in your jurisdiction regarding laws that are applicable to you.

Long-Term Elder Care

Long-term elder care is as important to those who are in their golden years as to their Adult Children, each for their own important reasons. In many jurisdictions, long-term elder care is a common component of an estate-planning portfolio and can also be a common component of a Prenuptial Agreement or divorce process. Because the possible need for long-term elder care is a foreseeable life event, and because of the impact that this can have on both sides of the parent–child relationship, I believe that it is especially important to consider this as a planning opportunity. Be sure to consult with an experienced attorney in your jurisdiction regarding laws that are applicable to you.

Currently in California, the Medi-Cal program can "recapture" benefits that were previously paid by making a claim against the decedent's assets that are subject to the jurisdiction of probate court (per Senate Bill #833). Assets owned by a Trust are not subject to the jurisdiction of the probate court in California, and thus are not subject to medical recapture. There may be opportunities for you to use similar planning tools in your jurisdictions. Be sure to consult with an experienced attorney in your jurisdiction regarding laws that are applicable to you.

13

TAKING THE WAR OUT OF OUR WORDS

Turning Conflict into Conversation

Sharon Strand Ellison,
author, speaker, and international consultant

"I left home one morning at 8 a.m., told my mother, who was vacuuming, goodbye on the run, and when I came home at noon, found a note on the kitchen table: 'I'm going to think things out. —Mama.' Her clothes were all gone from her closet. . . . After almost a month, Mama wrote a short note to my sister and me, told us she was in Las Vegas and she was going to divorce Dad. She didn't ask us how we were doing, or give a return address or a phone number. She asked us to try to understand."[1]

I can only imagine how many of us would feel rage at this young woman's mother. The shock. The abandonment. The lack of concern shown. Followed by her request for understanding.

In the shock of having our own parents get divorced, whether soon or long after we reach adulthood, our reactions can intensify the damage to everyone in the family, causing what too often becomes a splintering—even of relationships that were previously close—between parents and Adult Children, siblings, and extended family members.

When we feel hurt or want to protect someone we see being hurt, our reactions are most often defensive. We may withdraw, or defend one parent, and blame the other. It may seem impossible to resolve the myriad of issues that we face when parents divorce, including broken trust, loyalty conflicts, or a parent who becomes dependent for emotional or financial support. It can seem inevitable that the family has fallen apart and will never be the same again.

It won't be the same, but learning to be open and vulnerable about your feelings, along with being honest and direct with your parents and siblings, can transform a good share of the pain into a transformation of relationships that can bring healing, insight, and growth.

I can almost hear the protests. "You don't know my mom, dad, sister(s) brother(s)!" "They won't listen to reason!" "They just blame each other." "The whole family has taken up sides. It is like a battlefield. Nothing is going to change that!" Defensive reactions abound!

When we're hurt, as in war, we often don't want to show our vulnerability and pain. Plus, we've learned that defensiveness is hardwired, and it is. So, we often assume that we can't control our reactions. Unfortunately, defensiveness most often only creates and accelerates power struggle. And I believe that power struggle is the most pervasive and least recognized addiction on earth.

It has all the characteristics of addiction. The addiction here is winning, being right, controlling what others believe, think, or feel. Have you ever been in an argument with someone and you think, in response to one of their comments, "Well that's a good point, but I'm not going to tell you!" A sure sign that winning has become more important than the relationship, even someone you love, just as alcohol can become more important than relationships with loved ones.

We know a lot more about defensiveness now than in past generations. The hardwired part of defensive reactions is that when we feel a need to protect ourselves, others, or even an idea or a belief, the complex problem-solving part of the brain literally stops working. Scientists now have the technology needed to actually watch it "go dark," stop functioning. Simultaneously, the amygdala flairs, activating any one of the three primary defensive reactions of fight, flight, or freeze (surrender).

Efforts to talk people out of being defensive are worse than useless. Has anyone ever said to you, "Stop being so defensive!" Far from helping, it's like pouring gas on a fire. Even milder approaches to convince someone to "calm down" most often fail.

Historically, it's been assumed and verified that once a person gets defensive, the adrenaline rush lasts quite a while, from ten minutes to an hour. And, most of us can get defensive again, any time the same topic comes up. Divorced parents may react intensively a decade later at the mere mention of their ex's name by one of their own Adult Children or even a grandchild, and shatter what started out to be a pleasant family gathering.

It doesn't have to be that way. Imagine being able to turn a sarcastic comment or bitter conflict into a meaningful conversation. Have you ever been in a bad mood or feeling defensive when someone says something hysterically funny, and you burst out laughing? In that moment are you still experiencing the impact of the defensive adrenaline rush? Most people say "No." It vanished with the laughter. This means, we *can* learn how to communicate in ways that defuse defensiveness quickly, even in highly charged situations.

According to more recent scientific data, we can't talk someone out of being defensive—in fact trying to get someone to "calm down" usually only makes the situation worse. However, scientists have discovered that if we can communicate in any way so the other person feels safe enough to shift into any other *feeling* state, then their defensive reactions can disappear as autonomically as they appeared. The amygdala now goes dark in less than a nanosecond and the complex problem-solving cortex flares and comes alive. Now the person is more able to listen and reason, often instantly.

I realized decades ago that we'd been using the "rules of war," not just as a metaphor, but as the actual infrastructure for how we communicate with each other. It doesn't work to use the rules for one activity (war) for a completely different activity (communication).

What I call the *War Model* has shaped our methods of communication. *Questions* were for the purpose of interrogation. *Feedback* was given as criticism. *Stating* our own thoughts, feelings, and beliefs was based more on convincing others to agree than on simply telling our own story. *Predicting consequences* when setting limits with others was done with harsh, punitive attitudes. For centuries humans have been frequently using communication skills to manipulate and control others.

We can change all that by making simple changes in each form of communication I mention above. Below is a chart demonstrating the changes I made when developing the *Powerful Non-Defensive Communication™ (PNDC)* process. Using examples, I'll clarify how to use the skills needed to communicate with a combination of honesty and compassion, opening the door to reaching each other's hearts during the painful transitions involved in divorce.

SHIFTING FROM WAR MODEL TO POWERFUL NON-DEFENSIVE COMMUNICATION

Questions

In War Model Communication:

Inherent Nature: Interrogating

Tone: Harsh, entrapping, disbelieving, comes *up* at the end of the question

Body Language: Frowning, raising eyebrows, shrugging, shaking head

In Powerful Non-Defensive Communication:

Inherent Nature: Genuine curiosity

Tone: Relaxed, comes *down* at the end of the question

Body Language: Relaxed, present, but little expressive body language

Statements

In War Model Communication:

Giving Feedback to Others:

Inherent Nature and Intention: Critical, judgmental

Tone: Accusatory, directive, superior

Body Language: Frowning, finger pointing

Expressing Our Own Thoughts, Feelings, and Beliefs:

Inherent Nature and Intention: Convincing, persuading others to agree, judgmental if they don't comply

Tone: Sweetly cajoling, and/or harsh, blaming

Body Language: Frowning, finger pointing, shaking head at points of disagreement

In Powerful Non-Defensive Communication:

Giving Feedback to Others:

Inherent Nature and Intention: Descriptive—to let the other person know how we understand what they are saying

Tone: As with questions, relaxed, comes *down* at the end of the sentence

Body Language: Relaxed, present, but little expressive body language

***

Three Steps in Giving PNDC Feedback When Contradictions Exist:

(1) What I understand you to be saying to me;

(2) Any discrepancies I see (a) between what you are saying with your words and your tone or body language, (b) in my past experience with you, and (c) information I have from outside data; and

(3) My conclusions or assumptions about what the contradiction means, which often has to do with the person's motives or intentions.

***

Expressing Our Own Thoughts, Feelings, and Beliefs:

Inherent Nature and Intention: To fully express our own beliefs/values, thoughts/reasoning, and emotions/feeling, as well as discussing our own past, present, and/or future behavior

Tone: Can be anything from calm to passionate, which can include a range of emotions, such as: joy, sadness, anger, excitement, fear, depression, love

Body Language: Whatever body language is related to the feelings

***

Note of Caution: Whether giving feedback or expressing our thoughts, beliefs, and feelings, avoid slipping across the seductive, invisible line and trying in any way to convince the other person to agree.

Predictions

In War Model Communication:

Creating Boundaries/Limit Setting:

Inherent Nature and Intention: Controlling and punitive

Tone: Harsh, urgent (directives/orders, threats)

Body Language: Scowling, finger pointing, leaning forward

In Powerful Non-Defensive Communication:

If You Do X, Then I'll Do Y—If You Don't Do X, Then I'll Do Z:

Inherent Nature and Intention: Create security through predictability

Tone: Relaxed, comes *down* at the end of each side of the prediction

Body Language: Relaxed, present, but little expressive body language

The impact of making these three changes in how we ask *questions* and make *statements* and *predictions*, along with some phrasing, has the power to give people the kind of safety they need to move out of defensive reactiveness to a *feeling state* that opens the door to genuine, thoughtful, vulnerable, honest, respectful conversation. Even if the other person doesn't respond immediately (or ever) in the manner we'd like, we won't be trapped in power struggle and can respond with the kind of compassion and strength that carries wisdom.

WHICH DEFENSIVE MODES DOES EACH PERSON IN THE FAMILY USE?

It can be helpful to identify which of *six types of defensive reactions* each person in your family uses most frequently. Each parent, you, your own immediate family, siblings, any other extended family members who are involved.

We can shift between different defensive modes, depending on the situation or the person we are interacting with. However, I find that most of us have one or two "favorites." These defensive reactions are the primary ways the majority of us respond to conflict when we are triggered, angry, in pain and/or frustrated, and trying to figure out how to deal with stressful life situations and, in the case of divorcing parents, what is—or at least seems to be—the disintegration of our own, a spouse's, or partner's family of origin.

Being familiar with them can guide us in how we respond to others. It can also help any of us "catch ourselves" in the act of being defensive so we can learn to shift out of it.

The *six defensive modes* are in *three categories*, the same as in war: *Surrender*, *Withdrawal*, and *Counterattack*. In each category I've included a *passive* and an *aggressive* form.

Surrender-Betray: When using the *passive* form of surrender, you may respond, first and foremost, to all or most demands from one or both of your parents. If they are not treating you well, you still defend the necessity of doing so, even it means *betraying* your commitments to your own family's needs.

Surrender-Sabotage: When using the *aggressive* form of surrender, you may give in to a demand from a parent and then *sabo-*

tage in some way, perhaps by complaining to others, or not following through in a timely fashion.

Withdraw-Escape: When using the *passive* form of withdrawal, a family member might withdraw to *escape* from any conflict rather than trying to resolve it. At a gathering with one of the parents who is complaining about the other—or with siblings where there is conflict related to the parents' divorce—you or some other family member might seem pleasant but withdraw to play with children or do the dishes. Or you might find some reason to "just not show up."

Withdraw-Entrap: When using the *aggressive* form of withdrawal, you or another family member might use silence and disengagement, combined with sullen expressions and staring at others or off into space. A parent who has been asked to attend an event for a grandchild that the other parent is also attending might use this approach to silently throw a wet blanket of disapproval, *entrapping* others in their own "bad mood." Asking one or more questions that sets another person up for a zinger is another form of *Withdraw-Entrap*. For example, your brother asks you, "Do you think Mom has been demanding?" You say "Yes," feeling momentarily supported. He then says, "Then why do you keep doing everything she asks?"

Counterattack-Justify: When using the *passive* form of counterattack, you may *justify* why you continue to help a demanding parent, or your sister might justify why she hasn't "had time" to follow through on her commitment to sharing the responsibility for taking dad to his doctor appointments every other time. Your mom or dad may defend themselves to you with regard to what the other parent is saying about them.

Counterattack-Blame: When using the *aggressive* form of counterattack, one parent may level accusations at the other, hoping to get support from you. Or, your brother may accuse you of disloyalty for still even talking to the parent they see as having caused the divorce.

These *six defensive reactions* interface with each other. For example, if both parents are at a gathering and break into argument. You always did . . . ! I did not! It was you who . . . ! Are you kidding me? I never . . . ! You were always good at shifting the blame! Here is the classic argument, with each parent taking turns shifting back and forth between defending themselves and blaming the other.

USING NON-DEFENSIVE COMMUNICATION SKILLS TO DEFUSE DEFENSIVENESS

Rather than reacting defensively, we can use:

1. Questions: Ask genuinely curious questions.

2. Statements: Give feedback to others and express our own thoughts and beliefs.

a. Feedback: Give honest, but gentle feedback to the other person about:

(1) How we understand and see the person's position;

(2) Any contradictions we see between another person's words and body language or tone of voice; and

(3) Our conclusions or assumptions about the meaning of the contradiction.

b. Self-Expression: Say our own thoughts, beliefs, and feelings.

3. Predictions: Create clear, nonpunitive boundaries when needed. Being able to identify which defensive mode the other person is using can help guide how we respond.

These three nondefensive communication forms are sometimes used in the order listed—*questions*, *statements*, and *predicting consequences* if needed. However, they do not have to be used in a specific order.

As you read the examples below, it may seem "too simple" to get some of the shifts that the parents and/or siblings make. However, changes in intention, such as being genuinely curious about the other person's perspectives and experience, can make all the difference in the world.

For example, a single question a client of mine asked her husband opened the door to a conversation that saved their marriage. Mena came to a PNDC practice session in tears, and told us that her husband, Todd, had come home the night before and told her that he'd almost left her and their children. She felt totally betrayed and it was almost impossible for her to be able to ask a genuinely curious question. As we worked in the group to help her get there, people realized that if she asked the question from the place of her sense of betrayal and anger, he would surely get defensive. She practiced until she was able to ask the question in a more relaxed, neutral way. She came back the next week with the following story.

She said, "I asked Todd calmly, 'What made you want to leave me and the girls?'" *Her question was about his motives and intention.* "He told me, 'I know you had a hard time as a kid because your family was poverty-stricken, and it's been hard for you when I've wanted to quit my job and go back to school. Today at work, I was working at that new construction site and pounding what seemed like a thousand nails and I just lost it. I couldn't stand to do it for the rest of my life.' I realized I had been too afraid. We had a good talk. The girls are old enough now and in school, and I have good bookkeeping skills. So, I'm going to work part-time, and he's going to start by taking night classes."

SAMPLE CONVERSATIONS IN COMMON INTERACTIONS WITH DIVORCING PARENTS

Example 1

If Dad says, "*Why can't you just be happy for me that I am moving on with my life?*"

Instead of just withdrawing, or surrendering and listening, or getting angry, I can start with a question, such as: "Do you believe that it is, or should be, easy for me to be happy when you and Mom are going through a hard divorce?" *Form of Question: My assumption about how Dad sees my experience.*

Or: "What kind of impact do you think the divorce is having on me, Dad?" *Form of Question: How my parent sees the impact of the divorce on me.*

If I ask either of these first two questions with genuine curiosity—hard as it may seem—Dad might well shift, saying, "Oh, I know it must be hard. I guess I just feel so much happier, I wanted you to be happy for me too."

On the other hand, Dad might say, "I felt so trapped for years. I'd expect you to be *really happy* for me that I can get a life of my own now!" *Defensive Response: Blame.*

I might respond by saying, "What I hear you saying is that it should be easy for me to be happy in the way we'd normally be happy when everything is going well, like at a party or on a trip." *Statement—Feedback Part I: My understanding of what Dad is saying.*

"At the same time, the divorce was a shock to me, and you and Mom are telling me all sorts of things that made you unhappy that I never knew about, and I'm just beginning to deal with it." *Statement—Feedback Part II: Identifying what I see as a contradiction between Dad's expectation that I be able to respond supportively to his feelings and his unwillingness to understand and respond to mine.*

"So, it seems to me that you want me to be able to shift right away through my shock and just be happy for you." *Statement—Feedback Part III: My conclusions about Dad's motives.*

"I don't have my family to go home to any more. I want you to be happy, and Mom too, but I need time to grasp all this, and I'm in grief." *Statement—My Own Experience: Expressing my own thoughts, beliefs, and feelings.*

Dad has a second opportunity to shift and respond to my pain. In that case, he might just hug me and even apologize, saying, "Oh man, I'm sorry. Of course, this is a shock. I know you'd want me to be happy. That wasn't fair of me. I know you need time. I didn't tell you how unhappy I was, because I knew it would upset you. Of course, you were shocked."

Conversely, Dad might say, "Come on, you must have known we weren't happy. Even if you didn't, it's no reason not to be happy for me now." *Defensive response: Blaming*

In that case, rather than trying to convince him that I have legitimate feelings, or just walking off hurt and angry, I can set a limit, by making a *prediction* such as, "If you can't understand and respect that this is very hard for me and has shattered a huge part of my world, and trust that I do want both of you to be happy, then I will have a harder time feeling close to you." *Limit Setting: Predicting consequences.*

Followed by:

"If you can understand how hard this is for me and not judge me or blame me, and trust that I do want both of you to be happy, but need time to get through my own pain, then it will be easier for me to feel close to you." *Limit Setting: Predicting consequences.*

Using two "If-Then" phrases, I have let my parent know (1) how I will respond if he judges me for having a hard time, and conversely, (2) how I will respond if he can be understanding.

Example 2

If Mom says, "*I need to tell you about how badly your father has treated me when you weren't around. Why don't you ever want to listen?*"

I can ask, "What does it mean to you to tell me how badly he has treated you?" *Form of Question: What value would Mom be getting from being able to tell me how badly Dad has treated her.*

If Mom says, "I just need to have someone to talk to." *Defense: Justify.*

I might ask, "What's making you want to talk to me about it instead of some of your really good friends?" *Form of Question: Asking about her intention.*

Possibly followed by, "Have you talked with any of them?"

If Mom says, "I have, but I don't want to bother them all the time." *Defense: Justify.*

I might ask, "Is there any part of you that wants to tell me, so that I will know what a terrible person he is and be angry at him too?"

If Mom denies it, then I might say, "I hear you saying you just need me to listen, and you aren't doing it so that I will side with you and be angry at Dad." *Statement—Feedback Part I: My understanding of what Mom has said.*

"At the same time, you have asked me to listen to bad things about him and then said you don't want it to affect how I feel about him." *Statement—Feedback Part II: Identifying what seems to me to be a contradiction between Mom's request that I listen to her and her denial that her motive is to influence how I feel about Dad.*

"I can't know all of what happened between the two of you. I'm not in a place to want to hear you tell me how terrible he is. I want to be able to have my own relationship with each of you." *Statement—My Own Experience: Expressing my thoughts, beliefs, and feelings.*

I can go straight to my *prediction* here, without waiting for an answer.

"If you continue to try to tell me how rude and unresponsive he was to you, then I will simply ask you to stop, and let you know that I'm not willing to listen."

Followed by:

"If you can respect my wishes and not tell me how badly he treated you, then I will be able to enjoy my time with you and not feel stressed." *Prediction: How I will respond to each of the possible choices Mom might make.*

In each of the examples, if circumstances vary, it will alter the content of the conversation. For example, in some circumstances, one or the other parent might have been alcoholic, and/or verbally or physically abusive. In some of those cases, if the parent and Adult Child are close, the Adult Child might well want to support the parent.

Example 3

If Dad says, "*Don't count on me to be at your graduation if your mother is there.*"

I can ask, “Are you saying that I have to choose between you and Mom and I would have to tell Mom she can’t come, or else you’ll refuse to come?” *Form of Question: About Dad’s intention.*

An alternate or follow-up question I can ask: “Are you saying that it is more important to you not to see Mom than it is to you to see me graduate?” *Form of Question: About what Dad values most.*

If Dad doesn’t shift, I can say, “I hear you saying you will refuse to come if Mom is there.” *Statement—Feedback Part II: My understanding about what Dad is telling me.*

“At the same time, that means I’d have to be the one to tell Mom she can’t come.” *Statement—Feedback Part II: Contradiction that I see between Dad saying it’s just about not wanting to see Mom and what it would actually require of me.*

“I don’t think this is just about you not wanting to see Mom. I believe you want to make me chose between the two of you.” *Statement—Feedback Part III: My conclusion about Dad’s intentions.*

“I’m not willing to be put in the position of telling Mom that she can’t come. I would never do that. I don’t need you to sit together or even talk to each other. I also don’t want to have any hostile feelings and negative attitudes in the airwaves at my graduation. I don’t want my graduation ruined. This is a milestone in my life, and it would mean the world to me to have both of you there, just being happy for me.” *Statement—My Own Experience: Reasoning, beliefs, and feelings.*

In this case, I would certainly go immediately to my *prediction*, unless I felt an instant shift in Dad. Even at that, I’d want to be clear so I would make the *prediction* either way. If the shift is there, I’d start with, “I’m really happy to hear that because . . .”

If he doesn’t shift, I’d simply start with:

“If you can’t come and be gracious and happy about my graduation, then I don’t want you to come.”

Followed by:

“If you can come and be gracious and happy and celebrate my graduation with me, then I would love it.” *My prediction of consequences for either choice.*

Example 4

If my sibling says, "*When you still spend time with Mom after she had an affair and left, you're not being loyal. You're just betraying Dad. I don't know how he can even talk to you.*"

I might say, "I feel really sad for Dad, and I also know that lots of couples who love each other can end up with one or both drifting apart. What I know about both Mom and Dad is that they've always been good people. I don't like it that Mom got involved with someone else and left. I find it very painful. I also know Dad is a great guy and may end up finding someone he will be happy with, maybe happier. I have friends who were devastated over a breakup and ended up being thankful for it later. What worries me is that I'm afraid that you will judge me and just disconnect if I don't reject Mom. I don't want to lose Dad, Mom, or you. It's just so hard. I love you all so much." *Statement: My own thoughts, beliefs, and feelings.*

This is an example of going straight to my own experience without first asking questions or giving feedback. It's a bit risky because it's easy to slide into just "countering" the other person's position, which would lead to argument. However, if I share my own thoughts, reasoning, and feelings without defending Mom, who along with me is under attack, it can work. My sibling might not shift right away, or at all, but I have shared what I believe from my heart, without being adversarial.

Example 5

If one or both parents are putting a wet blanket on a holiday event—or worse, engaging in overt conflict.

Part I: Even though your mom or dad might be at a family gathering without the other parent present, their mood can still be a wet blanket on what would otherwise be a happy, fun birthday party or holiday dinner. The parent who is there may be grieving or sulking—or both—because being with family is a reminder of sadness and/or anger at the other, estranged parent.

Your reactions to your parent's mood may go through phases. You may start out trying to coax your parent out of their mood, perhaps making jokes that fall flat, or encouraging her or him to get involved. "Hey, Dad, come on out in the back yard and play catch with the grandkids. You love doing that!" Or, "Mom, can you come help me figure out if this turkey is done. You have always been able to tell better than I can! I either pull it out too soon or get it too dry."

When the coaxing doesn't work, you may try ignoring your parent but have a hard time getting out of the shadow of their mood, making it impossible to enjoy the day. Finally, frustrated, you may either withdraw into sullenness yourself, or just feel sadness and defeat. On the other hand, you might suddenly lash out in anger: "If all you wanted to do is sit and sulk all day, why did you even bother to come!?"

Of course, you're not the only family member being impacted, so you may disagree about how to respond. If the family gathering is at your house, you might be trying to gently coax and keep things light. Your sister might say, "Just leave her/him alone if she/he wants to sulk!" Your brother might say, "Tell her/him to get over it or go home!"

The problem here is that ignoring, coaxing, and making angry threats accomplish nothing more than creating power struggle. And it's an uphill battle from there. What you can do instead is to start with a genuine question. "Dad, are you having a hard time being here today?" If he denies, "Nope, just resting," you can say, "When I hear you say you are just resting, and at the same time, I see you frowning and not talking to anyone—which isn't usually like you unless you're upset—it seems to me that it is hard for you to be here without Mom, but you don't want to admit it."

The above three sentences include: *Statement—Feedback Part I: My understanding of what Dad is saying; Statement—Feedback Part II: Identifying what I see as a contradiction between what Dad is saying and what I know about his past behavior*; and *Statement—Feedback Part III: My conclusion about the meaning of the contradiction.*

"I know you've always loved being with the grandkids and playing catch with them or cards. Laughing, having fun. It makes me sad to see you here and not hanging out with them. I think they miss it too." *Statement—Feedback Part IV: Your own thoughts, beliefs, feelings.*

"If you just stay sitting here and don't spend any time with us or your grandkids, I think you'll just start feeling more and more isolated and alone. If you can go play with them, or maybe just watch them play, even if your heart isn't totally in it right this minute, then I think you might find that your mood changes and you start feeling free to have fun again." *Form of Prediction: Challenge-Choice.*

When making a *Limit-Setting Prediction*, you predict a consequence that you will implement, such as:

Side 1 of the prediction: "If you speak to me rudely, then I won't answer you."

Side 2 of the prediction: "If you speak to me respectfully, then I'm happy to answer you."

When making a *Challenge-Choice Prediction*, you predict what you *believe* the person will experience if they (a) make a certain choice or (b) do not make that choice. Life provides the consequence. This kind of prediction is more tentative:

Side 1 of the prediction: "If you do X, then I think you might experience . . ."

Side 2 of the prediction: "If you don't do X, then I think you might experience . . ."

Here, instead of letting your dad's mood rub off on you, you have stayed grounded, asked a gentle question, given feedback, expressed your own thoughts, beliefs, and feelings, and made a prediction—all without trying to convince him to do what you think best. He will be more likely to get past his own resistance instead of becoming entrenched in it. An added benefit is that this kind of grounded response can free you from being in bondage to your dad's mood.

Part 2: When both parents are at a family gathering, they may come out punching. Someone may bring a memory of some pleasant family event and your parents start arguing harshly over details about the event:

"Oh, yeah, that was the time you burnt the ribs to charcoal black!"

"The H . . . I did! Are you kidding me?! You're just trying to cover for having forgotten to pick up the birthday cake! You never did take responsibility when you screwed things up."

In other cases, the parents may have a softer veneer and be subtler:

"Oh, I remember that party, I think we had nicely charcoaled steak."

"Sweetheart, I think you have forgotten. That was the time you had to go get the birthday cake you forgot to pick up. Have you forgotten, or are you repeating another of your cleverly altered memories? It's such a talent of yours."

Either way, the joy of the original conversation has gone up in a whiff of smoke. Others in the family may disengage, leave the table, or grit their teeth and just keep eating. Or try to laugh it off. In the face of the harsher argument, you or a sibling might send the kids outside for a while, so they don't have to listen—or better yet, go out with them.

Getting angry or withdrawing is not going to solve the problem. It's time for calm, clear boundaries. You might say:

"Mom and Dad, I want to enjoy our time together and I don't want the kids or anyone else in the family to have to be part of an argument or dragged down by it." *Form of Statement—Part IV: Our own thoughts, beliefs, and feelings.*

"If you stay focused on your hurt and anger at each other, then I'd rather have you each visit separately with us and the kids sometime later. If you can be here without being at each other and just focus on enjoying being with us and the grandkids, then I'd love having you here." *Form of Prediction: Limit-Setting.*

Here you have made a clear, firm prediction that ends on what you'd like best, with an element of welcome at the same time, if the parents can "behave."

It might likely feel extremely hard to do this, especially without coming from a place of frustration and anger. At the same time, if you don't set calm, clear boundaries, the long-term impact on the family can be devastating. When we let the attitudes and behaviors of our parents (or anyone else) drag us down, we give away our power. When we can remember that we have a choice about being drawn into the power struggle and set clear boundaries, we don't "take the hook" thrown out by either parent, or anyone else.

I recall a friend who told me that many years ago when she was a child, her father, an alcoholic (who was not violent toward family members), had stormed out of the house on Christmas Eve. She was the oldest of four children and two of her young siblings were crying. She was very upset too. Then her mother said calmly, warmly, "Your dad will come home when he's ready. We have a choice. We can all be upset and ruin our Christmas Eve, or we can decide to enjoy it together." My friend said the impact of her mom making such a simple statement, focused on choice, had an amazing effect. Everyone shifted and had a wonderful time together.

Conscious decisions to stay out of the fray do not have to mean withdrawal. We can be both kind and firm. It protects our children, saves us a great deal of stress, and models a way of being that can take us out of needless cycles of trauma. Being both kind and firm is a crucial part of a way of being that brings our heart and spine together. Is it hard? Yes. Is it worth it? I believe it is. Absolutely. It can give us the wisdom and strength we need to free ourselves and leave a different legacy for our own children.

Some of you may wonder if longer statements would even be heard, especially without interruption. While you may well get interrupted sometimes, I've found that if my tone is not judging, urgent, or convincing, it is surprising how much better attention others will pay to what I'm saying.

THE THINGS WE DON'T SAY

Many of the things that adult children of divorcing parents hold back from telling their parents are the things that reflect their own pain and vulnerability. We may want to protect our parents.

We might hold back from telling our parents things like some of the comments from adult children of divorcing parents here in the book, such as: "I felt homeless." "My entire life changed in an instant." "I didn't know who I was anymore." "Had our whole family life together been smoke and mirrors?"

The impact of holding back can create a self-fulfilling prophecy, as seen in the following comment. "I've been questioning my ability to have a good relationship in the long term, and it's been causing my wife and me a lot of problems. I think she deserves a better man than me."

It's entirely understandable that this man might feel such fear without ever telling his wife about it. She might then think that the problems were because her spouse didn't love her anymore, when they were actually coming from *his* fear—fostered by his parents' divorce—that *he* wouldn't be good enough for *her*.

Often, we stuff our feelings, like Daniel, who felt caught in the middle between his parents. Then, it's only when we finally blow, that they come out. Finally, Daniel burst out in anger, "The other day I screamed at my mom and dad, 'Stop putting me in the middle! You both pull on me and expect me to be on your side against the other. I love you both. Can't you see that? I hate this! Leave me alone!'" He stormed out of the house.

When expressed from a vulnerable place, sharing the pain of our experience can be a vital part of healing for ourselves as well as our parents and other family members. We don't have to wait until we can't stand it anymore and blow up.

At the same time, sometimes if we haven't expressed our feelings before, and it comes out as a blowup, it can be what I call a "diamond in the rough." If we don't back away from it, perhaps feeling guilty and saying we didn't mean it, but rather honor that it's true, it can be the vehicle to a transition into a more in-depth, potentially healing conversation.

Sandra, a client of mine, told me a story about her related to her own recent divorce.

One night, her twenty-year-old daughter Alissa was angry at her and screamed at her, "I wish Cathy was my mother." Cathy was her ex-husband's current wife. Sandra was devastated, but she managed, with tears streaming uncontrollably down her face, to ask very gently, "Why do you wish Cathy was your mother?" She was calm, sounded curious, and her tone came down at the end of the sentence. Alissa also burst into tears, and they had what Sandra said was an incredible, healing conversation. Toward the end of the conversation, Alissa got a phone call from a friend. She told her friend, "I can't talk now. I'm talking to my mom." Sandra said that was a miracle in itself: her twenty-year-old daughter wanting to talk to her more than to one of her friends. What felt honest to Alissa in the moment of her anger was healed, and the healing was initiated by her mother's willingness to ask a most vulnerable question.

When we can be vulnerable and ask curious questions even if we're afraid to hear the answer, be more fully honest, not hold back in the name of protecting others, and set boundaries that help us keep our integrity, then we have the potential to turn crisis into healing. I think of it as having the heart and the spine together.

14

THERE IS HOPE AND HEALING

Hope is being able to see the light despite the darkness.
—Desmond Tutu, South African theologian and antiapartheid activist

Research indicates that even when adults have experienced myriad losses, physical and psychological disturbances, and grieving, after a period of time, most adults cope successfully with divorce.[1] In the previous chapters, we have included tools and skills that can assist Adult Children and their parents in having hope and healing. Following this chapter, we include additional resources that we have found helpful to Adult Children, their parents, and those who care about them.

The weak can never forgive. Forgiveness is the attribute of the strong.
—Mahatma Gandhi, Indian lawyer and activist

Forgiveness is a process that few people truly understand. We use the work of Dr. Fred Luskin, cofounder and director of the Stanford University Forgiveness Project, who has developed a forgiveness training methodology. Six research studies that the Stanford Forgiveness Project has conducted have validated his methodology. Below, from his book *Forgive for Good: A Proven Prescription for*

Health and Happiness, are some important points for Adult Children and their parents.

- Forgiveness is not forgetting that something painful happened, denying or minimizing your feelings, or giving up that you have feelings. Forgiveness does not mean reconciling with the one who hurt you.
- Forgiveness is: for you, not the one who hurt you; taking back your power; taking responsibility for how you feel; about your healing and not about the people who hurt you; a choice; and a trainable skill. Forgiveness helps you get control over your feelings and can improve your mental and physical health.[2]

He also writes, "In careful scientific studies, forgiveness training has been shown to reduce depression, increase hopefulness, decrease anger, improve spiritual connection, increase emotional self-confidence, and help heal relationships. Learning to forgive is good for both your mental and physical well-being and your relationships."[3]

His forgiveness training teaches that when people do not have the tools and skills to deal with their emotional pain of things not turning out the way they want, they create what he calls "grievance stories." If you answer yes to any of his four questions below, it is likely that you have created a grievance story about your parents' divorce.

1. Do you think about this painful situation more than you think about the things in your life that are good?
2. When you think about this painful situation, do you become either physically uncomfortable or emotionally upset?
3. When you think about this situation, do you do so with the same old repetitive thoughts?
4. Do you feel yourself telling the story about what happened over and over in your mind?[4]

His four questions above remind us about what we know from brain science—neurons that fire together, wire together. Neuropsychologist Donald Hebb first used this phrase in 1949, when he was describing how neural pathways in the brain form and grow stronger when they are stimulated through repetition. The tools in this chapter and throughout the book aid in healing, because they employ Hebb's concept that neurons that fire together, wire together. This is the reason practicing mindfulness meditation has so many benefits.[5] Mindfulness includes breathing from your diaphragm (belly), relaxing your muscles and entire body, awareness without judgment of what you are experiencing in the current moment, and mental imagery. Practicing mindfulness stimulates the neural pathways to become stronger with positive, not negative, images and emotions. Luskin prescribes a process he calls Positive Emotion Refocusing Technique (PERT) that is just such a mindfulness meditation.

When you are feeling the effects of an unresolved grievance or ongoing relationship problem, Luskin writes,

> Bring your attention fully to your stomach as you slowly draw in and out two deep breaths. As you inhale, allow the air to push your belly out gently. As you exhale, consciously relax your belly so that it feels soft.
>
> On the third full and deep inhalation, bring to your mind's eye an image of someone you love or of a beautiful scene in nature that fills you with awe and wonder. Often people have a stronger response when they imagine their positive feelings are centered in the area around their heart.
>
> While practicing, continue with *soft* belly breathing.
>
> Ask the relaxed and peaceful part of you what you can do to resolve your difficulty.[6]

Luskin points out that we impede the forgiveness process when we take things too personally, blame others for what we are feeling, and have unenforceable rules that are our expectations about how we think something should be—"Our parents should stay married for their lifetime," or how someone should think or behave—"My parents should not be dating and acting like giddy teenagers." Clearly, we do not have the power to make our unenforceable rules happen.[7] Instead of remaining stuck, being upset, and obsessively thinking about our unenforceable rule, he recommends practicing the above PERT exercise to calm your fight-flight-freeze response, and then state our strongest positive motivation for being in the grievance situation in the first place.[8] For example, instead of ruminating, "My parents should stay married for their lifetime," state, "I want a loving, intact family." Then accept that humans never get everything that they want.

Realizing that forgiveness is not a substitute for grieving also provides hope and healing. As chapter 4, "Shock and Then Grieving," explained, for many people, grieving is foundational for healing to occur. The timeframe for grieving significant losses like divorce can vary from months to years, and the phases that many theorists describe are not linear. Sometimes Adult Children can start the forgiveness process while they are still grieving. Embracing forgiveness enables you to begin practicing mindfulness, focusing on the present moment, and broadening your perspective. You can now see a different future than the one you imagined prior to your parents' divorce. We tell our clients that this is why car windshields are much larger than the rear- and side-view mirrors. When we are looking forward, we need a broader range of vision than the rear- and side-view mirrors provide.

> *What we have once enjoyed deeply we can never lose. All that we love deeply becomes a part of us.*
> —Helen Keller, American author, political activist, and lecturer

Speaking to this quote by Helen Keller and to the power of attachment bonds described in chapter 3, remembering what has happened helps Adult Children learn lessons that they can use in their lives going forward. For example, many Adult Children of gray divorce report that as painful as it was for them to experience their parents' divorce, there was a silver lining. They realized how fragile love relationships are, so they redoubled their commitments and efforts to build and keep their healthy love relationships. Or, some Adult Children who had distant relationships before their parents' divorce report that they began to have a close one-on-one relationship with their previously distant parents.

A study of Adult Children aged eighteen to fifty-four years old that we described in chapters 3 and 5 provides Adult Children and their parents hope for healing. Greenwood found that during their parents' divorce about half of them, whose parents divorced after they were eighteen years old, reported *not* having strained relationships with one or both parents. Those whose parents had divorced within the past five years were more likely to report having a strained relationship with their parents than those whose parents had divorced more than five years ago.[9] The Adult Children whose relationships with their parents were strained worked on mending their relationships over time.[10] In addition to indicating that parental divorce during adulthood is not necessarily a traumatizing event,[11] the results of this study are testament to what you learned in chapter 3—that the parent–child attachment bond is primal and endures "from the cradle to the grave," and in chapter 4, that when these attachment bonds are broken, grieving follows, and grieving can take time.

> *The best and most beautiful things in the world cannot be seen or even touched—they must be felt with the heart.*
> —Helen Keller, American author, political activist, and lecturer

DIVORCE RITUALS

Carol writes:

A decade ago, I attended a plenary session at a conference presented by Dr. Monza Naff, author of *Must We Say We Did Not Love? The Need for Divorce Rituals in Our Time.* She asked why our culture is lacking a ritual for couples who are ending their relationship in divorce to show each other the same respect and kindness that they showed each other in the beginning of their relationship. Her words resonated deeply with me. I immediately saw the value of her work, helping her clients through the divorce transition. As soon as the plenary ended, I made my way to the stage where she had delivered the plenary. I told her how her words had moved me and that I thought her process could help my clients. She is a true healer. In my practice, I use the tools that she developed and recommend her book to many of my clients and colleagues.

She writes that the ritual of a wedding ceremony and affirming vows before witnesses deepens the commitment of those getting married and marks a personal and communal passage. Yet, she says she knows of no culture or spiritual community that has a comparable, consistently practiced ritual for divorce, although traditions exist like funerals and wakes as ceremony for those experiencing the pain and loss that ensues from death.[12] She points out that our culture provides those who are divorcing or ending committed relationships "nothing to mark and aid the transition at the end of the commitment except embarrassment, shame, silence, pointed or indirect reproaches, active criticism, anger and despair, spoken or unspoken bitterness, and sadness."[13]

She has developed a ritual process that provides couples who are ending their long-held commitments to each other a divorce ritual ceremony. She describes that this ceremony captures the essence of what couples want to share with each other and with those who are dear to them.

1. Selecting a space for the ritual or ceremony that has special meaning,
2. Intentionally planning what we want to say and do in a time set apart just for that,
3. Making clear commitments that are set in a context of respect for ourselves and others, and
4. Using meaningful words and special objects to symbolize our commitments.

She states that the above components of ritual create a process that can engage a person's body, mind, spirit, and actions in ways that have great power,[14] and she affirms that in her work, she sees that the divorce ritual has heart, so much heart that it heals when nothing else can.[15] One person can perform divorce rituals, or they may include the couple, the nuclear family that includes the children, the extended family, and the couple's entire community. Her book is a treasure trove of ideas and tools for the varieties of families that exist, even divorcing step- and blended families. You can find videos of various divorce ritual ceremonies on YouTube. We encourage you and your parents to read her book and create your own divorce rituals that can facilitate healing for everyone involved.

> *Freedom is what you do with what's been done to you.*
> —Jean-Paul Sartre, philosopher

UNCONDITIONAL LOVE MEDITATION

Bruce writes:

More than twenty years ago, while visiting with a Unity minister in Maui, I experienced a version of the Unconditional Love Meditation. I am unable to give her attribution because I don't recall her name. For years I have used this meditation with my clients and found that it promotes their healing.

I taught this meditation to a group of family lawyers, therapists, and financial specialists several years ago. About two weeks later, one of the financial specialists told me she was in a meeting with an angry divorcing couple and their lawyers. They had reached an impasse. They were yelling, crying, and threatening. One of the lawyers called a time out and took her client into a room, where they did this exercise. The financial specialist said that when they emerged fifteen minutes later, everything had changed, and it was palpable. The meeting resumed, and the couple was able to make agreements for the benefit of their entire family. I was not surprised. That is a typical result. The meditation is below.

Get comfortable in a quiet place. Bring to your mind a face or faces of someone for whom you hold unconditional love. It can be one person, more than one, a pet, grandparents, and so on. In your mind, place their face or faces into your heart, seeing their face or faces. Imagine you are breathing unconditional love into their faces. Then as you exhale, donate that unconditional love back into the world. Repeat this. As you are breathing unconditional love right into their faces, watch their faces light up. Notice your heart space lighting up. Again, as you exhale donate that unconditional love back into the world. Continue doing this. Inhale unconditional love right into their faces. Because you are seeing the face of someone you love, when you look into their face, it is easy to generate feelings of unconditional love.

As you do this, you are changing the energy field around yourself and, eventually, the energy field of those around you. This is not just a metaphor. The heart is the most powerful generator of electromagnetic energy in our body, and we now have measuring devices that can measure it a number of feet away in all directions.[16] So there is a physical, tangible, measurable component to this. You are changing the energy field around you, and over time by extrapolation changing the energy field around those you love.

Repeat several times for about five minutes.

What did you notice?

If you do this for fifteen to twenty minutes, you may find yourself falling back into another space, connecting with your best self. Try it as a daily practice. The more you use it now, the less you will need it later. And, you will feel better as you do it. Years from now, when you are sitting around talking with people about how you got through these difficult times, you will know that perhaps you were doing the most powerful thing a person can do. You were generating unconditional love and donating it back into the world.

Changing the memories that form the way we see ourselves also changes the way we view others. Therefore, our relationships, job performance, what we are willing to do or are able to resist, all move in a positive direction.

—Francine Shapiro, American researcher and developer of EMDR

EYE MOVEMENT DESENSITIZATION AND REPROCESSING

Carol facilitated Atsuko's healing in chapter 3 by using Eye Movement Desensitization and Reprocessing (EMDR), and she referred her parents to EMDR therapists for the same reason. EMDR, developed by psychologist Francine Shapiro in the late 1980s, is an effective tool for healing. It is an integrative psychotherapy that activates the body's natural healing systems, thereby helping people heal from emotional distress that arises from painful life experiences. "There has been so much research on EMDR therapy that it is now recognized as an effective form of treatment for trauma and other disturbing experiences by organizations such as the American Psychiatric Association, the World Health Organization and the Department of Defense."[17] Research indicates that it can be an efficient and rapid treatment.[18] Dr. Shapiro's book, *Getting Past Your Past: Take Control of Your Life with Self-Help Techniques from EMDR Therapy*, is an excellent resource for healing.

MORE NEUROSCIENCE RESEARCH AND HOW TO USE IT IN HEALING

Dr. Amy Banks's book, *Wired to Connect: The Surprising Link Between Brain Science and Strong, Healthy Relationships*, describes her program that uses the latest research from neuroscience for creating healthy relationships. She says, "The science is clear. Social disconnection stimulates our brain's pathways and our stress response systems . . . we miss out on the richness of human experiences, of the empathic connections that are intricately tied to the depth and breadth of feeling and emotion. . . . There is plenty that you can do to nourish your neurological pathways for connection. If they are damaged, you can heal them."[19] Her book contains extensive exercises from her program that provide ways to heal your relationship with yourself and with others.

TWO MEN WITH HELPFUL IDEAS ABOUT HOPE AND HEALING

Bruce writes:

More than twenty years ago, while working on a project, Bruce interviewed two exceptionally interesting men. One was Stan Dale. He had been a radio personality and also had worked in television. He then returned to school and became a transactional analysis therapist and also continued his radio shows. From there he developed seminars on love and relationships. Stan led his seminars all over the United States and in many other countries. As part of his desire to promote peace, he took a group of Americans into the Soviet Union.

He explained to me that in his seminars, he asked this particular question: How do you feel when you are in love? Stan said that no matter where he was, Kansas or the Soviet Union, he always heard the same responses. Answers such as I feel more alive, more optimistic, happy, more connected. Colors are brighter. Stan said, "I then asked them, why do you ever take yourself out of love?"[20]

What a wonderful question that is. It implies that we have a choice about what mental and emotional states we want to experience. By bringing the option into present consciousness, we have the opportunity to make the choice.

The other man was Father Tom Allender, a Jesuit priest. I reinterviewed him in 2019. A question I asked him was a question I asked every person I interviewed. "If you were King or Queen of the world for one day and could tell people to do or not do one thing, what would it be?" Father Allender paused thoughtfully for a few moments and then said, "Any conflict we have with another there are always two sides of the street. The only side of the street we can sweep is our own. No matter how justified we are with our anger, anger is always our issue. We are not going to feel better about life no matter what the other person does until we release our anger. Our anger is our anger."[21]

I think both of these men describe the same thing. We are not solely reactive beings. These two processes can help you heal your wounds and take back control of your life.

> *It's not happiness that brings us gratitude. It's gratitude that brings us happiness.*
> —Unknown

GRATITUDE LISTS

For the next week, every evening before you go to sleep. Write down at least fifty things for which you are grateful; a hundred is even better! Keep reading, and you will learn why.

Human brains are wired for survival. Early humans were exposed to many physical dangers. They had to be on the lookout for potential trouble constantly. Today human brains still ensure that we pay more attention to bad things that MIGHT happen than to good things that are ACTUALLY happening. This heightens fear and anxiety.

Knowing you will be writing down fifty to a hundred things that you can feel grateful for, it becomes a task. It requires you to start noticing things that qualify. Here are examples: When you take a shower, instead of feeling it's a task because you are late, think of how you would feel if your shower didn't work, and allow yourself if only for a moment to feel grateful you can use it right now. Notice any part of your body that's working well. Is your back better today? Yes? Grateful! Are your eyes working? Yes? Is your hearing working? Yes? Grateful!

Those who make a serious effort to do this usually report a positive result. As you make this a daily practice, you will probably discover that even though there are problems, most of your life is working well. You can train your mind to notice the things in your life that are working. The change in focus changes your experience of life and dampens down your anxiety response. Give it a real try. You will be surprised how well it works to improve your self-talk, focus, and mood. Quoting numerous university studies, the article "7 Scientifically Proven Benefits of Gratitude"[22] explains why. The research found that gratitude:

- Opens the door to more relationships
- Improves physical health
- Improves psychological health
- Enhances empathy and reduces aggression
- Helps people sleep better
- Improves self-esteem
- Increases mental strength

REPAIRING UNHEALTHY ATTACHMENT STYLES

In her book, *Attachment: 60 Trauma-Informed Assessment and Treatment Interventions Across the Lifespan*, Dr. Christina Reese provides exercises to help repair dysfunctional attachment and improve relationships.

> *I'm not what happened to me, I am what I choose to become.*
> —Carl Jung, Swiss psychiatrist and psychoanalyst

INDIVIDUAL THERAPY

Francine Shapiro, developer of EMDR, said, "The past affects the present even without our being aware of it." Rollo May, American psychologist and author, opined, "Depression is the inability to construct a future." Over the years, many clients have said that they never realized how much being in individual therapy could benefit them until they experienced it. There are many benefits from individual therapy. In a May 2019 article, the associate editor of Psych-

Central.com writes, "Therapy isn't only for people with a diagnosis—or in crisis. Therapy is a great way to enhance your happiness."[23] She details eleven benefits of seeking professional help. Therapy:

- Provides perspective
- Sparks self-awareness
- Is objective
- Helps you change patterns
- Gives you "me" time
- Lets you unplug from electronic devices
- Cultivates connection
- Lets you unload—minus the hard feelings
- Is a place to be completely candid
- Teaches effective coping skills
- Is an opportunity for a positive ending

If you are feeling stuck in depression, anxiety, a general feeling of malaise, or simply want to improve your sense of well-being and want to learn how to move forward and construct a new, more positive future, individual therapy could assist you in doing so.

FAMILY THERAPY

John Bowlby, the developer of attachment theory that we detailed in chapter 3, said, "A main aim of family therapy is to enable all members to relate together in such a way that each member can find a secure base in his relationships within the family, as occurs in every healthy functioning family."[24] Atsuko and her parents in chapter 3 participated in individual and family therapy, and they were able to repair their broken attachment bonds, heal their distressed relationships, and become a healthy, loving restructured family.

IMPROVING COMMUNICATION AND RELATIONSHIPS

We consistently recommend the work of Bill Eddy, family lawyer, mediator, author, and social worker, to supplement individual, family, coparenting therapy. His website HighConflictInstitute.com is a goldmine for learning how to improve communication and relationships.

The poem below, written by François Garagnon, twentieth-century French jurist, captures why effective communication is fundamental to healing our relationships. Read and absorb it, then share with those with whom you most want to communicate effectively.

Nine Possibilities
Between what I think,
What I want to say,
What I believe I am saying,
What I say,
What you want to hear,
What you hear,
What you believe you understand,
What you want to understand,
There are at least nine possibilities
for misunderstanding.

Laughter is the tonic, the relief, the surcease for pain.
—Charlie Chaplin, English comic actor, composer, and filmmaker

HUMOR AND LAUGHTER HELP HEALING

Research substantiates that humor and laughter are therapeutic allies in healing.[25] So we close with these wise words:

Change is inevitable, except from a vending machine.
—Robert C. Gallagher, American sportswriter

Let the healing begin—and continue!

ADDITIONAL RESOURCES

BIFF: Quick Responses to High-Conflict People, Their Personal Attack, Hostile Email and Social Media Meltdowns, by Bill Eddy

Calling It Quits: Late-Life Divorce and Starting Over, by Deirdre Blair

Daring Greatly: How the Courage to Be Vulnerable Transforms the Way We Live, Love, Parent and Lead, by Brene Brown

Dating Radar: Why Your Brain Says Yes to "The One" Who Will Make Your Life Hell, by Bill Eddy and Megan Hunter

From Dating to Getting Serious, to Forming a "Blended Family," by Patricia Papernow

Gray Divorce: What We Lose and Gain from Mid-Life Splits, by Jocelyn Crowley

Healing the Woman Heart, by Monza Naff

I Don't Want to Talk about It: Overcoming the Secret Legacy of Male Depression, by Terrence Real

Love and Survival: 8 Pathways to Intimacy and Health, by Dean Ornish

My Father Married Your Mother: Writers Talk about Stepparents, Stepchildren, and Everyone in Between, edited by Anne Burt

Our Most Complicated Relationship: When You and Your Mother Can't Be Friends, by Victoria Secunda
Rising Strong: How the Ability to Reset Transforms the Way We Live, Love, Parent and Lead, by Brené Brown
Surviving and Thriving in Stepfamily Relationships: What Works and What Doesn't, by Patricia Papernow
The Good Divorce, by Constance Ahrons
The UCLA Mindful Awareness Research Center
We're Still Family, by Constance Ahrons
Women and Their Fathers: The Sexual and Romantic Impact of the First Man in Your Life, by Victoria Secunda

NOTES

INTRODUCTION

1. Susan L. Brown and I-Fen Lin, "The Gray Divorce Revolution: Rising Divorce Among Middle-Aged and Older Adults, 1990–2010," *Journals of Gerontology Series B: Psychological Sciences and Social Sciences* 67, no. 6 (2012): 731–41, doi:10.1093/geronb/gbs089.

2. Ibid., 735.

3. Colette Allred, "Age Variation in the Divorce Rate, 1990 and 2017," *Family Profiles*, FP-19-13 (Bowling Green, OH: National Center for Family and Marriage Research), https://doi.org/10/25035/ncfmr/fp-19-13.

4. Wendy Dennis, "How Grey Divorce Became the New Normal," everythingzoomer.com, June 3, 2016, https://www.everythingzoomer.com/sex-relating/2016/06/03/how-grey-divorce-became-the-new-normal/; Matthew Gray, David de Vaus, Lixia Qu, and David Stanton, "Divorce and Wellbeing of Older Australians," *Ageing and Society* 32 (2011): 475–98, https://doi.org/10.1017/S0144686X10001017; Fumle Kumagai, "The Fallacy of Late-Life Divorce in Japan," *Care Management Journals* 7, no. 3 (2006): 123–34, doi: 10.1891/cmj-v7i3a004; Mackenzie Stroh, "The 27-Year Itch," *Maclean's*, January 27, 2007, https://archive.macleans.ca/article/2007/1/29/the-27year-itch#!&pid=402.

5. Linda Nguyen, "Rising 'Grey Divorce' Rates Creates Financial Havoc for Seniors," *Globe and Mail*, September 19, 2012.

6. Sam Meadows, "Rise of the 'Silver Splitters': How Getting Divorced in Retirement Could Cost You Thousands," *Telegraph*, September 28, 2018, https://www.telegraph.co.uk/money/consumer-affairs/rise-silver-splitters-getting-divorced-retirement-could-cost/.

7. Dennis, "How Grey Divorce Became the New Normal."

8. I-Fen Lin, Susan L. Brown, and Anna M. Hammersmith, "Marital Biography, Social Security Receipt, and Poverty," *Research on Aging* 39, no. 1 (2017): 86–110, doi:10.1177/0164027516656139.

9. Martha M. Hamilton, "Divorce after 50 Can Destroy Even the Best Retirement Plans," *Washington Post*, December 11, 2016, https://www.dailyherald.com/article/20161211/business/161219961/.

10. Stephen G. Anderson, "The Very Idea of 'Lawyer Assisted Negotiation' Is a Misnomer," *Start Mediation*, 2015, http://www.startmediation.co.uk/the-very-idea-of-lawyer-assisted-negotiation-is-a-misnomer/.

1. DIVORCE IS A NEVER-ENDING CHAIN OF EVENTS

1. Wendy Dennis, "How Grey Divorce Became the New Normal," everythingzoomer.com, June 3, 2016, https://www.everythingzoomer.com/sex-relating/2016/06/03/how-grey-divorce-became-the-new-normal/.

2. Susan L. Brown and I-Fen Lin, "The Gray Divorce Revolution: Rising Divorce Among Middle-Aged and Older Adults, 1990–2010," *Journals of Gerontology: Series B: Psychological Sciences and Social Sciences* 67, no. 6 (2012): 731–41, doi:10.1093/geronb/gbs089.

3. Ibid., 735.

4. "Lawsuit Stress: The Dark Side of Litigation," *Mental Healthy*, http://www.mentalhealthy.co.uk/anxiety/anxiety/lawsuit-stress-the-dark-side-of-litigation.html.

5. Walter Kirn, "My Parents' Bust-Up, and Mine," *New York Times Magazine*, October 8, 1995, https://www.nytimes.com/1995/10/08/magazine/my-parents-bust-up-and-mine.html.

2. IT'S ALL ABOUT THE RELATIONSHIPS

1. Louis Cozolino, *The Neuroscience of Human Relationships: Attachment and the Developing Social Brain*, second edition (New York: Norton, 2014).

2. Amy Banks, *Wired to Connect: The Surprising Link Between Brain Science and Strong, Healthy Relationships* (New York: Jeremy P. Tarcher/Penguin, 2016), 3.

3. Ibid., 16–17.

4. Ibid.

5. Debra Umberson, "Relationships Between Adult Children and Their Parents: Psychological Consequences for Both Generations," *Journal of Marriage and Family* 54 (1992): 664–74, doi:10.2307/353252.

6. Joleen Greenwood, "Parent–Child Relationships in the Context of Mid- to Late-Life Parental Divorce," *Journal of Divorce and Remarriage* 53 (2012): 1–17, https/doi.org/10.1080/10502556.2012.635959.

7. Daniel Siegel, "Relationship Science and Being Human," Dr. Dan Siegel blog, December 17, 2013, https://www.drdansiegel.com/blog/2013/12/17/relationship-science-and-being-human/.

8. Alan Booth and Paul R. Amato, "Parental Marital Quality, Parental Divorce, and Relations with Parents," *Journal of Marriage and the Family* 56 (1994): 21–34, doi:10.2307/352698; William Aquilino, "Later Life Parental Divorce and Widowhood: Impact on Young Adults' Assessment of Parent–Child Relations," *Journal of Marriage and Family* 56 (1994): 908–22, doi:10.2307353602; Kate Hughes, "Mothering Mothers: An Exploration of the Perceptions of Adult Children of Divorce," *Australian Journal of Social Issues* 42, no. 4 (2007): 563–79, doi:10.1002/j.1839-4655.2007.tb00078.x; Adam Shapiro, "Later-Life Divorce and Parent–Adult Child Contact and Proximity: A Longitudinal Analysis," *Journal of Family Issues* 24 (March 2003): 264–85, doi:10.1177/0192513X02250099; Maaike Jappens and Jan Van Bavel, "Parental Divorce, Residence Arrangements, and Contact Between Grandchildren and Grandparents," *Journal of Marriage and Family* 78 (December 2015), doi:10.1111/jomf.12275; Sarah Katharina Westphal, Anne-Rigt Poortman, and Tanja Van der Lippe, "What about the Grandparents? Children's Post-divorce Residence Arrangements and Contact with Grandparents," *Journal of Marriage and Family* 77, no. 2 (April 1, 2015): 424–40, doi:10.1111/jomf.12173; Teresa M. Cooney, "Young Adults' Relations with Parents:

The Influence of Recent Parental Divorce," *Journal of Marriage and the Family* 56 (1994): 45–56, doi:10.2307/352700.

9. William S. Aquilano, "Later Life Parental Divorce and Widowhood: Impact on Young Adults' Assessment of Parent–Child Relations," *Journal of Marriage and the Family* 56 (November 1994): 913–15, doi:10.2307/353602.

10. Sylvia L. Mikucki-Enyart, Sarah E. Wilder, and Hayden Barber, "'Was It All Smoke and Mirrors?': Applying the Relational Turbulence Model to Adult Children's Experience of Late-Life Parental Divorce," *Journal of Social and Personal Relationships* 34, no. 2 (February 4, 2016): 209–34, doi:10.1177/0265407516629226; Denise Haunani Solomon and Leanne K Knobloch, "A Model of Relational Turbulence: The Role of Intimacy, Relational Uncertainty, and Interference from Partners in Appraisals of Irritations," *Journal of Social and Personal Relationships* 21, no. 6 (December 1, 2004): 795–816, doi:10.1177/0265407504047838.

3. ATTACHMENT AND ABANDONMENT

1. Ariann E. Robino, "The Human–Animal Bond and Attachment in Animal-Assisted Interventions in Counseling," PhD dissertation (Virginia Polytechnic Institute and State University, 2019), 116–18.

2. Mary S. Ainsworth and John Bowlby, "An Ethological Approach to Personality Development," *American Psychologist* 46, no. 4 (1991): 333–41, doi:10.1037/0003-066X.46.4.333.

3. These three attachment styles were described in 1970 by Ainsworth and Bell: Mary S. Ainsworth and Sylvia M. Bell, "Attachment, Exploration, and Separation: Illustrated by the Behavior of One-Year-Olds in a Strange Situation," *Child Development* 41 (1970): 49–67, doi:10.2307/1127388. The fourth attachment style, Disorganized-Disoriented, was introduced in 1986 by Main and Solomon: Mary Main and Judith Solomon, "Discovery of a New Insecure-Disorganized/Disoriented Attachment Pattern," in Michael W. Yogman and T. Berry Brazelton, eds., *Affective Development in Infancy* (Norwood, NJ: Ablex, 1986), 95–124.

4. Joseph J. Campos et al., "Socioemotional Development," in Marshall M. Haith and J. J. Campos, eds., *Handbook of Child Psychology: Vol. 2. Infancy and Psychobiology* (New York: Wiley, 1983), 783–915.

5. Cindy Hazan and Phillip Shaver, "Romantic Love Conceptualized as an Attachment Process," *Journal of Personality and Social Psychology* 52, no. 3 (1987): 518, doi: 10.1037/0022-3514.52.3.511.

6. Ibid., 516 and 518.

7. Phillip Shaver and Cindy Hazan, "A Biased Overview of the Study of Love," *Journal of Social and Personal Relationships* 5, no. 4 (1988): 484–86, doi:10/1177/0265407588054005.

8. Jude Cassidy, Jason Jones, and Phillip Shaver, "Contributions of Attachment Theory and Research: A Framework for Future Research, Translation, and Policy," *Development and Psychopathology* 25 (2013): 141, doi:10.1017/S0954579413000692.

9. John Bowlby, *The Making and Breaking of Affectional Bonds* (London: Tavistock, 1979), 103.

10. Jude Cassidy and Phillip Shaver, *Handbook of Attachment: Theory, Research, and Clinical Applications*, third edition (New York: Guilford Press, 2016), 942.

11. John Bowlby, *Loss: Sadness and Depression* (New York: Basic Books, 1980), 40.

12. John Bowlby, *Attachment and Loss: Vol. 1. Attachment*, second edition (New York: Basic Books, 1969, 1982); John Bowlby, *Attachment and Loss: Vol. 2. Separation: Anxiety and Anger* (New York: Basic Books, 1973); John Bowlby, *Attachment and Loss: Vol. 3. Loss: Sadness and Depression* (New York: Basic Books, 1980).

13. Debra J. Zeifman and Cindy Hazan, "Pair Bonds as Attachments: Mounting Evidence in Support of Bowlby's Hypothesis," in Judy Cassidy and Philip R. Shaver, eds., *Handbook of Attachment: Theory, Research, and Clinical Application*, third edition (New York: Guilford Press, 2016), 430.

14. Ibid., 419.

15. Mario Mikulincer and Phillip R. Shaver, *Attachment in Adulthood: Structure, Dynamics, and Change*, second edition (New York: Guilford Press, 2018), 67–68.

16. Ibid., 61.

17. Brooke C. Feeney and Joan K. Monin, "Divorce Through the Lens of Attachment Theory," in Jude Cassidy and Phillip R. Shaver, eds., *Handbook of Attachment: Theory, Research, and Clinical Application*, third edition (New York: Guilford Press, 2016), 945.

18. Ibid.

19. Mario Mikulincer and Phillip R. Shaver, "Adult Attachment and Emotion Regulation," in Jude Cassidy and Phillip R. Shaver, eds., *Handbook of Attachment: Theory, Research, and Clinical Application*, third edition (New York: Guilford Press, 2018), 526.

20. Ibid., 521.

21. Feeney and Monin, "Divorce Through the Lens of Attachment Theory," 946.

22. Bowlby, *Loss: Sadness and Depression*; Tamara L. Fuller and Frank D. Fincham, "Attachment Style in Married Couples: Relation to Current Marital Functioning, Stability over Time, and Method of Assessment," *Personal Relationships* 92, no. 2 (1995): 17–34, doi:10/1111/j.1415-6811.1995.tb00075.x; Jeffry A. Simpson, W. Andrew Collins, Sisi Tran, and Katherine C. Hayden, "Attachment and the Experience and Expression of Emotions in Romantic Relationships: A Developmental Perspective," *Journal of Personality and Social Psychology* 92, no. 2 (2007): 363–65, doi:10.1037/0022-3514.92.2.355.

23. Louis Cozolino, *The Neuroscience of Human Relationships: Attachment and the Developing Social Brain*, second edition (New York: Norton, 2014), 4.

24. Joleen Greenwood, "Parent–Child Relationships in the Context of Mid- to Late-Life Parental Divorce," *Journal of Divorce and Remarriage* 53, no. 1 (2012): 5–6, doi:10.1080/10502556.2012.635959.

25. Ibid., 6–7.

26. Rick Shoup, Robert M. Gonyea, and George Kuh, "Helicopter Parents: Examining the Impact of Highly Involved Parents on Student Engagement and Educational Outcomes," paper presented at the 49th Annual Forum of the Association for Institutional Research, Atlanta, Georgia, June 1, 2009, 2, 14, 21.

4. SHOCK AND THEN GRIEVING

1. William Shatner, retrieved from https://www.brainyquote.com/quotes/william_shatner_459183.

2. D. A. Wolf, "Death or Divorce: Which Is Worse?" *Huffington Post*, January 16, 2012, https://www.huffpost.com/entry/death-or-divorce-which-is_b_1101346.

3. Merriam-Webster.com.

4. Jane Gordon Julien, “Never Too Old to Hurt from Parents’ Divorce,” *New York Times*, April 21, 2016, https://www.nytimes.com/2016/04/24/fashion/weddings/never-too-old-to-hurt-from-parents-divorce.html.

5. Todd M. Jensen and Gary L. Bowen, “Mid- and Late-Life Divorce and Parents’ Perceptions of Emerging Adult Children’s Emotional Reactions,” *Journal of Divorce and Remarriage* 56, no. 5 (July 4, 2015): 419, doi:10.1080/10502556.2015.1046795.

6. Joshua Ehrlich, *Divorce and Loss: Helping Adults and Children Mourn When a Marriage Comes Apart* (New York: Rowman & Littlefield, 2018), 74.

7. Anthony Papa and Nicole Lancaster, “Identity Continuity and Loss after Death, Divorce, and Job Loss,” *Self and Identity* 15, no. 1 (2016): 47–61, doi:10.1080/15298868.2015.1079551.

8. Elisabeth Kübler-Ross, *On Death and Dying* (New York: Scribner, 1969).

9. John Bowlby, “Grief and Mourning in Infancy and Childhood,” *Psychoanalytic Study of the Child* 15 (1960): 9–39, doi:10/1080/00797308.1960.11822566.

10. John Bowlby, *Attachment and Loss, Vol. 3: Loss: Sadness and Depression* (New York: Basic Books, 1980), 85.

11. Colin Murray Parkes, *Bereavement: Studies of Grief in Adult Life*, third edition (Philadelphia: Taylor and Francis, 1996), 30.

12. John Bowlby and Colin Murray Parkes, “Separation and Loss within the Family,” in E. James Anthony, ed., *The Child in His Family* (New York: Wiley-Interscience, 1970), 198.

13. John Bowlby, *The Making and Breaking of Affectional Bonds* (London: Tavistock/Routledge, 1979).

14. George A. Bonanno, “Loss, Trauma, and Human Resilience: Have We Underestimated the Human Capacity to Thrive after Extremely Aversive Events?” *The American Psychologist* 59, no. 1 (2004): 23, doi:10.1037/0003-066x.59.1.20.

15. “Complicated Grief,” Mayo Clinic, https://www.mayoclinic.org/diseases-conditions/complicated-grief/symptoms-causes/syc-20360374.

16. Colin Murray Parkes, “The Effects of Bereavement on Physical and Mental Health: A Study of the Case Records of Widows,” *British Medical Journal* 2 (1964): 274–79, doi:10.1136/bmj.2.5404.274.

17. Paul K. Maciejewski, Baohui Zhang, L. Susan Block, and Holly G. Prigerson, “An Empirical Examination of the Stage Theory of Grief,”

Journal of the American Medical Association 297, no. 7 (2007): 716–24, doi:10.1001/jama.297.7.716.

18. J. William Worden, *Grief Counseling and Grief Therapy*, fifth edition (New York: Springer Publishing Company, 2018).

19. George Bonanno and Dacher Keltner, "Facial Expressions of Emotion and the Course of Conjugal Bereavement," *Journal of Abnormal Psychology* 106, no. 1 (1997): 126–37, doi:10.1037//0021-843x.106.1.126.

20. Bonanno et al., "Resilience to Loss and Chronic Grief: A Prospective Study from Preloss to 18-Months Postloss," *Journal of Personal and Social Psychology* 83, no. 5 (2002): 1150–64, doi:10.1037//0022-3514.83.5.1150.

21. W. Thomas Boyce, *The Orchid and the Dandelion: Why Some Children Struggle and How All Can Thrive* (New York: Knopf, 2019).

22. Robert Emery, *Renegotiating Family Relationships* (New York: Guilford Press, 2012), 40–61.

23. For example, see the grief theories of Mardi Horowitz, "Stress-Response Syndromes: A Review of Posttraumatic and Adjustment Disorders," *Hospital Community Psychiatry* 37, no. 3 (1986): 241–49, doi: 10.1176/ps.37.3.241; Robert Neimeyer, *Meaning Reconstruction and the Experience of Loss* (Washington, DC: American Psychological Association, 2001); George Bonanno and Stacey Kaltman, "Toward an Integrative Perspective on Bereavement," *Psychological Bulletin* 125, no. 6 (1999): 760–86, doi:10.1037/0033-2909.125.6.760; Margaret Stroebe and Henk Schut, "The Dual Process Model of Coping with Bereavement: Rationale and Description," *Death Studies* 23, no. 3 (1999): 197–224, doi:10.1080/074811899201046.

5. STAGES OF ADULT DEVELOPMENT

1. Frank F. Furstenberg and Kathleen E. Kiernan, "Delayed Parental Divorce: How Much Do Children Benefit?" *Journal of Marriage and Family* 63, no. 2 (May 1, 2001): 449, doi:10.1111/j.1741-3737.2001.00446.x.

2. Thomas H. Holmes and Richard H. Rahe, "The Social Readjustment Rating Scale," *Journal of Psychosomatic Research* 11, no. 2 (1967): 213–18, doi:10/1016/0022-3999(67)90010-4.

3. See the theories of Erik Erikson, Carl Jung, and Daniel Levinson.

4. Dr. Lorraine Fleckhammer, "Adulthood Age Group Growth and Development" (Hawthorn, Victoria, 2017), https://web2.aabu.edu.jo/tool/course_file/lec_notes/1001242_AdulthoodAgeGroupGD.pdf.

5. Paul R. Amato and Tamara D. Afifi, "Feeling Caught Between Parents: Adult Children's Relations with Parents and Subjective Well-Being," *Journal of Marriage and Family* 68, no. 1 (2006): 222, doi:10/1111/j.1741-3737.2006.00243.x.

6. Krista K. Payne, "Young Adults in the Parental Home, 1940–2010," *Family Profiles*, 2012, http://ncfmr.bgsu.edu/pdf/family/family_profiles/file98800.pdf.

7. Ibid.

8. Amato and Afifi, "Feeling Caught Between Parents," 224.

9. Catherine C. Ayoub, Robin M. Deutsch, and Andronicki Maraganore, "Emotional Distress in Children of High-Conflict Divorce: The Impact of Marital Conflict and Violence," *Family and Conciliation Courts Review* 37 (1999): 297–315, doi:10.1111/j.174-1617.1999.tb01307.x; Edward Mark Cummings and Patrick T. Davies, "Effects of Marital Conflict on Children: Recent Advances and Emerging Themes in Process-Oriented Research," *Journal of Child Psychology and Psychiatry and Allied Disciplines* (January 2002): 31–63, doi:10.1111/1469-7610.00003.

10. Amato and Afifi, "Feeling Caught Between Parents," 232.

11. Judith S. Wallerstein and Julia M. Lewis, "The Unexpected Legacy of Divorce: Report of a 25-Year Study," *Psychoanalytic Psychology* 21, no. 3 (2004): xii, doi:10.1037/0736-9735.21.3.353.

12. Collaborative Divorce is a family-focused divorce process that offers couples a respectful, nonadversarial way to reach balanced, respectful, and lasting agreements, without court intervention. For more information, visit the website of the International Academy of Collaborative Professionals at www.collaborativepractice.com.

13. Jude Cassidy and Phillip Shaver, *Handbook of Attachment: Theory, Research, and Clinical Application*, third edition (New York: Guilford Press, 2016), 180.

14. Joleen Greenwood, "Effects of a Mid- to Late-Life Parental Divorce on Adult Children," *Journal of Divorce and Remarriage* 55 (2014): 540, doi:10.1080/10502556.2014.950903.

15. Ibid., 542.

16. Ibid., 543.

17. Ibid., 543–44.

18. Ibid., 545.
19. Ibid., 545–46.
20. Ibid., 546.
21. Ibid., 546–47.
22. Joleen Greenwood, "Parent–Child Relationships in the Context of Mid- to Late-Life Parental Divorce," *Journal of Divorce and Remarriage* 53 (2012): 11, doi:10.1080/10502556.2012.635959.
23. Ibid., 14.
24. Leo Averbach, "The High Failure Rate of Second and Third Marriages," *Pyschology Today*, 2012, https://www.psychologytoday.com/us/blog/the-intelligent-divorce/201202/the-high-failure-rate-second-and-third-marriages.

6. COMMUNICATION

1. Larry Galvin, "Early Childhood Experiences Shape the Brain's Physical Architecture," *Evanston Round Table*, 2009, https://evanston-roundtable.com/main.asp?SectionID=16&subsectionID=27&articleID=2888.
2. Center on the Developing Child–Harvard University, *The Science of Early Childhood Development*, 2007, developingchild.harvard.edu, https://46y5eh11fhgw3ve3ytpwxt9r-wpengine.netdna-ssl.com/wp-content/uploads/2007/03/InBrief-The-Science-of-Early-Childhood-Development2.pdf.
3. Rick Hanson and Richard Mendius, *Buddah's Brain: The Practical Neuroscience of Happiness, Love and Wisdom* (Oakland, CA: New Harbringer Publications, 2009), 41.
4. Louann Brizendine, "Love, Sex and the Male Brain," CNN.com, March 25, 2010, http//www.cnn.com/OPINION/03/23/brizendine.male.brain/index.h.
5. Wray Herbert, "Review of Delusions of Gender," *Washington Post*, September 12, 2010, http://www.washingtonpost.com/wp-dyn/content/article/2010/09/10/AR2010091002678.html.
6. Deborah Tannen, *You Just Don't Understand: Women and Men in Conversation* (New York: William Morrow Paperbacks, 2007).

7. Warren Farrell, *Why Men Are the Way They Are: The Male–Female Dynamic*, first edition (New York: McGraw-Hill, 1986); Warren Farrell, *The Myth of Male Power* (New York: Simon & Schuster, 1993).

7. BOUNDARIES

1. Janet G. Woititz, *Healthy Parenting: How Your Upbringing Influences the Way You Raise Your Children, and What You Can Do to Make It Better for Them*, first edition (New York: Simon & Schuster/Fireside, 1992).

2. Claudia Black, *It Will Never Happen to Me: Growing Up with Addiction as Youngsters, Adolescents, Adults*, second edition (Center City, MN: Hazelden Publishing, 2009).

8. CHANGING FAMILY ROLES AND RULES

1. Susan L. Brown and I-Fen Lin, "The Gray Divorce Revolution: Rising Divorce among Middle-Aged and Older Adults, 1990–2010," *Journals of Gerontology Series B: Psychological Sciences and Social Sciences* 67, no. 6 (2012): 731–41, doi:10.1093/geronb/gbs089.

2. Kathy McCoy, "7 Surprising Facts about Gray Divorce: What You Thought You Knew Might Not Be True," *Psychology Today*, September 25, 2018.

3. Claudia Black, *It Will Never Happen to Me: Growing Up with Addiction as Youngsters, Adolescents, Adults*, second edition (Center City, MN: Hazelden Publishing, 2009); Sharon Wegscheider-Cruse, *Another Chance: Hope and Health for the Alcoholic Family* (Palo Alto, CA: Science and Behavior Books, 1988).

4. Andy Hinds, "Messages of Shame Are Organized around Gender," *The Atlantic*, April 26, 2013, https://www.theatlantic.com/sexes/archive/2013/04/messages-of-shame-are-organized-around-gender/275322/.

5. Ibid.

6. Prachi Singh, "Summing Up: Inside the Big Fat Global Wedding Industry," *Fashion United*, 2016, https://fashionunited.uk/news/business/summing-up-inside-the-big-fat-global-wedding-industry/2016062420874.

7. Sarah Schmidt, "The Wedding Industry in 2017 and Beyond," MarketResearch.com, 2017, https://blog.marketresearch.com/the-wedding-industry-in-2017-and-beyond.

8. Hinds, "Messages of Shame."

9. Sally Dickerson, Margaret E. Kemeny, Najib Aziz, Kevin Kim, and John L. Fahey, "Immunological Effects of Induced Shame and Guilt," *Psychosomatic Medicine* 66, no. 1 (2004): 124–31, https://www.ncbi.nlm.nih.gov/pubmed/1474764.

9. RELATIONSHIPS WITH SIBLINGS, EXTENDED FAMILY, FRIENDS, AND COMMUNITY

1. Deborah Tannen, *You Just Don't Understand: Women and Men in Conversation* (New York: William Morrow and Company, 1990), 44.

2. Joleen Greenwood, "Adult Sibling Relationships in the Context of a Mid- to Late-Life Parental Divorce," *Journal of Divorce and Remarriage* 55, no. 5 (2014): 391–407, doi:10.1080/10502556.2014.920686.

10. FAMILY TRADITIONS AND RITUALS

1. Maureen Culkin Rhyne, "The Effects of Parental Mid-Life Divorce on Young Adult Development," presented at the National Council on Family Relations Annual Conference, Seattle, Washington, November 14, 1990, https://files.eric.ed.gov/fulltext/ED330952.pdf.

2. "Why It's So Hard for Adults When Their Parents Divorce," youbeauty.com, May 15, 2014, https://www.youbeauty.com/life/why-grey-divorce-sucks-for-adult-children/.

3. Rhyne, "The Effects of Parental Mid-Life Divorce on Young Adult Development."

4. Ibid.

5. Ibid.

6. Marjorie A. Pett, Nancy Lang, and Anita Gander, "Late-Life Divorce: Its Impact on Family Rituals," *Journal of Family Issues* 13, no. 4 (1992): 526–52, doi:10.1177/019251392013004008.

7. Ibid.

8. Remy Smidt, "These Parents Threw a Lit 'Divorce Party' to Make Their Split Less Awkward," BuzzFeed News, December 19, 2016, https://www.buzzfeednews.com/article/remysmidt/happily-never-after.

11. PARENTAL DATING, REPARTNERING, AND REMARRIAGE

1. Ruth Kinniburgh-White, Claire Cartwright, and Fred Seymour, "Young Adults' Narratives of Relational Development with Stepfathers," *Journal of Social and Personal Relationships* 27, no. 7 (2010): 890–907, doi:10.1177/0265407510376252.

2. Constance R. Ahrons, "Family Ties after Divorce: Long-Term Implications for Children," *Family Process* 46 (2007): 53, doi:10.1111/j.1545-5300.2006.00191.x.

3. Ibid., 60.

4. Ibid., 64.

5. Visit the websites of the International Academy of Professionals at www.collaborativepractice.com and the Association of Family and Conciliation Courts at www.afccnet.org for referrals for professionals experienced in assisting families experiencing these difficult family transitions and restructuring.

6. Adam Shapiro and R. Corey Remle, "Generational Jeopardy? Parents' Marital Transitions and the Provision of Financial Transfers to Adult Children," *Journal of Gerontology: Social Sciences* 665B, no. 1 (2010): 99–109, doi:10.1093/geronb/gbq010.

12. HOW PARENTS OF GRAY DIVORCE CAN HELP THEIR ADULT CHILDREN

1. Sarah L. Canham, Atiya Mahmood, Sarah Stott, Judith Sixsmith, and Norm O'Rourke, "'Til Divorce Do Us Part: Marriage Dissolution in

Later Life," *Journal of Divorce and Remarriage* 55, no. 8 (2014): 592, doi:10.1080/10502556.2014.959097.

2. Marjory Campbell, "Divorce at Mid-Life: Intergenerational Issues," *Journal of Divorce and Remarriage* 23, nos. 1–2 (1995): 200, doi:10.1300/J087v23n01_12.

3. Joan Kelly, "Developing Beneficial Parenting Plan Models for Children Following Separation and Divorce," *Journal of the American Academy of Matrimonial Law* 19 (2005): 237–54; Catherine C. Ayoub, Robin M. Deutsch, and Andronicki Maraganore, "Emotional Distress in Children of High-Conflict Divorce: The Impact of Marital Conflict and Violence," *Family and Conciliation Courts Review* 37 (1999): 297–331, doi:10.1111/j.174-1617.1999.tb01307.x; Robert Emery, *Marriage, Divorce, and Children's Adjustment*, second edition (Thousand Oaks, CA: Sage, 1999).

4. Paul R. Amato and Tamara D. Afifi, "Feeling Caught Between Parents: Adult Children's Relations with Parents and Subjective Well-Being," *Journal of Marriage and Family* 68 (2006): 232, doi:10.1111/j.1741-3737.2006.00243.x.

5. Lori Anne Shaw, "Divorce Mediation Outcome Research: A Meta-Analysis," *Conflict Resolution Quarterly* 27 (June 1, 2010): 447–67, doi:10.1002/crq.20006.

6. Constance R. Ahrons, "Family Ties after Divorce: Long-Term Implications for Children," *Family Process* 46 (2007): 62, doi:10.1111/j.1545-5300.2006.00191.x.

7. Ibid., 59.

8. Susan L. Brown, I-Fen Lin, Anna M. Hammersmith, and Matthew R. Wright, "Repartnering Following Gray Divorce: The Roles of Resources and Constraints for Women and Men," *Demography* 56 (2019): 503, doi: 10.1007/s13524-018-0752.x.

9. Patricia Papernow, "Recoupling in Mid-Life and Beyond: From Love at Last to Not So Fast," *Family Process* 57 no. 1 (2018): 60, doi:10.1111/famp.12315.

10. Kali S. Thomas and Robert Applebaum, "Long-Term Services and Supports (LTSS): A Growing Challenge for an Aging America," *Public Policy and Aging Report* 25, no. 2 (April 29, 2015): 56–62, doi:10.1093/ppar/prv003.

11. US Senate Commission on Long-Term Care (2013), *Final Report to Congress*, September 12, 2013, http://ltcocommission.org/.

12. * Brian Don Levy is an attorney at law, licensed to practice law in the State of California (SBN 57614) and in no other jurisdiction. The opinions expressed herein and some of the subject matter of this article are specific references to, and/or governed by, California law. No attorney–client relationship is created as a result of the content of this article. The information provided herein is general in nature, and is not specific to any person or family, and is *not* intended as legal advice. Be sure to consult with an experienced local-to-you lawyer regarding your own unique circumstances.

13. Leo Averbach, "The High Failure Rate of Second and Third Marriages," *Psychology Today*, February 6, 2012, https://www.psychologytoday.com/us/blog/the-intelligent-divorce/201202/the-high-failure-rate-second-and-third-marriages.

13. TAKING THE WAR OUT OF OUR WORDS

1. Monza Naff, *Must We Say We Did Not Love? The Need for Divorce Rituals in Our Time* (Deadwood, OR: Wyatt-MacKenzie Publishing, 2008), 1–2.

14. THERE IS HOPE AND HEALING

1. Paul R. Amato, "The Consequences of Divorce for Adults and Children," *Journal of Marriage and Family* 62 (2000): 1269–87, doi:10.1111/j.1741-3737.2000.01269.x.; Constance R. Ahrons, "Family Ties after Divorce: Long-Term Implications for Children," *Family Process* 46, no. 1 (2007): 55, doi:10.1111/j.1545-5300.2006.00191.x.

2. Fred Luskin, *Forgive for Good: A Proven Prescription for Health and Happiness* (New York: HarperCollins, 2002), vii–viii.

3. Ibid., xv.

4. Ibid., 10.

5. Daphne M. Davis and Jeffrey A. Hayes, "What Are the Benefits of Mindfulness?" *Monitor on Psychology* 43, no. 7 (July/August 2012): 7–8, doi:10.1037/e584442012-022; Daphne M. Davis and Jeffrey A. Hayes, "What Are the Benefits of Mindfulness? A Practice Review of Psychother-

apy-Related Research," *Psychotherapy Theory Research Practice Training* 48, no. 2 (2011): 198–208, doi: 10.1037/a0022062.

6. Luskin, *Forgive for Good*, 120.

7. Ibid., 51.

8. Ibid., 211.

9. Joleen L. Greenwood, "Parent–Child Relationships in the Context of Mid- to Late-Life Parental Divorce," *Journal of Divorce and Remarriage* 53 (2012): 6, doi:10.1080/10502556.2012.635959.

10. Ibid., 10.

11. Joleen L. Greenwood, "Effects of a Mid- to Late-Life Parental Divorce on Adult Children," *Journal of Divorce and Remarriage* 55 (2014): 554, doi:10.1080/10502556.2014.950903.

12. Monza Naff, *Must We Say We Did Not Love? The Need for Divorce Rituals in Our Time* (Deadwood, OR: Wyatt-MacKenzie Publishing, 2008), 9–10.

13. Ibid., 12.

14. Ibid., 15.

15. Ibid., 18.

16. Heart Math Institute, http://www.information-book.com/biology-medicine/biofields-heart-electromagnetic-field/.

17. EMDR Institute, "What Is EMDR?" http://www.emdr.com/what-is-emdr/.

18. EMDR International Association, "Treatment Guidelines," http://www.emdria.org/page/treatmentguidelinesnew.

19. Amy Banks, *Wired to Connect: The Surprising Link Between Brain Science and Strong, Healthy Relationships* (New York: Jeremy P. Tarcher/Penguin, 2016).

20. Stan Dale, interview by Bruce Fredenburg, January 10, 1997.

21. Tom Allender, interview by Bruce Fredenburg, January 10, 1997.

22. Amy Morin, "7 Scientifically Proven Benefits of Gratitude That Will Motivate You to Give Thanks Year-Round," Forbes.com, November 23, 2014, https://www.forbes.com/sites/amymorin/2014/11/23/7-scientifically-proven-benefits-of-gratitude-that-will-motivate-you-to-give-thanks-year-round/#1896d116183c21.

23. Margarita Tartakovsky, "National Psychotherapy Day: Therapists Reveal What Therapy Can Do for You," PsychCentral.com, n.d., https://psychcentral.com/blog/national-psychotherapy-day-therapists-reveal-what-therapy-can-do-for-you/.

24. John Bowlby, *The Making and Breaking of Affectional Bonds*, second edition (New York: Routledge Classics, 1979).

25. William B. Strean, "Laughter Prescription," *Canadian Family Physician* 55, no. 10 (2009): 965–67.

REFERENCES

Ahrons, Constance R. 2007. "Family Ties after Divorce: Long-Term Implications for Children." *Family Process* 46:53–65. doi:10.1111/j.1545-5300.2006.00191.x.

Ainsworth, Mary S., and Sylvia M. Bell. 1970. "Attachment, Exploration, and Separation: Illustrated by the Behavior of One-Year-Olds in a Strange Situation." *Child Development* 41: 49–67. doi:10.2307/1127388.

Ainsworth, Mary S., and John Bowlby. 1991. "An Ethological Approach to Personality Development." *American Psychologist* 46 (4): 333–41. doi:10.1037/0003-066X.46.4.333.

Allred, Colette. 2017. "Age Variation in the Divorce Rate, 1990 and 2017." *Family Profiles*, FP-19-13. Bowling Green, OH: National Center for Family and Marriage Research. doi:10.25035/ncfmr/fp-19-13.

Amato, Paul R. 2000. "The Consequences of Divorce for Adults and Children." *Journal of Marriage and Family* 62:1269–87. doi:10.1111/j.1741-3737.2000.01269.x.

Amato, Paul R., and Tamara D. Afifi. 2006. "Feeling Caught Between Parents: Adult Children's Relations with Parents and Subjective Well-Being." *Journal of Marriage and Family* 68 (1) 222–35. doi:10.1111/j.1741-3737.2006.00243.x.

Anderson, Stephen. 2015. "The Very Idea of 'Lawyer Assisted Negotiation' Is a Misnomer." *Start Mediation.* http://www.startmediation.co.uk/the-very-idea-of-lawyer-assisted-negotiation-is-a-misnomer/.

Aquilino, William. 1994. "Later Life Parental Divorce and Widowhood: Impact on Young Adults' Assessment of Parent–Child Relations." *Journal of Marriage and Family* 56: 908–22. doi:10.2307/353602.

Averbach, Leo. 2012. "The High Failure Rate of Second and Third Marriages." *Psychology Today*, February 6. https://www.psychologytoday.com/us/blog/the-intelligent-divorce/201202/the-high-failure-rate-second-and-third-marriages.

Ayoub, Catherine C., Robin M. Deutsch, and Andronicki Maraganore. 1999. "Emotional Distress in Children of High-Conflict Divorce: The Impact of Marital Conflict and Violence." *Family and Conciliation Courts Review* 37:297–315. doi:10.1111/j.174-1617.1999.tb01307.x.

Banks, Amy. 2016. *Wired to Connect: The Surprising Link Between Brain Science and Strong, Healthy Relationships*. New York: Jeremy P. Tarcher/Penguin.

Black, Claudia. 2009. *It Will Never Happen to Me: Growing Up with Addiction as Youngsters, Adolescents, Adults*. Second edition. Center City, MN: Hazelden Publishing.

Bonanno, George. 2004. "Loss, Trauma, and Human Resilience: Have We Underestimated the Human Capacity to Thrive after Extremely Aversive Events?" *The American Psychologist* 59 (1): 20–28. doi:10.1037/0003-066x.59.1.20.

Bonanno, George, and Stacey Kaltman. 1999. "Toward and Integrative Perspective on Bereavement." *Psychological Bulletin* 125 (6): 760–86. doi: 10.1037/0033-2909.125.6.760.

Bonanno, George A., and Dacher Keltner. 1997. "Facial Expressions of Emotion and the Course of Conjugal Bereavement." *Journal of Abnormal Psychology* 106 (1): 126–37. doi:10.1037//0021-843x.106.1.126.

Bonanno, George A., Camille B. Wortman, Darrin R. Lehman, Roger G. Tweed, Michelle Haring, John Sonnega, Deborah Carr, and Randolph M. Nesse. 2002. "Resilience to Loss and Chronic Grief: A Prospective Study from Preloss to 18-Months Postloss." *Journal of Personal and Social Psychology* 83 (5): 1150–64. doi:10.1037// 0022-3514.83.5.1150.

Booth, Alan, and Paul R. Amato. 1994. "Parental Marital Quality, Parental Divorce, and Relations with Parents." *Journal of Marriage and the Family* 56: 21–34. doi:10.2307/352698.

Bowlby, John. 1960. "Grief and Mourning in Infancy and Early Childhood." *Psychoanalytic Study of the Child* 15:9–39. doi:10/1080/00797308.1960.11822566.

———. 1973. *Attachment and Loss: Vol. 2. Separation: Anxiety and Anger*. First edition. New York: Basic Books.

———. 1979. *The Making and Breaking of Affectional Bonds*. Second edition. New York: Routledge Classics.

———. 1980. *Attachment and Loss: Vol. 3. Loss: Sadness and Depression.* New York: Basic Books.

———. 1980. *Loss: Sadness and Depression.* New York: Basic Books.

———. 1982. *Attachment and Loss: Vol. 1. Attachment*. Second edition. New York: Basic Books.

Bowlby, John, and Colin Murray Parkes. 1970. "Separation and Loss within the Family." In *The Child in His Family*, edited by E. James Anthony. New York: Wiley-Interscience.

Boyce, W. Thomas. 2019. *The Orchid and the Dandelion: Why Some Children Struggle and How All Can Thrive*. New York: Knopf.

Brizendine, Louann. 2010. "Love, Sex and the Male Brain." CNN.com. http// www.cnn.com/OPINION/03/23/brizendine.male.brain/index.h.

Brown, Susan L., and I-Fen Lin. 2012. "The Gray Divorce Revolution: Rising Divorce Among Middle-Aged and Older Adults, 1990–2010." *Journals of Gerontology Series B: Psychological Sciences and Social Sciences* 67 (6): 731–41. doi:10.1093/geronb/ gbs089.

———. 2019. "Repartnering Following Gray Divorce: The Role of Resources and Constraints for Women and Men." *Demography* 56:503–23. doi: 10.1007/s13524-018-0752-x.

Campbell, Marjory. 1995. "Divorce at Mid-Life: Intergenerational Issues." *Journal of Divorce and Remarriage* 23, (1–2): 185–202. doi:10.1300/J087v23n01_12.

Campos, Joseph, Karen C. Barrett, Michael E. Lamb, Hill H. Goldsmith, and Luz C. Stenberg. 1983. "Socioemotional Development." In *Handbook of Child Psychology, Vol 2. Infancy and Psychobiology*, edited by Marshall M. Haith and J. J. Campos. New York: Wiley.

Canham, Sarah L., Atiya Mahmood, Sarah Stott, Judith Sixsmith, and Norm O'Rourke. 2014. "'Til Divorce Do Us Part: Marriage Dissolution in Later Life." *Journal of Divorce and Remarriage* 55 (8): 591–612. doi:10.1080/10502556.2014.959097.

Cassidy, Jude, Jason Jones, and Phillip Shaver. 2013. "Contributions of Attachment Theory and Research: A Framework for Future Research, Translation, and Policy." *Development and Psychopathology* 25:19–52. doi:10.1017/S0954579413000692.

Cassidy, Jude, and Phillip Shaver. 2016. *Handbook of Attachment: Theory, Research, and Clinical Application*. Third edition. New York: Guilford Press.

Center on the Developing Child–Harvard University. 2007. *The Science of Early Childhood Development*. https://46y5eh11fhgw3ve3ytpwxt9r-wpengine.netdna-ssl.com/wp-content/uploads/2007/03/InBrief-The-Science-of-Early-Childhood-Development2.pdf.

"Complicated Grief." n.d. The Mayo Clinic.https://www.mayoclinic.org/diseases-conditions/complicated-grief/symptoms-causes/syc-20360374.

Cooney, Teresa M. 1994. "Young Adults' Relations with Parents: The Influence of Recent Parental Divorce." *Journal of Marriage and the Family* 56: 45–56. doi:10.2307/352700.

Cozolino, Louis. 2014. *The Neuroscience of Human Relationships: Attachment and the Developing Social Brain*. Second edition. New York: Norton.

Cummings, Edward M., and Patrick T. Davies. 2002. "Effects of Marital Conflict on Children: Recent Advances and Emerging Themes in Process-Oriented Research." *Journal of Child Psychology and Psychiatry and Allied Disciplines* (January): 31–63. doi:10.1111/1469-7610.00003.

Davis, Daphne, and Jeffrey Hayes. 2011. "What Are the Benefits of Mindfulness? A Practice Review of Psychotherapy-Related Research." *Psychotherapy Theory Research Practice Training* 48 (2): 198–208. doi:10.1037/a0022062.

———. 2012. "What Are the Benefits of Mindfulness?" *Monitor on Psychology* 43 (7): 7–8. doi:10.1037/e584442012-022

Dennis, Wendy. 2016. "How Grey Divorce Became the New Normal." everythingzoomer.com, June 3. https://www.everythingzoomer.com/sex-relating/2016/06/03/how-grey-divorce-became-the-new-normal/.

Dickerson, Sally, Margaret E. Kemeny, Najib Aziz, Kevin Kim, and John L. Fahey. 2004. "Immunological Effects of Induced Shame and Guilt." *Psychosomatic Medicine* 66 (1): 124–31. https://www.ncbi.nlm.nih.gov/pubmed/1474764.

Ehrlich, Joshua. 2014. *Divorce and Loss: Helping Adults and Children Mourn When a Marriage Comes Apart*. Lanham, MD: Rowman & Littlefield.

Ellison, Sharon S. 2007. *Taking the War Out of Our Words: The Art of Powerful Non-Defensive Communication*. Deadwood, OR: Wyatt-MacKenzie Publishing.

EMDR Institute. n.d. "What Is EMDR?" http://www.emdr.com/what-is-emdr/.

EMDR International Association. n.d. "Treatment Guidelines." http://www.emdria.org/page/treatmentguidelinesnew.

Emery, Robert. 1999. *Marriage, Divorce, and Children's Adjustment*. Second edition. Thousand Oaks, CA: Sage.

———. 2012. *Renegotiating Family Relationships: Divorce, Child Custody, and Mediation*. New York: Guilford Press.

Farrell, Warren. 1986. *Why Men Are the Way They Are: The Male–Female Dynamic*. First edition. New York: McGraw-Hill.

———. 1993. *The Myth of Male Power*. New York: Simon & Schuster.

Feeney, Brooke C., and Joan K. Monin. 2016. "Divorce Through the Lens of Attachment Theory." In *Handbook of Attachment: Theory, Research, and Clinical Application*. Third edition. New York: Guilford Press.

Fleckhammer, Lorraine. 2017. "Adulthood Age Group Growth and Development." Hawthorn, Victoria. https://web2.aabu.edu.jo/tool/course_file/lec_notes/1001242_Adulthood Age Group GD.pdf.

Fuller, Tamara L., and Frank D. Fincham. 1995. "Attachment Style in Married Couples: Relation to Current Marital Functioning, Stability over Time, and Method of Assessment." *Personal Relationships* 92 (2): 17–34. doi:10/1111/j.1415-6811.1995.tb00075.x.

Furstenberg, Frank F., and Kathleen E. Kiernan. 2001. "Delayed Parental Divorce: How Much Do Children Benefit?" *Journal of Marriage and Family* 63 (2): 446–57. doi:10.1111/j.1741-3737.2001.00446.x.

Galvin, Larry. 2009. "Early Childhood Experiences Shape the Brain's Physical Architecture." *Evanston Round Table*. https://evanstonroundtable.com/main.asp?SectionID=16&subsectionID=27&articleID=2888.

Gray, Matthew, David De Vaus, Lixia Qu, and David Stanton. 2011. "Divorce and the Wellbeing of Older Australians." *Ageing and Society* 31 (3): 475–98. doi:10.1017/S0144686X10001017.

Greenwood, Joleen. 2012. "Parent–Child Relationships in the Context of Mid- to Late-Life Parental Divorce." *Journal of Divorce and Remarriage* 53 (1): 1–17. doi.10.1080/10502556.2012.635959.

———. 2014. "Adult Sibling Relationships in the Context of a Mid- to Late-Life Parental Divorce." *Journal of Divorce and Remarriage* 55 (5): 391–407. doi:10.1080/10502556.2014.920686.

———. 2014. "Effects of a Mid- to Late-Life Parental Divorce on Adult Children." *Journal of Divorce and Remarriage* 55 (7): 539–56. doi:10.1080/10502556.2014.950903.

Hamilton, Martha. 2016. "Divorce after 50 Can Destroy Even the Best Retirement Plans." *Washington Post*, December 11. https://www.dailyherald.com/article/20161211/business/161219961/.

Hanson, Rick, and Richard Mendius. 2009. *Buddha's Brain: The Practical Neuroscience of Happiness, Love and Wisdom*. Oakland, CA: New Harbringer Publications.

Hazan, Cindy, and Phillip Shaver. 1987. "Romantic Love Conceptualized as an Attachment Process." *Journal of Personality and Social Psychology* 52 (3): 511–24. doi:10.1037/0022-3514.52.3.511.

Herbert, Wray. 2010. "Review of Delusions of Gender." *Washington Post*, September 12. http://www.washingtonpost.com/wp-dyn/content/article/2010/09/10/AR2010091002678.html.

Hinds, Andy. 2013. "Messages of Shame Are Organized Around Gender." *The Atlantic*, April 26. https://www.theatlantic.com/sexes/archive/2013/04/messages-of-shame-are-organized-around-gender/275322/.

Holmes, Thomas H., and Richard H. Rahe. 1967. "The Social Readjustment Rating Scale." *Journal of Psychosomatic Research* 11 (2): 213–18. doi:10/1016/0022-3999(67)90010-4.

Horowitz, Mardi. 1986. "Stress-Response Syndromes: A Review of Posttraumatic and Adjustment Disorders." *Hospital Community Psychiatry* 37 (3): 241–49. doi:10.1176/ps.37.3.241

Hughes, Kate. 2007. "Mothering Mothers: An Exploration of the Perceptions of Adult Children of Divorce." *Australian Journal of Social Issues* 42 (4): 563–79. doi:10.1002/j.1839-4655.2007.tb00078.x.

Jappens, Maaike, and Jan Van Bavel. 2015. "Parental Divorce, Residence Arrangements, and Contact Between Grandchildren and Grandparents." *Journal of Marriage and Family* 78 (2). doi:10.1111/jomf.12275.

Jensen, Todd M., and Gary L. Bowen. 2015. "Mid- and Late-Life Divorce and Parents' Perceptions of Emerging Adult Children's Emotional Reactions." *Journal of Divorce and Remarriage* 56 (5): 409–27. doi:10.1080/10502556.2015.1046795.

Julien, Jane Gordon. 2016. "Never Too Old to Hurt from Parents' Divorce." *New York Times*, April 21. https://www.nytimes.com/2016/04/24/fashion/weddings/never-too-old-to-hurt-from-parents-divorce.html.

Kelly, Joan. 2005. "Developing Beneficial Parenting Plan Models for Children Following Separation and Divorce." *Journal of the American Academy of Matrimonial Law* 19:237–54.

Kinniburgh-White, Ruth, Claire Cartwright, and Fred Seymour. 2010. "Young Adults' Narratives of Relational Development with Stepfathers." *Journal of Social and Personal Relationships* 27 (7): 890–907. doi:10.1177/0265407510376252.

Kirn, Walter. 1995. "My Parents' Bust-Up, and Mine." *New York Times Magazine*, October 8. https://www.nytimes.com/1995/10/08/magazine/my-parents-bust-up-and-mine.html.

Kübler-Ross, Elisabeth. 1969. *On Death and Dying*. New York: Scribner.

Kumagai, Fumle. 2006. "The Fallacy of Late-Life Divorce in Japan." *Care Management Journal* 7 (3): 123–34. doi:10.1891/cmj-v7i3a004.

"Lawsuit Stress: The Dark Side of Litigation." n.d. http://www.mentalhealthy.co.uk/anxiety/anxiety/lawsuit-stress-the-dark-side-of-litigation.html.

Lin, I-Fen, Susan L. Brown, and Anna M. Hammersmith. 2017. "Marital Biography, Social Security Receipt, and Poverty." *Research on Aging* 39 (1): 86–110. doi:10.1177/0164027516656139.

Luskin, Fred. 2000. *Forgive for Good: A Proven Prescription for Health and Happiness*. New York: HarperCollins.

Maciejewski, Paul K., Baohui Zhang, Susan D. Block, and Holly G. Prigerson. 2007. "An Empirical Examination of the Stage Theory of Grief." *Journal of the American Medical Association* 297 (7): 716–24. doi:10.1001/jama.297.7.716.

Main, Mary, and Judith Solomon. 1990. "Procedures for Identifying Infants as Disorganized/Disoriented During the Ainsworth Strange Situation." In *Attachment in the Preschool Years: Theory Research and Intervention*. Chicago: University of Chicago Press.

McCoy, Kathy. 2018. "7 Surprising Facts About Gray Divorce: What You Thought You Knew Might Not Be True." *Psychology Today*, September 25.

Meadows, Sam. 2018. "Rise of the 'Silver Splitters': How Getting Divorced in Retirement Could Cost You Thousands." *Telegraph*, September 28. https://www.telegraph.co.uk/money/consumer-affairs/rise-silver-splitters-getting-divorced-retirement-could-cost/.

Mikucki-Enyart, Sylvia L., Sarah E. Wilder, and Hayden Barber. 2016. "'Was It All Smoke and Mirrors?': Applying the Relational Turbulence Model to Adult Children's Experience of Late-Life Parental Divorce." *Journal of Social and Personal Relationships* 34 (2): 209–34. doi:10.1177/0265407516629226.

Mikulincer, Mario, and Phillip Shaver. 2016. "Adult Attachment and Emotion Regulation." In *Handbook of Attachment: Theory, Research, and Clinical Application*, edited by Jude Cassidy and Phillip R. Shaver. New York: Guilford Press.

———. 2016. *Attachment in Adulthood: Structure, Dynamics, and Change*. Second edition. New York: Guilford Press.

Morin, Amy. 2014. "7 Scientifically Proven Benefits of Gratitude That Will Motivate You to Give Thanks Year-Round." Forbes.com, November 23. https://www.forbes.com/sites/amymorin/2014/11/23/7-scientifically-proven-benefits-of-gratitude-that-will-motivate-you-to-give-thanks-year-round/#1896d116183c21.

Naff, Monza. 2008. *Must We Say We Did Not Love? The Need for Divorce Rituals in Our Time*. Deadwood, OR: Wyatt-MacKenzie Publishing.

Neimeyer, Robert. 2001. *Meaning Reconstruction and the Experience of Loss.* Washington, DC: American Psychological Association.

Nguyen, Linda. 2012. "Rising 'Grey Divorce' Rates Creates Financial Havoc for Seniors." *Globe and Mail*, September 19.

Papa, Anthony, and Nicole Lancaster. 2016. "Identity Continuity and Loss after Death, Divorce, and Job Loss." *Self and Identity* 15 (1): 47–61. doi:10.1080/15298868.2015.1079551.

Papernow, Patricia. 2017. "Recoupling in Mid-Life and Beyond: From Love at Last to Not So Fast." *Family Process* 57. doi:10.1111/famp.12315.

Parkes, Colin Murray. 1964. "The Effects of Bereavement on Physical and Mental Health—A Study of the Medical Records of Widows." *British Medical Journal* 2 (5404): 274 LP–279. doi:10.1136/bmj.2.5404.274.

———. 2001. *Bereavement: Studies of Grief in Adult Life*. Philadelphia: Taylor and Francis.

Payne, Krista K. 2012. "Young Adults in the Parental Home, 1940–2010." National Center for Family and Marriage Research. http://ncfmr.bgsu.edu/pdf/family/family_profiles/file98800.pdf.

Pett, Marjorie A., Nancy Lang, and Anita Gander. 1992. "Late-Life Divorce: Its Impact on Family Rituals." *Journal of Family Issues* 13 (4): 526–52. doi:10.1177/019251392013004008.

Rhyne, Maureen Culkin. 1990. "The Effects of Parental Mid-Life Divorce on Young Adult Development." Presented at the National Council on Family Relations Annual Conference. Seattle, WA, November 14. https://files.eric.ed.gov/fulltext/ED330952.pdf.

Robino, Ariann E. 2019. "The Human–Animal Bond and Attachment in Animal Assisted Interventions in Counseling." PhD dissertation. Virginia Polytechnic Institute and State University.

Schmidt, Sarah. 2017. "The Wedding Industry in 2017 and Beyond." MarketResearch.com. https://blog.marketresearch.com/the-wedding-industry-in-2017-and-beyond.

"Science of the Heart." n.d. HeartMath.org. https://www.heartmath.org/resources/downloads/science-of-the-heart/.

Shapiro, Adam. 2003. "Later-Life Divorce and Parent–Adult Child Contact and Proximity: A Longitudinal Analysis." *Journal of Family Issues* 24. doi:10.1177/0192513X02250099.

Shapiro, Adam, and R. Corey Remle. 2010. "Generational Jeopardy? Parent's Marital Transitions and the Provision of Financial Transfers to Adult Children." *Journal of Gerontology: Social Sciences* 665B (1): 99–109. doi:10.1093/geronb/gbq010.

Shatner, William. n.d. "Untitled Quote." brainyquote.com. https://www.brainyquote.com/quotes/william_shatner_459183.

Shaver, Phillip, and Cindy Hazan. 1987. "Romantic Love Conceptualized as an Attachment Process." *Journal of Personality and Social Psychology* 52 (3): 511–24. doi:10.1037/0022-3514.52.3.511.

———. 1988. "A Biased Overview of the Study of Love." *Journal of Social and Personal Relationships* 5 (4): 473–501. doi:10.1177/0265407588054005.

Shaw, Lori Anne. 2010. "Divorce Mediation Outcome Research: A Meta-Analysis." *Conflict Resolution Quarterly* 27:447–67. doi:10.1002/crq.20006.

Shoup, Rick, Robert M. Gonyea, and George Kuh. 2009. "Helicopter Parents: Examining the Impact of Highly Involved Parents on Student Engagement and Educational Outcomes." In 49th Annual Forum of the Association for Institutional Research. Atlanta, GA.

Siegel, Daniel. 2013. "Relationship Science and Being Human." Dr. Dan Siegel blog, December 17. https://www.drdansiegel.com/blog/2013/12/17/relationship-science-and-being-human/.

Simpson, Jeffry A., W. Andrew Collins, Sisi Tran, and Katherine C. Haydon. 2007. "Attachment and the Experience and Expression of Emotions in Romantic Relationships: A Developmental Perspective." *Journal of Personality and Social Psychology* 92 (2): 355–67. doi:10.1037/0022-3514.92.2.355.

Singh, Prachi. 2016. "Summing Up: Inside the Big Fat Global Wedding Industry." Fashion United. https://fashionunited.uk/news/business/summing-up-inside-the-big-fat-global-wedding-industry/2016062420874.

Smidt, Remy. 2016. "These Parents Threw a Lit 'Divorce Party' to Make Their Split Less Awkward." Buzzfeed News, December 19. https://www.buzzfeednews.com/article/remysmidt/happily-never-after.

Solomon, Denise Haunani, and Leanne K. Knobloch. 2004. "A Model of Relational Turbulence: The Role of Intimacy, Relational Uncertainty, and Interference from Partners in Appraisals of Irritations." *Journal of Social and Personal Relationships* 21 (6): 795–816. doi:10.1177/0265407504047838.

Strean, William B. 2009. "Laughter Prescription." *Canadian Family Physician* 55 (10): 965–67.

Stroebe, Margaret, and Henk Schut. 1999. "The Dual Process Model of Coping with Bereavement: Rationale and Description." *Death Studies* 23 (3): 197–224. doi: 10.1080/074811899201046.

Stroh, Mackenzie. 2007. "The 27-Year Itch." *Maclean's*, January 27. https://archive.macleans.ca/article/2007/1/29/the-27year-itch#!&pid=402.

Tannen, Deborah. (1990) 2007. *You Just Don't Understand: Women and Men in Conversation*. New York: William Morrow Paperbacks.

Tartakovsky, Margarita. n.d. "National Psychotherapy Day: Therapists Reveal What Therapy Can Do for You." PsychCentral.com. https://psychcentral.com/blog/national-psychotherapy-day-therapists-reveal-what-therapy-can-do-for-you/.

"The Science of Early Childhood Development." n.d. https://www.developingchild.harvard.edu.

Thomas, Kali S., and Robert Applebaum. 2015. "Long-Term Services and Supports (LTSS): A Growing Challenge for an Aging America." *Public Policy and Aging Report* 25 (2): 56–62. doi:10.1093/ppar/prv003.

Umberson, Debra. 1992. "Relationships Between Adult Children and Their Parents: Psychological Consequences for Both Generations." *Journal of Marriage and Family* 54: 664–74. doi:10.2307/353252.

US Senate Commission on Long-Term Care. 2013. *Final Report to Congress*. September 12. http://ltcocommission.org/.

Wallerstein, Judith S., and Julia M. Lewis. 2004. "The Unexpected Legacy of Divorce: Report of a 25-Year Study," *Psychoanalytic Psychology* 21 (3): 353–70.

Wegscheider-Cruse, Sharon. 1988. *Another Chance: Hope and Health for the Alcoholic Family*. Second edition. Palo Alto, CA: Science and Behavior Books.

Westphal, Sarah Katharina, Anne-Rigt Poortman, and Tanja Van der Lippe. 2015. "What about the Grandparents? Children's Postdivorce Residence Arrangements and Contact with Grandparents." *Journal of Marriage and Family* 77 (2): 424–40. doi:10.1111/jomf.12173.

"Why It's So Hard for Adults When Their Parents Divorce." 2014. Youbeauty.com. https://www.youbeauty.com/life/why-grey-divorce-sucks-for-adult-children/.

Woititz, Janet G. 1992. *Healthy Parenting: How Your Upbringing Influences the Way You Raise Your Children, and What You Can Do to Make It Better for Them*. First edition. New York: Simon & Schuster/Fireside.

Wolf, D. A. 2012. "Death or Divorce: Which Is Worse?" *Huffington Post*, January 16. https://www.huffpost.com/entry/death-or-divorce-which-is_b_1101346.
Worden, J. William. 2018. *Grief Counseling and Grief Therapy*. Fifth edition. New York: Springer Publishing Company.
Zeifman, Debra M., and Cindy Hazan. 2016. "Pair Bonds as Attachments: Mounting Evidence in Support of Bowlby's Hypothesis." In *Handbook of Attachment: Theory, Research and Clinical Applications*, edited by Judy Cassidy and Philip R. Shaver. New York: Guilford Press.

INDEX

ABOUT THE AUTHORS

Carol R. Hughes, PhD, LMFT, holds her doctoral degree in clinical psychology and her master's degree in counseling psychology, achieving both summa cum laude and Phi Beta Kappa honors. She is also a two-time Fulbright Scholar. Carol served for ten years as an associate professor of human services at Saddleback College. In her practice in Laguna Hills, California, as a California-licensed marriage and family therapist and family-focused divorce professional, for more than thirty years she has assisted hundreds of divorcing families as a therapist, child and coparenting specialist, divorce coach, and mediator.

Bruce R. Fredenburg, MS, LMFT, has been a California-licensed marriage and family therapist for more than thirty years and is board certified in clinical hypnosis. He was a college instructor in human services at Saddleback College and at the National Medical Review School in Southern California. He also created and taught parenting classes for adoptive and foster parents. Trained and experienced in chronic pain management, trauma, addictions, mediation, and collaborative divorce, Bruce helps families as a therapist, divorce coach, child and coparenting specialist, and mediator in his practice in Laguna Hills, California.

In addition, in 2003, Carol and Bruce were founding members of Collaborative Divorce Solutions of Orange County, an interdisciplinary practice group of divorce professionals dedicated to respectful, peaceful divorce solutions for families.

CPSIA information can be obtained
at www.ICGtesting.com
Printed in the USA
BVHW031017240520
580224BV00002B/3